Author Biography

(Photo by Pattie Boyd)

Sally Arnold grew up on a Wiltshire farm in the 1950s and trained as a Norland Nurse. An early client took her far from this world: Mick Jagger, who hired her to look after his daughter Jade. She then switched to minding grown-ups. As rock's first female tour manager, she worked for The Who, the Rolling Stones, Mike Oldfield, Peter Gabriel and Lynyrd Skynyrd, and developed a second career organising the first Comic Relief shows. Alongside Pete Townshend, she went on to run The Who's Double O Charity, which funded therapies for addiction. Sally was named one of the Women of the Year in 1997 for her charity work.

She sustained her lifelong love of classical music, singing with the London Symphony Orchestra (LSO) Chorus, and as Concert Manager for Classic FM, along with her passion for travel. This included a pioneering trip to China by train in 1973.

Through the years Sally has met and worked with royals – from Prince Charles and Princess Diana to the late Duke of Edinburgh – Poet Laureate Ted Hughes, world leaders such as Mikhail Gorbachev and Chou En-lai, and great musicians such as Anne-Sophie Mutter. She now lives in Devon.

Find out more at www.rocknrollnanny.co.uk

D1460632

Rock N Roll Nanny

A Memoir by
Sally Arnold

SilverWood

Published in 2022 by SilverWood Books

SilverWood Books Ltd
14 Small Street, Bristol, BS1 1DE, United Kingdom
www.silverwoodbooks.co.uk

This work depicts actual events in the life of the author as truthfully as recollection permits. Some dialogue has been retold in a way that accurately evokes the meaning and feeling of what was said. The story, the experiences, and the words are the author's alone.

ISBN 978-1-80042-149-3 (paperback)

British Library Cataloguing in Publication Data
A CIP catalogue record for this book is
available from the British Library

Page design and typesetting by SilverWood Books

This book is dedicated to those who died far too young:
my beloved sister, Jane; my soul-mate Dean Kilpatrick;
my dear friends, Cassie and Steve Gaines;
and my hero, dearest friend and mentor, the unique genius,
Ronnie Van Zant

Contents

List of Photographs

The author has made all reasonable efforts to trace the current holders of the copyright of material used in this book. If any copyright holder believes that their material has been used without due credit, the author will make arrangements to correct omissions in any future re-printing. To see these and many other photographs in full colour, please visit the author's website www.rocknrollnanny.co.uk and sign up for updates.

Front cover: Sally with Roger Daltrey of The Who; Sally with Ronnie Van Zant of Lynyrd Skynyrd; Sally's Rolling Stones TOE (Tour of Europe) 1976 Access all Areas pass; Lynyrd Skynyrd backstage pass; Sally's WTP (Who Touring Party) pass; Sally in her Norland Uniform; Stones ad from 1976 Tour of Europe; Sally with her fiance, Dean Kilpatrick, stage manager of Lynyrd Skynyrd; Sally with Princess Diana.

Back cover: Allen Collins and Dean Kilpatrick on the Lynyrd Skynyrd Tour bus; Allen Collins, Ronnie Van Zant, Artimus Pyle and Billy Powell of Lynyrd Skynyrd; Sally with John Entwistle of The Who; Sally with Gary Rossington of Lynyrd Skynyrd; Dean Kilpatrick and Steve Gaines of Lynyrd Skynyrd; Sally with Pete Townshend of The Who.

A Note from Sally

I have written this book many years after the events, and should explain that it can be quite difficult to look back, recall and remember conversations and events absolutely accurately. Although some of them are still extremely vivid in my memory, others are less clear. Where possible I have checked with many who were there and with other sources to make this memoir as accurate as possible. But as someone once said: "Recollections may vary." So, if anything in this book is remembered differently by others, then I apologise for my memory.

Sally Arnold
Devon, England, 2022

Introduction

How did a farmer's daughter from rural Wiltshire end up meeting, and working with, some of the most famous people of our times: from Russian President Mikhail Gorbachev and Chinese Premier Chou En-lai to Mick Jagger, Poet Laureate Ted Hughes and HRH Prince Philip? All I remember from childhood is that I didn't want to follow the normal route of marriage and children. And being a nanny totally fulfilled that potential vestige of any vague maternal feelings. I wanted to be free to live a good life and travel the world.

As a child I never dreamt I would fulfil that dream, but I travelled widely – to all the usual places, like Europe and the United States, and to much more unusual ones like Russia, China, Nepal, Afghanistan, Fiji, and Iran.

Now, as I pore over old letters and diaries, I realise the same thread winds through all these very different phases and adventures: my free, selfish life has actually been one of looking after other people. First as a Norland Nurse, and then as rock's first female tour manager.

This is my story...

Prologue

Oh my God…oh shit…oh my God…what was I going to do? A riot was in the offing…

The support band had finished their set. We'd had the usual 30-minute break – but now we were up to fifty minutes. The band, all but one, was ready to go on stage. The crowd was roaring, whooping, shouting, "Skynyrd…! Skynyrd…! Free Bird…! Free Bird…!" and clapping like crazy in anticipation. The atmosphere was heated – but becoming threatening as the band were running so late…

And it was all my fault…

We had no drummer – no Artimus. We waited and waited. Skynyrd couldn't possibly go on without a drummer. Artie's fantastic, dynamic drumming – sometimes like a train throb, throb, throbbing down the line – was so vital to that Skynyrd sound.

Oh, shit – what to do? I felt utterly sick. That morning, the tour bus had been ready to leave the hotel at the specified time. Everybody had packed their bags and was on the bus ready to go – except Artimus. So, I did what I had always threatened to do if someone was late. I told the driver to leave. Without Artimus…

I wouldn't have done it without knowing that it wasn't far to the next gig, and I knew that Artimus had his itinerary with the landline phone numbers of the next hotel and venue (no mobile/cell phones then).

But no call came…not to the hotel nor to the venue. Had he got lost in the wilds of middle England…? Or taken umbrage and decided not to turn up…?

We'd done the soundcheck that afternoon without a drummer.

The band's leader, Ronnie Van Zant, totally understood why I had done what I'd done, thank goodness, and the others all backed me up too. We'd all been getting sick of Artie's antics. He'd been taking acid at inappropriate moments (although when is appropriate?!) and had been generally disruptive.

Now, I was waiting outside the stage door in a state of utter panic. I thought I might have a heart attack or, at the very least, faint into peaceful oblivion. My nausea was getting worse by the minute. My head was throbbing. The crowd was hollering by now, and the venue's manager was panicking alongside me too.

"Where is he?" he asked in desperation.

"I really don't know," I replied, silently praying.

Then – then…a taxi came screeching towards us – with Artie. At last! I could barely look at him, just grabbed his arm and marched him inside. I violently shoved him onto that stage, hissing angrily, "We'll talk about this later!"

I stood at the side of the stage that night in a puddle of utter and palpable relief, but shooting regular angry looks at Artimus every time he glanced over at me.

It was such a close shave, but it proved to the band that they had to – just had to – obey my instructions at all times. It's the same with children. You have to be consistent and carry out any threat or punishment, otherwise they will just run rings around you.

And of course the band all realised that the only reason I had rules was for them. It was vital – *of the utmost importance* – that they always got to the next venue. That's what my job was as tour manager: to get the band, by hook or by crook, to the next gig, regardless of what dramas or problems we'd had previously.

Lynyrd Skynyrd were by far the most difficult band I had to deal with, over and above all my other bands put together. They were such naughty boys that I was frequently pleading with hotel managers and the police on their behalf, and usually at around 3am or some such ungodly hour.

But the other side of this was the sheer excitement mixed with relief when the band, be it the Stones, The Who, Skynyrd, Mike Oldfield or Peter Gabriel, got on that stage for a live gig. I could feel the intoxication coming from the roar of the crowd, combined with the volume, and the vibrations that were visceral and literally throbbed through my whole body. And to know that I was, in part, responsible for making this thrilling and exciting event happen.

Despite all the arguments or delays, here they were. My boys. On that stage. Playing their amazing music.

How lucky I was...

But how *on earth* had I got here...?

PART ONE

BECOMING

Chapter 1

My Family – and Other Animals

My background is like that of many middle-class English women growing up in the 1950s. I was brought up on a dairy farm in Wiltshire. We lived in a large Tudor farmhouse on the edge of Salisbury Plain, which Cromwell had used during the Civil War. I remember being given a wind-up record player, but it only played 78rpm shellac records, which broke easily. I was given some records by Elvis Presley, which opened my eyes and ears, as he did for so many people at that time.

I was the eldest of four, with two younger sisters and then, at last, a boy, who came along when I was eleven. We happily spent hours messing about on the farm, playing under and around the cows' legs and walking for miles up to the plains to fish in the dew ponds. No worries about children wandering around alone in those days. It was bliss.

After kindergarten, I went to our local village school in Easterton. However, I wasn't there for long, as – horror of horrors – I quickly picked up the broad Wiltshire accent of the other kids. That just *would not do* – I couldn't possibly visit my grandparents with such a broad West Country accent!

My father trained as an engineer before WW2, then became a farmer after the war. As the only boy, he seemed to have had quite an austere life, as his father was very Victorian and strict. He fought in the Royal Signals Corps in the war, part of Montgomery's 8th Army. My mother was training to be an actress at the Royal Academy of Dramatic Art (RADA) before the war, then she joined the Entertainments National Service Association (ENSA), which entertained the troops during the war.

My parents moved into the farm in 1948, but after twenty years there, my grandfather forced my father to move to London and work at his company, MK Electric, which made electric plugs and sockets, ostensibly to take over the business. My father ended up having three heart attacks within just a year or so of starting, having gone from being a farmer to working 9 to 5 in an office, with a horrendous 45-minute drive to commute there and back every day.

My childhood was lived in the aftermath of WW2, and I vaguely remember my mother using a ration book, which each family had until 1954. These coupons, used mainly for sugar for us, had to be stamped by the shopkeeper. Bread was purchased in the village bakery, and I loved picking off the crust of the freshly baked loaf to eat on my walk back home – absolutely delicious for me, but to the great annoyance of my mother! We produced our own eggs, bacon, milk, butter and cream on the farm. The large bacon joints would hang in the cellar, which my father would cut slices off as needed. I think back on it now, and bizarrely this was where I used to nurse and feed the runts of the piglet litters that needed fattening up; little did I know these were for slaughter, but that's the necessity of farm life, of course.

Left: Sally's Arnold grandparents, and right: Sally's father and mother on their wedding day
(Photos from author's personal collection)

I also remember the excitement when the first oranges and bananas arrived. Although they hadn't been part of the rationing, they were just not imported. Never had I tasted such wondrous things. My mother would push a sugar lump deep into an orange and I'd spend hours wandering around the farm sucking on this scrumptious snack!

Our Tudor farmhouse had no bathroom initially, just a loo with a tatty old sink in an outhouse. My father quickly installed a bathroom, and basins in each bedroom. He was very capable at everything to do with electrics, mechanics, and general building handiwork. There was a large log fire permanently blazing away in the dining room, which was where we mainly congregated. It was one of those massive inglenook fireplaces with nooks and crannies, and hooks for hanging pots on, which were often put to good use.

There was no central heating for a good few years, and the house was bitterly cold in the winter. Our bedroom sometimes even had icicles *inside* the windows...! There would be massive 2-foot-long ones outside hanging down from the thatch. My sisters and I had a small chimney-style electric heater in our bedroom which we would put our clothes on top of – just for a few minutes – to try to warm them up a little...it was only a very little, though! It was always a big rush to dress as quickly as possible and try to warm up during those bitterly freezing cold winters.

My paternal grandfather, Charles Arnold, known as Leonard, was an inventor and founded MK Electric in 1919. He invented the three-prong safety socket, which was used worldwide in his lifetime. (See Appendix.) He even showed me how to change a plug when I was about six years old.

My grandmother was from Cornwall. I know very little about the Cornish side of the family, other than an uncle of my grandmother, Mabel Symons, was the Very Reverend Charles Douglas Symons CB, MC, DD, MA, and was an eminent man of the cloth, having been Chaplain-General to the forces 1933–44. He was then made a Chaplain of the Order of St John and Jerusalem and, finally, Honorary Chaplain to the King from 1944 to his death in 1949, serving as Chaplain at the Tower of London.

MK Electric went public in the 1960s, making my grandfather a multi-millionaire. Taxes at that time were eye-wateringly high, reaching 83% on investment income and peaking at an incredible 98%. Despite this, when he died in 1969, he was the sixth richest man in the country. But he didn't believe in inherited wealth, so the majority of his estate went in death duties and to charity. He was also not interested in avoiding taxes and always said he would abide by the law of the land, hence he had over £4 million ready in his account just to pay the inland revenue on his death (apparently, £4 million would be in the region of a third of a billion pounds now).

Their large mansion in Enfield, north London, was bequeathed to the Cheshire Homes Charity. Renamed Arnold House, it ran for some fifty years as a Cheshire Home, but in 2020 had to close due to necessary health and safety regulations, which were too expensive to rectify. My parents were presented to the Queen there at her visit in February 1983. There were rumours that my grandfather turned down a knighthood, but I don't know how true that is. He certainly never talked about it, being famously modest.

The residue of the estate was used to set up the Arnold Foundation Charity, a grant-giving trust. It gave away over many hundreds of thousands of pounds to numerous good causes over the years, then closed down in

Margaret and Jim Arnold (L) with Leonard Cheshire (R)
on the visit of Her Majesty the Queen to Arnold House Cheshire Home, 1983
(Photo from author's personal collection)

2001. The capital was donated to Bristol University to fund a bursary in the electrical and electronic engineering department – The Arnold Scholarship.

My grandfather had not always been this saintly, though. After training as an electrical engineer, and doing a course in telegraphy, he went to work for the Marconi Company in Liverpool, where he got into trouble. He said in a tape recording:

> I got into trouble because I'm very fond of experimental work, and another lad and myself erected aerials in our respective digs, and constructed some wireless apparatus and communicated with each other. One night, when several ships and liners were coming in, we picked up their messages, and very foolishly we answered them! Well, the authorities tracked down who was doing this and we were called up before the Manager the next morning and dismissed on the spot! After this, an application was then made to the authorities that no one would be allowed to use experimental wireless apparatus without a licence. That's how that law came about!

He then worked for Sir Henry Hozier (Lady Churchill's father/Winston Churchill's father-in-law) at Lloyds of London, for whom he erected a wireless station at the Lizard in Cornwall. Then to Egypt, where he set up another wireless station at Suez. Unfortunately, however, Lloyds had a law case against Marconi and lost it, so their wireless division went bust.

On returning to England, my grandfather shared digs with Charles Belling, and they started Belling and Co. However, he had to sell out when WW1 started and obviously couldn't carry on at the company while he was in the army. After the war, he set up MK Electric and was one of the first employers to give workers paid holidays and pension schemes in the 1920s. MK workers were a happy lot. As a child, he would often take me for a visit to the factory, and I would love hearing everybody say how fond they were of 'the old man'. He had absolutely no ego, and refused to have a Rolls Royce or Bentley as he found them far too ostentatious. So, he had Armstrong Siddeleys instead. I always thought they were magnificent cars! He was always courteous and honourable, showing an old-fashioned politeness to everybody, especially his staff. And, despite smoking his pipe non-stop, he was never ill and just dropped dead from a heart attack at eighty-four (there is more about him, in his own words, in the Appendix).

When staying with these grandparents, the routine was extremely strict. We were never allowed to mix with the staff. There were many rules and regulations we had to abide by: for example, a gong would be rung by one of the maids fifteen minutes before a meal, then again five minutes before, and woe betide you if you were late. We children were never allowed into the drawing room and were confined to the nursery – a large, cold, forbidding room. As children, we usually ate there, only occasionally having a meal in the dining room with the whole family. The large cellar, which I frequently explored, had been used as an air-raid shelter during WW2.

My maternal grandfather, Charles Marques MBE, came over from Australia at just eighteen years old with his father to fight with the Anzacs in WW1, and both, amazingly, survived Gallipoli. He married a Welsh girl, Edna Lewis, who had been a teacher of Home Economics, and who was his senior in the army ranks during the war. This high position for a woman was very unusual for the times. He lost an eye just after the war, so had a glass one which he would hide under his pillows for me to find as a little girl.

He started up his company, Concrete Utilities, in Hertfordshire making concrete lamp-columns and farm buildings. The company, in turn, passed to my uncles and is now run by my male cousins. He was a member of the Royal Institution, where an annual lecture is still given in his memory, usually given by eminent scientists on various scientific topics.

These grandparents were far less strict than the Arnolds, and we could wander around their huge estate unhindered. One of the early owners had planted a specimen of each tree that would grow in England. There was also a working farm on the estate, and all the estate workers had cottages, too, and I was allowed to mix with these staff and their families.

I am still in touch with the gardener's daughter, who recently told me my grandfather had a mistress...to say I was shocked would be an understatement, especially as he often said he would 'horsewhip' my father if he was unfaithful to my mother. And yet, there he was, betraying my grandmother, who was kindness personified. It would have torn the whole family apart if we had ever found this out.

One of my uncles on my mother's side was David Marques, the famous rugby player who played for the Harlequins and was even captain of the

England team. He was my godfather and, on my confirmation, he brought a girlfriend along who was a Norland Nurse and travelling around the world in her job. This meeting was fortuitous because it's what helped me decide my future career.

After the local village school in Easterton, I went to boarding school at the tender age of seven – which to some may seem cruel, as not many children went at such an early age, but I absolutely loved it. The main reason I was sent there was because the village school was 'no longer appropriate', apparently – my continual use of the broad Wiltshire accent was given as one reason!

My boarding school, Knighton House, was run by the wonderful Peggy and John Booker (parents to Christopher Booker, the brilliant journalist and co-founder of *Private Eye*). The uniform was red dungarees over grey shorts with yellow Aertex shirts – what fun, and so different from any other school uniform. I stayed friends with the Bookers well into my adult years. I was never a bookish girl, as many there were, but the Bookers would tell me frequently that they knew I was destined for special things as I had so much common sense and was so bright. I hope I've lived up to that and I'd certainly say I've experienced some special things throughout my life.

In my last year at Knighton, at the age of thirteen, I was made a prefect. I was self-assured and had always pushed the boundaries and broken rules at every opportunity. However, the school seemed to recognise that this was an energy that could be channelled for the better into responsibility and leadership. Later, at Norland, as I went through the ranks and became a senior nurse, again that self-assurance came to the fore in helping the junior nurses. This natural authority was extremely helpful later – even necessary – in my job as a tour manager to rock bands. I also needed a certain amount of tenacity in order to deal with the many egos in the rock world, as well as resilience and humour. I made sure the boys knew they had to listen to me and obey my instructions for the good of the tour, and of the whole band. Although, of course, in the 70s and 80s a woman was always 'bossy' whereas a man was always 'assertive'. That was more than annoying.

I went on to two more boarding schools after Knighton. Byculla School was based in a beautiful Tudor house in Hampshire that was used in the film *The Happiest Days of Your Life* with Margaret Rutherford. This was where I met Sally Wood, still a close friend to this day, whose father was Ken Wood, of Kenwood food mixers. We often used to complain that our families made such boring things – mine: electric plugs and concrete lamp-columns, and hers: food mixers. If only they had made something exciting like clothes or shoes or make-up!

At Byculla, Sally and I were nearly seduced and raped by a French teacher. We'll call him Mr N. During private 'Italian' lessons in the science lab, he would stroke our hands and try to persuade us to go to his bungalow at night. We refused for months. His methods were astonishing. One day, he gave us some verses typed on *gold* paper. They were from Carmina Burana: extremely erotic poetry written in Latin by medieval monks, which was set to music by Carl Orff. We had never, ever come across such sophisticated things and became more and more fascinated by this worldly, exciting man.

Eventually, we agreed to go to his bungalow. Why, I wonder now? We were both fifteen, and horribly curious about this charismatic and handsome man, who we thought looked just like Dirk Bogarde. We prepared ourselves by putting on about two bras, three pairs of knickers and four shirts under three cardigans. Then we climbed out of our dormitory window, dug our way under the surrounding 20-foot-high wire fence and got to Mr N's bungalow, which he shared with the maths teacher. Goodness only knows how this man didn't know what was going on next door.

What shocked us initially was that, on looking through Mr N's bedroom window, we saw him dishevelled – not the man with slicked-back hair, all neat and smart, we were used to. This was utterly off-putting and quite disgusting. Especially as what had initially tempted us was how suave, handsome, charming and charismatic he was. Suddenly seeing him as a normal scruffy old man made us instantly regret going.

Although it was not enough to stop us…but we suddenly realised this was no joke. He plied us with horrible weak orange squash and dried-up sandwiches, and then tried to fondle and kiss us. When we rejected him, he said, "You can either stay three minutes or three hours."

We immediately jumped up and, in unison, shrieked, "Three minutes!" We then clambered out of his window as quickly as we could, and ran away.

We later discovered this had happened with a number of other girls, and that one of the more senior girls had even become pregnant by him. At some point, he was asked to leave the school, but I think he just went to another girls' boarding school. Thankfully, times have changed and that situation surely wouldn't happen now – and, if it did, I hope the #MeToo movement would have something to say about it!

Other strange and naughty things went on at Byculla, too. Nearby lived a very strange man who would stand at his first-floor window, masturbating in full view of any girls who happened to be walking by. We'd often go there on purpose and call for him, because he would throw us sweets wrapped in newspaper. On one occasion, he came downstairs and took three of us into his garden shed and let us touch his erect penis! Of course, we reacted like the little girls we were, and ran off shrieking and laughing. It all seemed so naughty and slightly exciting – and we never for a moment thought it was dangerous. Given how naive we all were in those days, it just seemed funny.

Did our parents ever realise that this sort of thing went on in boarding schools in England? Also, that we girls had to do all the cleaning and housework? Here they were, paying sizable fees for us to attend this prestigious school, yet we were used as skivvies. The food was dire, too, so we were permanently hungry.

That school went bankrupt – right in the middle of studying for my O levels – which was terribly disruptive. Most of us amalgamated with St Vincent's Academy for Young Ladies at Walton Hall in Warwickshire, the house made famous in the film about Georgiana, Duchess of Devonshire. It was built by the Mordaunt family, became a home for injured soldiers after WW2 and is now a hotel. It was a strange school – the headmistress was, allegedly, a heroin addict. Thank goodness for the music teacher. He gave me the confidence to believe I was good at something, at last. And that was singing. I also started studying music theory with him and passed the various grades quickly. I loved, absolutely loved, the theory lessons – they opened up a whole new dimension for me, especially in mathematics.

Writing now, I realise there was a lot of privilege in my upbringing and education. I feel lucky to have been to boarding school, then secretarial college and then Norland College. It gave me advantages, and a confident attitude that stood me well in my later working life. I never took any of this for granted and capitalised on it by working my utmost at every single job I undertook. My parents and grandparents always stressed the importance of giving back as well, so I have always, since my teenage years, done a great deal of voluntary charity work. It was drummed into me from an early age that we should all help as much as possible, wherever possible, and I've carried that through my life.

Chapter 2

The 1960s – London and Freedom

In the spring of 1965, when I was sixteen, I went off to London to the St James's Secretarial College in Kensington, mainly to fill in time before going off to the Norland Nursery Training College that September. I was a paying guest with a young family in Holland Park. There was another girl staying there, who, being a little older than me, taught me many necessary things about living in London – like how to find a private gynaecologist!

At that time, London was quite dismal in many ways, especially visually, as many of the buildings were black and grimy, still covered in filth from the war, with areas still showing bomb damage. But that summer was a fantastically exciting time to be there, with all the 60s fashions and music. I was often mistaken for Twiggy or Mia Farrow as I looked a little like them – petite and blonde, with a pixie haircut.

While at college, I worked at the Marquee Club in Wardour Street for a short while, in the cloakroom on Friday and Saturday nights, so that I could get in for free. The Marquee Club had started off in Oxford Street but moved to its famous Wardour Street location not long before I arrived in London. It was right in the middle of Soho's busy nightlife, and a huge draw for rock bands and fans. All the best musicians played there, many of whom I got to meet. I particularly remember Eric Clapton with his frizzy perm – not an attractive look, although it was very popular back then. Another memory is of Pink Floyd and their psychedelic backdrops. I also saw Jimi Hendrix play there. All utterly fascinating and exciting. I was such a country bumpkin and had never seen or heard anything like this before, but I soon caught up – in every sense!

I met Chris Squire there, the bass player of a group called Syn.

He would later join Yes and become mega-famous. We dated for the whole summer, and I would often stay with him and his family in north London, then rush back on the first bus to my digs in Holland Park, sneaking in so nobody knew I'd stayed out all night. Unmarried sex was so frowned upon in those days. The other places we frequented were Alexandra Palace (Ally Pally) for concerts, The Cromwellian and The Whisky A Go Go and Speakeasy clubs. All great fun.

Around this time, I would frequently visit a friend from secretarial college at her parents' home in St John's Wood. There, I met some of the neighbours, namely the families of Clement Freud, the TV personality, and of Brian Duffy, one of the famous photographers of the time. Duffy and his wife asked me to be the au pair to their four children. So I did, as I was becoming rather fed up with studying secretarial stuff and wanted to earn some money. Thank goodness my typing and bookkeeping still come in handy – although, sadly, I've forgotten all my shorthand.

I made friends with the au pair who looked after Clement Freud's children, as the families lived near each other, and I would often pop into their house. The eldest child and I became friends as we were close in age, and I also occasionally babysat the two youngest children.

In 2016, two women spoke to the ITV 'Exposure' programme accusing Sir Clement Freud of abuse. It was further covered in the press that he was an habitual abuser of young girls. Now it's in the public domain, I can write about what happened between him and me.

Clement, or Clay as most friends knew him, was a shock to me. I had only ever met men who were decent and kind, like my uncles, or my friends' fathers. None of them were like Clay. I'd probably known him for a few months when he forced me to give him a blow job. I was just sixteen years old. I was visiting one day when he said he wanted to see me in his study. So I went in and he beckoned me over to his desk, grabbed my arms and pushed my head down with great force under his desk. I had no idea I could complain or ask him to stop forcing me to perform this sickening act on him.

Despite this, Clay and I did stay friends and occasional lovers over the years. He became something of a mentor and I found him clever, erudite, and fun to be with. I could go to him for help when I didn't dare ask my father, or any of my uncles. He'd take me out to meals and teach me how to eat caviar and other exotic food and drink. One day, he came to my flat when I was ill and cooked scrambled eggs with truffles for me. There was a dark side, too, obviously, and he often used to intimidate others on purpose. He seemed to relish making people uneasy around him. He had this weird way of lowering his head, then looking up at you with his hooded eyes. He'd speak in a little-boy-lost type of voice, very soft and quiet, trying to be menacing and intimidating. I used to just laugh at him when he was like that with me.

Clay frequently took me to parties at Victor Lownes' house in Connaught Square. Victor was manager of the London Playboy Club and I became quite friendly with his girlfriend at the time. On one occasion there, in 1969, when I was twenty, Roman Polanski tried to get us both into bed – but we weren't prepared to play ball. He was a horrible little man with bad breath who seemed to think all women found him devastatingly attractive – well, we didn't, so he promptly left in a high dudgeon. This incident was just a few weeks before his wife, Sharon Tate, was killed by the Charles Manson gang in Los Angeles.

I suppose the reason for sharing this is to show how – even before I had gone on the road with rock bands and saw their shenanigans – I was seeing men betray their wives and have affairs. This quickly made me realise that some men were just not to be trusted. Even if they were in love with their wives, they had no compunction about betraying them. These experiences convinced me at an early age that I never wanted to be a 'wife'. Why go through such emotional pain because of a man? It was something I made clear vociferously, just before I did eventually get married – that I didn't want to be a 'wife' because wives get cheated on. In fact, now that I'm in my seventies, I look at all my friends and contemporaries, and only about three couples I know are still together and truly happy.

In the autumn of 1968, I started the two years' training at Norland Nursery Training College. It was an obvious choice for me as I knew I was good with children, and I wanted to travel. The college was residential and based in a beautiful old mansion, Denford Park, just outside Hungerford in Berkshire – although it is now based in Bath, is not residential and even takes young men, which I think is great. It was exactly the same as being at boarding school, which I was used to, but some of the girls were very homesick, never having left home before.

The training covered everything to do with looking after a child from birth to seven years old. It included nutrition, cooking and health, including all the childhood diseases, the incubation periods and how to treat them. Other important areas were literacy and language, nursery rhymes and, obviously, play time. Learning and development were also vital and, of course, the teaching of good manners.

We had practical supervised care of children of all ages, as the college used to take in babies and children while parents went away (often, they were the children of diplomats). On one horrendous occasion, a baby died at the college, of what we now call sudden infant death syndrome. When I was training, any unexplained death of an infant was known as 'cot death', probably because it usually happened during sleep. The exact cause was, and remains, unknown and, sadly, this remains one of the leading causes of infant mortality in the Western world. The death of the baby at the college was a massive shock to all of us there, and affected us for many years afterwards. It seems to be more understood these days, thank goodness, and there is strong evidence that putting babies to sleep on their backs and not allowing them to overheat helps enormously.

When I was training, the college was quaintly old-fashioned. We had to learn to use a mangle for wet clothes! That was silly, as none of the families we were going to work for would have a mangle – they would all have spin dryers. We even had to starch our uniform collars and aprons. So antiquated. We did a great deal of fine needlework, knitting and crocheting. Part of our exams included making a dress with a smock front. Most of the girls chose pink or pale blue, but I decided on dark bottle-green, with white smocking – and, even though I say so myself, it looked great, with every stitch neat and minuscule. Cooking, along with preparation of food and special diets for children, was another important aspect.

My training also included six months in Farnborough Hospital in Kent, in the children's ward and the premature unit. I loved those few months working in the hospital and being part of a wonderful team of doctors and nurses. I even enjoyed working in the sluice room, emptying and cleaning the bedpans. I also had a lovely affair with a trainee gynaecologist who was a rather gorgeous guy – all the other nurses fancied him, but I got him! At one point, I was even allowed into the operating theatre to watch a total hip replacement, which I found fascinating.

We had to take difficult exams at the end of each term, and if we failed even one of them then we were out. At one stage, I was being rather naughty, going out too often etc, so my grandfather threatened to disinherit me. I pulled my socks up and managed to get my diploma. Diploma presentation day was very exciting for all of us who were graduating. My parents and Arnold grandparents came, too, and for once they all actually seemed to be proud of me!

With my Norland and National Nursery Examination Board (NNEB) diplomas in hand, I got my first job – with Georgia Brown, the jazz singer and actress, looking after her baby boy in London. That was an eye-opener. She set very strict rules. I was instructed to call her 'Miss Brown', and told I was not to have any boyfriends in the house. I wasn't allowed out or to see my friends, and had very little time off, so ultimately it didn't work out. My next job was with the most wonderful family in Kensington Square, Mr and Mrs Clayton and their sons Olaf and Alexander, both of whom I immediately fell in love with. I am still in touch with Mrs Clayton to this day and hear about the boys and their families.

At around this time I was dating Nicky Chinn, the record producer who I'd met through a Norland chum who was engaged to Mike Chapman, Nicky's songwriting partner. They were famously known as Chinnichap, and made a fortune writing pop songs. One of their first bands was The Sweet. This led to me dating Brian Connolly, The Sweet's lead singer, who I ended up being 'engaged' to for about two months – why, I can't imagine, as we had absolutely nothing in common. I think he was just impressed by what he called my 'upper-class ways'. I use the word 'engaged' lightly, as even though he asked me to marry him, it really wasn't an official engagement.

We all had great fun in those days, going to clubs like the Speakeasy and the Revolution, and then the Picasso Coffee Bar in Kings Road for breakfast after an all-nighter. I used to shop regularly at Quorum, the Chelsea Cobbler and Granny Takes a Trip in World's End.

Much as I loved my job with the Clayton family, after a year I wanted a change and took a job with the photographer Clive Barda, who specialised in portraits of classical musicians. My main passion throughout my life has been classical music, so that really attracted me. Through Clive I met the most wonderful people: the pianist Daniel Barenboim and his cellist wife Jacqueline Du Pré, who invited me to their house in Hampstead; the American pianist Micha Dichter, who became a good friend; I dated the Dutch conductor Edo de Waart and the fascinating Chinese pianist Fou Ts'ong. I also met Terry Harrison and Jasper Parrott, who had just started up a management company, Harrison/Parrott, for classical performers, and I helped them out by looking after some of their artists' day-to-day affairs – doing errands for the violinist Kyung Wha Chung and the pianist Cristina Ortiz.

I enjoyed the job with Clive Barda, but I really wanted to go travelling. None of my friends could come with me so, in the spring of 1971, I put an ad in *The Times*, requesting a 'Travelling companion to share the costs'.

And so my next adventure began.

Chapter 3

Adventures Abroad

I had many replies to that advert in *The Times*, even one from a member of the Romanov family, but I eventually chose a lovely girl, Caroline. I think it's better to travel with someone you don't know very well, as you both have to be just that bit more polite and thoughtful.

So off we set in my little Triumph Spitfire sports car for France, the beginning of a trip round the hotspots of Europe, via Versailles, the Loire Valley, Tours, all in youth hostels, until we got to the Côte d'Azur. We stayed at a friend's house in Antibes, staying in a tiny room right over the sea. This friend was an old girlfriend of my rugby playing uncle, David Marques. There we met her aunt, Mme Renee Laporte, who ran the Picasso Gallery – and learned she had been Picasso's lover in her youth.

My French friend was working on the Cannes Film Festival and, through her, we were invited to a party on a yacht hired by the film producer Jean-Pierre Rassam. Strangely, this connection would also lead me to Mick and Bianca Jagger, and thence to my tour managing.

Jean-Pierre immediately made a play for me. He was so charming and persuasive that I gave in to his wiles, still thinking it would only be a bit of fun. But we ended up becoming totally obsessed with each other. He was the most charismatic man I'd ever met. I was twenty-two to his thirty, which he thought was a massive age gap, but I didn't! I found him to be unlike any previous boyfriends. He was amazingly intelligent, erudite, quick and witty, and massive fun to be with.

We spent the next five days together, one day sailing across the bay to St Tropez in extremely rough seas. I was violently seasick, vomiting over the side of the boat, but even this didn't put him off me. If anything, he seemed to adore me even more. This was my first great true love and passion. I never knew before that sex could be so all encompassing, like being taken somewhere else, an out-of-body experience as some of the great writers and poets have written about.

But when I told him that we must go, Jean-Pierre wouldn't let us leave. The situation got so bad that we had to escape from the boat very early one morning without him noticing. It broke my heart to leave him, but I couldn't let Caroline down. And, anyway, he was going back to Paris soon. When I later tried phoning the boat from a phone box to apologise, I was told Jean-Pierre had left early as he was so upset about me leaving. Luckily, he had given me a phone number for his company in Paris, Sine Qua Non, so I could arrange to meet up with him there at some point in the future.

Caroline and I motored on to Italy, taking in Florence, Rome and Naples. There were some frightening incidents, like kids trying to steal stuff out of the car and even attempting to wrench the mirrors off the car bonnet. We certainly learned a lot about how to take care of ourselves!

From Brindisi we took the car ferry to Corfu where we rented a room in a tiny cottage from a farmer, which was just above the beach in Paleokastritsa. There was hardly anyone else there, just a few other very poor travellers like us on the beaches. It was so lovely and cheap that we stayed there for about ten days. On Corfu I was taught another big lesson, this time about cars: my Spitfire, being so low on the ground, got stuck in a rough country lane. We couldn't budge it, and thought we'd be stuck there forever. Eventually some farmers came along, laughed mightily at our predicament, and just picked up the car.

Greece was very different in those days, as it was still under military control, after the overthrow of the monarchy. Yugoslavia, too, was no picnic. We nearly ended up in prison – or worse…

We were driving north towards Dubrovnik, happily cruising along with the roof down and enjoying the balmy weather, when we joined a queue of traffic. Suddenly a few cars in front of us stopped dead, with no warning. Thankfully I managed to screech to a halt, only just missing the car in front, but – on looking in my rear-view mirror, certain my little car would be smashed into – I saw the car behind swerve to miss me, but so violently that it ended up upside down in the ditch beside us...

Caroline and I immediately jumped out of my car to see if we could help, as the car was packed with five rather large adults. But they all turned on us, gesturing that it was my fault for causing their accident, raising their hands and fists at us. It was terrifying – we were convinced we were going to be attacked. By this time the rest of the traffic had moved on, so it was just us, with Caroline and I trying desperately to explain that we'd had no option but to stop, but they either didn't understand or didn't want to.

I reached a point where I couldn't keep arguing, so I said flatly, "Let's call the police."

One of them, a huge burly man, straightened himself up as he climbed out of the car and said, "I *am* the police."

Caroline and I looked at each other in horror.

"We don't want to end up in prison for something we haven't done," whispered Caroline.

I nodded.

In that moment we seemed to speak to each other without words. For a second or two time seemed to stand still. Then we both turned, raced back to the car, and leapt in. There was a shout behind us. I know my heart was thumping and I'm sure Caroline's was too. One of the men dashed forward and tried to grab the keys out of the ignition. At the same moment, a big angry woman loomed up on the other side of the car and tried to snatch Caroline's bag. I frantically turned the key in the ignition, praying the car would start, and – hallelujah – it did! We screeched off with Caroline hanging on for dear life to her bag, as it contained her passport and cash.

Luckily the straps broke, leaving Caroline with the bag and the woman with just the straps. I put my foot down and drove as fast as I could. We didn't look back.

Thankfully they couldn't chase us, but they had our description and that of the car, probably even the number plate. After a while, we pulled over, put the roof up and put scarves on – trying to disguise ourselves. It seems funny now, but it wasn't at the time. It was probably hours before we stopped shaking.

We continued north via Skopje, Mitrovica, Budva, Kotor. The

countryside here was quite bleak, and we only ever saw farmers and people working in the fields. As usual we attracted a lot of attention from the children and, as in Naples, they were quite frightening, trying to steal from us whenever we stopped.

In Dubrovnik, we parked the car outside the main city, hiding it as much as possible under some trees, then walked into town and found a good B&B built into the old wall. We stayed there a few days, taking in the amazing culture. It should have been a lovely stay, because the architecture was stunning and there were so many beautiful ancient sites but, after the incident with the car, our visit was marred by the continual fear of being arrested, or found and beaten up. I think we spent most of our waking moments looking over our shoulders for burly men and a woman with broken handbag straps in her fist!

Eventually, we wound our way back through Vienna and Salzburg to civilisation. Caroline went back to the United Kingdom, while I was reunited with Jean-Pierre in Paris. I realised how deeply I felt for him, and him for me, so I moved in with him.

Jean-Pierre Rassam and his mother (Photo from author's personal collection)

Jean-Pierre always lived in hotels, so when I arrived in Paris we lived in the penthouse suite of the Hôtel de l'Université (the first hotel he lived in as a young film producer; later moving to the much grander Plaza Athénée Hôtel) in Saint-Germain, on the Left Bank, and ate breakfasts at the Café de Flore and dinners at the Brasserie Lipp, often with French film stars like Jean Yanne and Anna Karina. Brasserie Lipp was the famous hang-out for the artistic and intellectual crowd, and I met some fascinating people with Jean-Pierre. Thankfully I had my car in Paris, so I could regularly visit my chums there. I became very close to JP's mother, and his sister Anne-Marie (who was married to the famous film director and producer Claude Berri). Both told me they had never seen JP so much in love as he was with me.

And we *were* in love. Jean-Pierre was charisma personified and I was dazzled by him – and the sex was out of this world. But I soon learned that he played horrendous mind games. He would declare undying love one minute, then change his mind. He'd beg me to marry him, over and over again. I had no thoughts of marriage, but I eventually said yes because the passion and the intensity was so strong. He'd literally swept me off my feet. But the minute I said I would marry him, he changed his mind again!

What is it with these men who seek to take over your very soul? It feels dark, not loving – more like a determination to possess… I'd never been treated in such a way before and I think this coloured my lack of trust with future boyfriends. Some men seem to love the chase but aren't prepared for the reality of marriage.

I really was on an emotional rollercoaster, but the good times more than made up for the moving floor beneath my feet when I was with Jean-Pierre.

Then one evening we went to a party and met Mick and Bianca Jagger…

From my 1971 diary:

20th September: Met Mick Jagger and his wife Bianca. She's very pregnant. Someone told them I'm a Norland Nurse so they asked me to be their nanny. Bianca said she was fed up with interviewing so many unsuitable nannies and really wanted me. I said no, I was happy with my boyfriend, but gave them my number at the hotel in case I got fed up with Jean-Pierre.

22nd September: Had tea with Mick and Bianca Jagger on the terrace of their suite on the top floor of L'Hôtel. If I take the job it will start in about 2 months' time. I gave them details for my previous employer so they can get a reference. Bianca seemed to have no idea when the baby was due and kept clutching her stomach saying, "Meek, Meek, ze baby is coming," when nothing of the sort was happening!

Mick Jagger and Bianca Pérez-Mora Macías, taken on their engagement, 1970
(© Patrick Lichfield, with kind permission) (Photo was a gift to Sally from Mick and Bianca)

I sometimes wonder about fate and how it brings people together. Mick told me that he'd written to the Norland Nursery Training College saying he had previously had a Norland Nurse when he was with Marianne Faithfull, for her son. He told them that, now his wife was expecting a baby, he'd like another Norland Nurse. He then showed me a letter from Norland's principal, Miss Keymer, saying she 'would like to recommend a nurse called Sally Arnold, and I am trying to find her'. What a coincidence!

Mick said, "Look, it's fate. You've got to come and work for us!"

I learned later he phoned one of my previous employers. She told me recently that she was so surprised when he called because he didn't give his name and spoke to her in a rather uncouth way, and she wondered, how can Sally work for somebody who speaks like that? Strangely, Mick spoke the Queen's English in private and with only a couple of people around, but the minute there were more or he was on the phone, he'd switch to the sort of Mockney accent we all know today.

My impression at the time was how normal Mick and Bianca seemed. He was very attentive, pouring tea, carrying and fetching things for her. She was so beautiful. I had never seen a woman with such perfect skin, teeth, hair, figure – everything.

I still didn't want the job, though – mainly because of Jean-Pierre. But fate kept bringing me back into the Jaggers' orbit. In September of that year I met up with my friend Judi, another Norlander. We went to L'Hôtel, where we bumped into Mick. He said he would phone me later that evening, and so we kept in touch. He kept saying that he and Bianca really wanted me as their nanny.

Meanwhile, things were deteriorating with Jean-Pierre. As summer turned towards autumn, I spent quite a bit of time with Mme Rassam, his mother, at her beautiful apartment in Neuilly-sur-Seine, a very upmarket suburb to the west of Paris (where the Duke and Duchess of Windsor lived). We had always got on really well and she began to confide in me. She was so worried about him and showed me piles of bills for thousands of dollars that he owed. As I was now beginning to get extremely annoyed with the emotional games JP was playing, I eventually drew on my reserves of self-confidence to tell him I didn't love him any more. He was devastated and begged me to reconsider, but I was firm. I think it was at that point that I made the decision to take the job with the Jaggers.

I couldn't stay with JP any more, so quickly packed and phoned the Jaggers: "I'll take the job," I said. "But I have to go back to England to sort things out first, but I'll be back soon."

Mick and Bianca were delighted, and we agreed to stay in touch – and that I'd be back to take up the position as their nanny after the baby was born.

Back at home with my parents in England in late October, I was woken up at about 3am by my sister. She came running into my bedroom shouting, "You've got a little girl! You've got a little girl!"

"What?" I rubbed the sleep out of my eyes, heart pounding at the suddenness of being jerked out of a deep sleep. "What are you talking about?"

"It was on the radio!" she cried.

The Jaggers had had a baby girl on the 21st. My new job was about to begin.

Chapter 4

Life with the Jaggers

From my 1971 diary:

> 23rd October: Well, it was in the papers today. I phoned the clinic in Paris and spoke to Bianca. Phoned again in the evening and spoke to both of them. I received my travelling expenses from the Stones' accountant, £3 for my train ticket from Dorset to London, and £12.90 for my air ticket to Paris. He wrote: 'The above expenses, I am informed, relate to your new post with Mr and Mrs Mick Jagger.'

Mick phoned and said he'd get a room somewhere for me and that maybe his driver would meet me. So, I caught an 8pm flight from London to Paris. I arrived at Orly Airport, but nobody met me, so I took a taxi to L'Hôtel, where Mick had left a message for me to go to Hotel Danube. I phoned him to say I'd arrived. I think I put something pithy in my diary that night: *He's bloody lucky that I'm confident enough to find my own way around Paris.* Too right!

The next day Alan Dunn, Mick's driver, phoned to say hello and make plans for driving me to the clinic. When I got close to Bianca's private room, I could hear a baby crying and crying. The plaintive sounds echoed all along the corridors. And there she was, little Jade, in a separate room all on her own, with the sun streaming in, right on her. It was blazing hot. No wonder she was in such distress. I scooped her up in my arms and told her I would look after her from now on. She was the sweetest baby, very petite with darkish hair.

I stayed there for a few hours with the baby and Bianca. Later, Mick and his brother, Chris, turned up, and Mick gave me money to buy some necessary things for the baby. The next few days were a busy blur of shopping for baby supplies, being in and out of the clinic, feeding and changing Jade, Mick lunching with Bianca and then racing off to register the baby's birth.

I packed and by 3.30pm on 29ᵗʰ October we were ready to leave the clinic. I carried the baby out, only to be faced with a wall of noise and flashing lights. Fans and photographers were everywhere! In between signing records and pictures for the fans, Mick kept telling me to hide Jade's face as he wanted to take the pictures himself for the press.

Letter to my parents, 29ᵗʰ October, L'Hôtel, 13 Rue des Beaux-arts, Paris V:

Mick and Bianca are both very nice and have been super to me so far – and – contrary to our ideas – they are really crazy about each other. I did some shopping for the baby in the afternoon, and in the evening went out with Alan and Chris. And onto a club with Chris. Don't worry, I won't have an affair with my boss's brother!

We're now here at the hotel and when Mick goes to Antibes tomorrow we're going to stay at Nathalie Delon's apartment 'til next weekend – then we're going to a chateau in Antibes. Apparently we're only going to be there for a couple of months.

Alan told me that it's impossible to plan more than a few weeks in advance, because things are always changing. He also told me that we're going to America soon – he thinks – and he wouldn't be surprised if we spent Christmas with Bianca's parents in Nicaragua. So – it all sounds exciting, doesn't it? He also mentioned maybe going to Japan and Russia.

Jade's very good so far. She's with them at the moment and has just had her 6pm feed. So I'll go and get her at about 8pm – wash her and feed her again at 9pm. The clinic's routine was 3-hourly feeds, but I'm hoping to change that to 4-hourly soon.

Judi (my nanny chum) is back in Paris now, but I don't think she's too happy in her job with a Greek shipping family – who treat her like a servant. At least I'm thought of as one of the family – in fact, Alan just said that the family hadn't increased by one, but by two – which made me feel very happy. Even though Alan's the driver, he's also Mick's right-hand man.

Living in a small hotel room with a baby wasn't easy. I had to wash the nappies (diapers) in the bath, then dry them by spreading them around the bedroom and bathroom. There were no disposable nappies then, just the terry towelling outer ones, with the softer muslin inner ones. I also had to use a strange metal contraption for boiling the bottles, when Norland had taught us to use Milton for sterilisation. Never mind. I managed.

On 31st October we went to Nathalie Delon's apartment where we would be staying for a while, a luxurious living space filled with white suede-covered sofas and chairs. Nathalie was a sweet and thoughtful lady and a good friend of Bianca's. When they were together they reminded me of giggling children enjoying each other's company.

Sleep had become a distant memory with the baby waking throughout the night, but I quickly slipped into the routine of feeds, bath time, and nappies.

Working with a small baby meant I was often covered with regurgitated milk, which was one of the reasons I chose to wear my Norland uniform. The pale beige dress with its crisp white collar was hard-wearing and practical. It also meant I didn't have to compete with the gorgeous outfits Bianca wore. However, I hadn't appreciated the fascination my uniform held for men until Omar Sharif walked in one day. He was there to visit Nathalie but was quite taken by my outfit and kept trying to sit next to me on the sofa!

During the short time we spent at Nathalie's, we formed a friendship. One where I felt comfortable asking her opinion on JP.

"I like Rassam a lot, although…" she trailed off and I knew what she was going to say next. "He's completely mad and dreadful to people, so be careful. Don't get your heart broken."

From my 1971 diary:

> 6th November: V. busy. We were supposed to be leaving – but didn't! Bianca went out in the afternoon. Had quite a heart-to-heart with Alan about Mick & Bianca and their relationship. Spoke to Jean-Pierre for the first time in ages. He said everything was alright and that he doesn't enjoy sex with anyone except me! He's only saying this as he knows I'm leaving Paris soon!

We left Nathalie's a day later than expected and, even then, nearly missed our flight because Bianca forgot her massive, beautiful engagement ring!

As abrupt, violent shifts rocked the plane, Bianca and I clung onto each other until we were on solid ground. It was like riding a rollercoaster without breaking for sudden twists and drops. This was a normal, regular, daily flight from Paris to Nice, not a private plane.

Mick met us at the airport. "How was your flight?"

"It was terrible!" cried Bianca. "Sally and I clung to each other the entire time. I didn't know if we were going to make it. What would you do if I died?"

"I'd cry," he said, sweet and full of love.

Despite the house's address being Bastide du Roi in Antibes, it was on a hill three miles inland in the middle of nowhere. It was owned by the Comte and Comtesse Polignac, relatives of the Monaco royal family. It was a typical French chateau, very large and imposing outside, and the numerous rooms inside were quite difficult to navigate.

I worked hard to get into a routine with Jade. Up early, bathe the baby, weigh her, give her a feed at 9am. Then downstairs to breakfast. I always seemed to eat on my own, as everyone else was always asleep until about

Sally with Mick, Bianca and baby Jade
(Photo from author's personal collection)

2pm. Then I seemed to spend hours rushing from one end of the house to the other, washing clothes and nappies, hanging them out to dry, and ironing them. I had a different room for doing different things. It felt a very difficult house to work in. I had lunch at 1pm, alone again although the housekeeper, Mme Villars, was very sweet to me. Then Mick and Bianca would get up. Bianca fed Jade at 3pm, 6pm and 9pm. I did her last feed at 11.30pm and she regularly slept through the night. At midnight I was ready to fall exhausted into my bed, and then it was up again at dawn. No wonder I was always so tired!

Jade and I stayed on the top floor alongside Alan. There must have been at least eight more rooms on our floor alone. We each had our respective bedrooms and private bathrooms with a little sitting room that we shared. The view from my bedroom window showed snow-capped mountain tops, and the weather was crisp and fresh like spring.

Outside my room was an ornate marble staircase that led to the Jaggers' floor below which had five bedrooms and five bathrooms for the two of them. They seemed to use different rooms every night – and separate ones sometimes. A massive, elegant spiral staircase led downstairs to the ground floor.

Having separate rooms for laundry, cleaning, and ironing made working difficult. I spent my days rushing from one end of the house to the other. After eight hours of hustle and bustle before the Jaggers had even gotten out of bed, I was exhausted. Sometimes in the evenings Bianca would take over feeding the baby.

No matter how unpredictable the days were, like clockwork I'd be up at about 7am and the routine of running around remained a constant. When I realised I couldn't remember the last time I got to bed before midnight, I decided to change Jade's routine.

From my 1971 diary:

11th November: Busy day again. Alan up at midday. Others up around 2pm. Bianca told me to bring Jade indoors at midday – regardless of weather. Such a pity, as the weather at this time of year in this area is wonderful and perfect for a baby to be out in for a short while.

Mme Villars, the housekeeper, got upset when Bianca accused her of feeding the cats wrong, so she vowed never to work with the 'catsees' again. So my responsibilities as nanny had expanded to include caring for the cats and goldfish as well. I had to feed them all now, and change the water in the fish tank. Also give eye drops to the cats…which was quite a performance!

Jade was already a month old by mid-November and so much had happened in a short period. We had a lovely day celebrating, taking Polaroid and cine cameras out in the garden. Bianca looked so elegant in her dark brown velvet gown over her nightclothes. It was stunning – not like a normal dressing gown at all. Later Bianca told me that Mick didn't want me to have a baby alarm, but he told me I could have one. Like many couples, sometimes they contradicted each other, which I found quite confusing.

A few days later, Bianca approved my request for a few hours off, which I spent in Cannes with Alan. Apparently, he spoke with them about my needing a proper day off, which I really appreciated.

The Côte d'Azur wasn't the most exciting place this time of year and Bianca was starting to feel the effects of being in the middle of nowhere with nothing to do, especially as Mick was out so much making *Exile on Main Street* with the rest of the band over at Keith Richards' chateau. She buzzed me one night to say we might be going to Paris for the next week or so. I didn't mind at all since I might get to see Jean-Pierre.

He had been busy working on a new movie with Jane Fonda and Yves Montand, *Tout Va Bien* but, the last time we spoke, he promised not to marry anybody else and invited me to stay on the yacht with him in Cannes next May.

Bianca didn't say anything more about going to Paris, just that it was very cold there. She and Mick went down with a bad cold, then a couple of days later the doctor came to give Jade her BCG jab for tuberculosis, as we might be going to Nicaragua. Fortunately, everyone recovered quickly since I found out at the last minute we'd be leaving for Los Angeles in three days. That's how things operated, plans that were often made at the last minute.

I managed to get everything packed and ready to leave on such short notice, leaving everything neat and tidy in my area. From the amount of hand luggage we had, anyone would have thought we packed every item from the chateau. Admittedly, I had a lot myself, but that was mostly bottles and nappies to last for sixteen hours of travelling.

Early mornings were routine for me so, when the day came, I made sure everyone else was up and ready on time. We had a 9.30 flight to catch!

Chapter 5

To Los Angeles

Once again, Bianca and I were terrified because of the turbulence. This time Mick was there, trying to calm us down, despite being just as frightened and telling us that take-off is the most dangerous part! First, we flew to Paris, then dense fog in London caused our flight to be delayed. Mick Taylor and his family joined us in the Pan Am VIP lounge for a couple of hours. It seems their au pair thought I was a snob for wearing a uniform, but when it came to working with an infant, practicality trumped fashion.

For the flight from London to Los Angeles, Jade and I would travel tourist class while everyone else, including Keith Richards' and Anita Pallenberg's nanny, would travel first class. I didn't mind at all, as I'd prefer to be on my own for such a long flight.

During the flight Mick got into a row with the stewardess when he asked if Jade and I could upgrade to first class. There were empty seats there, but he refused to pay the extra cost, so we couldn't move. Mick just shrugged; he wasn't that bothered, and neither was I. Later there were newspaper headlines that exaggerated the whole thing, which made me realise for the first time how people like Mick are regularly misquoted. There was only a little arguing, and certainly no fisticuffs, as the papers claimed.

We eventually arrived in Los Angeles on 30th November, and exhaustion doesn't begin to describe the level of tired I was feeling. Fortunately, Jade was wonderful during the entire ordeal. The Beverly Wilshire Hotel was our new temporary 'home' until Mick and Bianca found a house they liked. This was meant to take a few days, but it actually took a few weeks.

America was a whole new world to me. I was in Beverly Hills, California! We had rooms at the Beverly Wilshire Hotel on Wilshire Boulevard on the east side of South Rodeo Drive. Rod Stewart and the Faces were in the rooms opposite mine and I'd often bump into Warren Beatty in the lift, as he lived in a suite on the top floor. But I was most fascinated by the television – here there were ten films each day, dozens of other shows each morning, and thirteen channels. Then again, every time I looked up, it was an advert. The programmes were shorter than the ads! In those days, there were only three channels in England, and they all went off by 11pm.

The first night wasn't the greatest. Poor baby Jade was jet-lagged after such a long flight, crying at odd hours, and sleeping sporadically. I also found it difficult to adjust, but for different reasons. The transition from having separate rooms for different chores to a single hotel room proved difficult – the bedroom and bathroom were strewn with nappies for a while, just as at L'Hôtel in Paris.

"Pack up Jade's things," Bianca suddenly announced. "We're going to New York. I'm tired of this place!"

It had only been a day since we checked into the Beverly Wilshire Hotel. I phoned Mick at the studio, as I was concerned about Jade flying again so soon after such a long transatlantic flight. She was only a few weeks old and, in my professional opinion, it was not good for such a young baby to be travelling yet again. Fortunately Mick understood.

When I asked Bianca why she wanted to go to New York, she said, "Mick's always busy, either recording with the band, or eating with them so I hardly ever see him." She was bored without him.

In the end, we didn't go, which was a relief.

From my 1971 diary:

> 3rd December: Still in the hotel. Took Jade up onto the roof garden for a while – but it was rather cold. Met Charlie Watts, who seems very nice.

> 4th December: Fans and people calling all day today! Saw Stewart Granger and Carol Channing in the hotel. Went for a walk in Rodeo Drive, but had to carry Jade as I still had no pram. I didn't wear my uniform as I didn't want to be stared at!

On 10th December, Mick and Bianca started to look at houses. One of them was a house William Randolph Hearst, aka Citizen Kane, built for his mistress, Marion Davies. However, Bianca said it was old and falling to pieces. Life in such a famous household could feel chaotic at times. There were so many comings and goings, urgent meetings, late night phone calls, and a variety of visitors – Genevieve Waite, the soon-to-be wife of John Phillips of the Mamas and the Papas, came in with Bianca one day. Sometimes we seemed to be about to leave for New York, but then trips were called off at the last minute. There were flurries of house-hunting activity but we still stayed in the hotel. This might feel exciting for some people, but I found I craved stability, especially for the baby. I felt I had to learn to survive the drama and uncertainty.

As soon as one fire was put out, another arose. Mick's guitar and coat were stolen from the studio and his ex-girlfriend and mother of his daughter Karis, Marsha Hunt, called from London asking for money. That same day, Mick had sent Nancy – a girl who worked for the Stones' record producer – to collect his harmonica from the hotel suite. There was no sign of it anywhere, despite a thorough search. We never did find the harmonica, but I did find a friendship when Nancy offered to show me around LA if I ever had any free time. Nancy is still a very good friend of mine and has helped me with these memoirs. She has reminded me that we overheard Mick shouting at Allen Klein when he visited, reminding him that he'd been sacked, and they wanted nothing more to do with him.

From my 1971 diary:

> 16th December: Jade is 8 weeks old. I phoned Nancy about a day off and she suggested either a weekend or Boxing Day – that's if I can get some time off.

Letter to my parents, 21st December, Beverly Wilshire Hotel:

> Well – we're still in this wretched hotel & I don't know when we're moving, but here's an address you can write to me: c/o Marshall Chess (of Chess Records). I sent you a telegram the other day – just to say that I'll be phoning soon. In fact I'm going to try & book the call.

It had been a while since I'd spoken to my family. Back then, long-distance calls had to be booked through the international operator, and I was still waiting for the 'okay' to call home. It took a lot of back and forth before Mick and Bianca finally agreed to let me call at Christmas, which was just around the corner.

There were also still a lot of questions about when and where we'd be moving. One day, Mick said we'd be moving into the Citizen Kane house, but we had to wait until the previous occupants moved out. The next day, there was talk of moving into the actor Laurence Harvey's house, and then Elvis Presley's house was offered to them. Honestly, I was hoping we'd move into Elvis's house!

On 23rd December, Mick told me we'd be moving the next day, after we'd been in the hotel nearly a month. We spent Christmas Eve moving into 414 St Pierre Road, Bel Air (aka the Citizen Kane house). Mick and Bianca weren't kidding when they called this place the 'mad house'. It was huge and guarded behind large wooden gates, not locked, nor electric as they are nowadays. With Buddha statues, altars, painted ceilings, sculptures, and Chinese hangings everywhere…the word 'strange' doesn't cover it. This vast property was falling to pieces, covered in dust, with ants everywhere. Apart from that, it had a lot of charm.

Once through the front door, there was a huge kitchen to the right, and a massive dining room directly ahead, where large French windows opened onto a terrace. Another set of French windows opened onto the terrace in the hallway that ran the length of the house. Directly to the left of the front door was an imposing wooden staircase. The hall led into a large, but cosy, drawing room/library with a massive fireplace with a gas fire. This was the first time I had ever seen a fireplace like this – no need to worry about starting a fire, just turn on the gas and load the logs!

A smaller, private staircase led up to Mick and Bianca's suite of rooms at that end of the house. I had my choice of bedroom and, of course, I chose the one farthest away from theirs. My smaller suite was above the kitchen, accessed by the big staircase. Between my room and theirs was the guest room where Alan would stay when he visited, as well as others like Charlie Watts, with another guest room next to mine. Interestingly I've noticed that many authors who have written Mick Jagger's biographies, even the renowned Philip Norman, have stated this house had something like twenty bedrooms. It didn't. It had five, each with an adjoining bathroom.

There was a jungle-like garden full of rocks and pools, and the swimming pool itself was incredible – two enormous pools were connected by a river and a waterfall, which had two bridges crossing it. Apparently, it hadn't been filled since 1930 because it was too expensive to run.

Rochelle, the housekeeper, had worked there for twenty-two years and I can't imagine how difficult it must have been for one person to clean such a massive house. She was a warm and friendly African-American lady who told Mick about the term Tumblin' Dice – from her games of dice with her friends – which he mentions in a documentary.

Late on Christmas Eve Mick and Bianca went shopping and came back with masses of food: a turkey, a ham, dates, nuts, even an English Christmas pudding. Plus, a tree, decorations and lights.

On Christmas Day, the scent of simmering onions and spices filled the air as Mick and I prepared a traditional English Christmas lunch. Bianca thought we were crazy for making everything as English as possible, but I was happy to have a sense of 'home' after all the upheaval.

It was quite surreal – the three of us sitting at one end of the massive dining table to enjoy our turkey, roast potatoes, bread sauce, and Christmas pudding. The couple was smiling, loving, and affectionate to one another.

When it came to presents, I was astonished at the sophisticated way they had wrapped the presents – in black tissue paper with white satin ribbons. At home, we'd just reuse old Christmas wrapping paper again and again, year after year. They gave Jade a gold ring and a jade egg, and me a Gucci leather wallet, one of Bianca's old jackets from Yves Saint Laurent, and a cowboy shirt.

They went out that evening, leaving me in that big, creepy mansion alone with the baby. I tried to be brave but with every creak my imagination ran wild. I was resolute at first, but then got the horrors and went to bed.

I was allowed a few hours off on Boxing Day, so I took Nancy up on her offer to hang out. After doing the laundry and fighting a colony of ants that morning, it was nice to take a lunch break at a restaurant in Malibu. It was great to have some time off, and Nancy and I discovered that we had so many things in common, like horseback riding.

My routine now was up at 8am, bathe the baby, weigh her and feed her at 9am. Usually I would try to take her through to Bianca so she could feed her, but she was often still asleep. Then I would have my own breakfast, and the rest of the day was washing clothes and nappies, hanging them out to dry, and ironing them. Then Mick and Bianca would start getting up and she would sometimes do the next feeds, unless she was going out or was away. I would do the last feed at 11.30pm, and Jade would sleep through the night by this time, thank goodness.

The 'mad house' had some regular guests that I had the pleasure of getting to know. When Keith Richards and Anita Pallenberg would come by, Anita would spend a long time with me and Jade in the upstairs nursery. Genevieve, John Phillips' fiancée, called about bringing a pram soon, which I was grateful for. I still didn't have a pram or pushchair, so I had to carry Jade everywhere and, at two months old, she was getting a bit heavy.

(Around this time Genevieve and John Phillips mentioned their nine-month-old son and said that they were looking for a nanny. The monthly salary was $350, and I almost took the job – especially since I still hadn't been paid properly – but instead I said I'd reach out to two of my Norland friends.)

Thankfully, I didn't have to wait too long for the pram as Genevieve and John soon came around with an English Pedigree, which had belonged to Mama Cass herself. John stayed behind and helped me set up the pram while everyone else went out. He was the first person ever to offer me cocaine, plus some grass, both of which I declined. I had never tried coke before and was quite scared, especially as I had a baby to care for. He also invited me to his New Year's Eve party, and that I wanted to go to, if I was allowed.

Along with offering me the drugs, John also showed me where a gun was hidden. Cocaine was one thing, but a gun in the house? Bloody hell! The small, loaded handgun was tucked away on top of some books on the bookshelf.

He and Mick went out to buy a guitar later that evening, and Bianca disappeared, leaving Genevieve alone. Seeing how upset she was, I stayed with her, and we talked for quite a while. To say it was awkward would be an understatement. Genevieve was sweet but we really had nothing in common, so it was quite an effort for me to keep her occupied.

Mick came into my room at 9am the next day, which surprised me. It was the first time I had seen him up so early, or maybe he hadn't even gone to bed. My first thought was that he and Bianca were having another argument, but instead, he asked, "Can you show me how to change nappies and how to bathe Jade?"

Delighted, I said, "Of course!"

Watching him trying to hold a wriggling baby was a sight to see.

He was fantastic and wanted to figure out a way for me to go to John and Genevieve's party, but Bianca wasn't too keen, although I ended up going. I think Mick just said something to Bianca like, "Come on, why not let Sally go?" But I didn't really enjoy it, as I didn't know anybody.

From my 1972 diary:

> New Year's Day 1972: Mick is quite poorly with a sore throat, so Bianca and I had a look, and his throat really was very red and swollen.

It's well documented that Mick and Bianca's relationship was volatile. They were both young, beautiful people living in the lens of celebrity. There was so much pressure on them, and that would put a strain on any relationship. In early January, things became intense. One day, Bianca packed her bags. I wasn't sure if Jade and I were supposed to go with her. Mick seemed tired of the games, and assured me he wouldn't let Bianca take Jade. Hearing that was a relief, as I could imagine us getting to New York and coming right back again.

Poor Mick. Bianca did go to New York, and he was terribly unhappy. One morning, I sat on the stairs with a teary-eyed Mick as he strummed his guitar, with him recalling how he met Bianca. Eddie Barclay had taken her to a Stones' concert, and at the after-party Mick had a *coup de foudre* and fell in love with her instantly. He even told me he had kept the piece of paper on which she had written her name and phone number. I couldn't believe he kept it for so long. That was so romantic. I don't think she ever knew how deeply in love he was with her.

He also told me he was thinking of having his tonsils out, as he kept getting tonsillitis, but he was worried it might change his singing voice.

He also told me he was thinking of having a gemstone put in one of his teeth. Not an emerald, as that would look too much like spinach…and a ruby was too dark and would look like a rotten tooth! I think he eventually opted for a diamond.

While Bianca was away, Mick and John decided to have a party just a few days later, which lasted until 3am. What a noise! Nancy had brought her friend Pat, who spent the night with Mick. Again, this was what proved to me that no matter how much a man loves his wife, he will still sleep with someone else; thus reaffirming my decision never to be a wife. I didn't join in with the party, as I had Jade to look after.

Rumours spread like wildfire; some even suggested Bianca had gone off to be with Ryan O'Neal. None of us knew what the truth was. Later, of course, it became part of the divorce proceedings, in which I testified, but at the time we didn't know what was happening. It was a terrible time for Mick, but Bianca did come back a few days later.

In early January, when Bianca got back, we all went to John and Genevieve's house on Malibu beach for lunch. On our return home, Donald Cammell was waiting for Mick (Cammell was director of the film *Performance*, which Mick and Anita were in).

With the Stones' tour coming up, it was time to start the visa process. Downtown Los Angeles was an eye-opener for me, being nothing like London. It was just so modern, so different from the ancient buildings of London, and busy, busy, busy with massive cars, buses and trucks – a contrast to the peace and quiet up the hill in Bel Air. Although Bel Air was rather boring, with nothing to do, it was very calm and had fresh air. There was nowhere to walk, only along the roads, although there was what some called a local 'park', but it was just a bit of grass in the middle of the road junction – called Dog Shit Park!

Going to the visa office with Mick and Bianca was quite an experience. It was a typically stark, open-plan, bureaucratic office with nasty strip lighting, very cold and clinical. Everybody was staring at them, and probably at me too in my Norland uniform.

But we were too late and couldn't get the visas that day. Mick and Bianca didn't seem to realise that some places wouldn't stay open just for them, as it had closed just before we got there. So we went back a few days later, and afterwards Bianca and I took a stroll down Sunset Boulevard and had lunch at The Source. She and I were getting along really well at this time, giggling together while shopping and eating. At this stage I was really enjoying the job.

From my 1972 diary:

> 9th Jan: At last I got some time off. Nancy picked me up at 3pm, we went to see a film, and I stayed the night at her lovely apartment. It was bliss to have a good long sleep. We went to a fabulous shop, Mister Frank on Santa Monica Boulevard, then went horse-riding in the Hollywood hills. A day off at last!

> 11th Jan: A prospective temporary nanny came for an interview. Not much good. Bianca keeps changing her mind about what she wants. I suggested a friend of Rochelle's, but when we'd arranged it, Bianca said no – so I give up. Charlie Watts arrived today. I'd originally met him at the chateau in France, and he was always one of the few people who was always really friendly and nice to me. We just chatted about normal everyday things – how's the baby doing etc.

The early months of 1972 brought a noticeable change in the way things were. For various reasons, it began to feel as if the job might not work out for the long term. I wasn't unhappy with my work, and I adored Jade, but issues kept popping up.

As the days went on, the stranger things became. One evening Bianca and I were watching TV when we were interrupted by the unexpected sound of the doorbell echoing throughout the mansion. Since we weren't expecting any visitors, we were startled by the noise. Keeping quiet, Bianca crept over to the bookcase and grabbed the loaded gun. My nerves were frayed as I followed her to the door. I wasn't sure who or what I expected to see but was relieved when no one was there.

"Don't worry, Sally. It was nothing."

Still, it was a bit frightening seeing Bianca shaking like a leaf while holding a gun, and I was thankful the new bodyguard would be arriving soon. Tony, our last bodyguard, didn't work out too well. To say he was horrible would be an understatement. Bianca refused to get into the car with him, and his arrogant and rude behaviour spread to Genevieve and other guests. He would go around the house acting like he owned it, drinking Mick's whisky and wine, and smoking Bianca's cigarettes. I wasn't scared of him, but I disliked him; he thought he was irresistible, and I had a hard time convincing him otherwise!

From my 1972 diary:

> 14th Jan: Went shopping with Rochelle. I'm in a very bad mood 'cos still no temp for Sunday. An Italian woman phoned for the temp position – she sounded nice, but Bianca didn't call her back.

> 15th Jan: The Italian woman came for an interview & was very fussy & soppy over Jade, but she came anyway, so I got my evening off. Mad rush to get ready.

On the 19th Charlie Watts took me and Jade shopping at Century City. He helped me order a baby seat and bouncer. We were supposed to be going to the doctor in the afternoon, but Bianca didn't return in time. She wasn't very happy about our shopping trip, saying she didn't want Jade in the smog of LA, although we'd been nowhere near the smog of downtown.

The next day, Bianca and I took Jade to the doctor for her triple antigen (for diphtheria, tetanus, and whooping cough) and polio vaccinations. The doctor said, "Whoever has been looking after this baby has made a wonderful job of it."

I had recently discovered the Jaggers' secretary knew my friend, Jack Oliver, when they worked at Apple Records together in London. Jack was an old friend and a member of the Chocolate Watch Band with my good friend Gary Osborne (the songwriter who went on to write with Elton John). So, luckily, I now had two chums to hang out with on my days off, with Nancy at the Troubadour, and with Jack at the Aware Inn and the Whisky a Go Go.

The only drawback to taking a day off was the new temporary nanny. Even after I showed her everything, she *still failed* to follow Jade's routine. I would come back to find Jade hadn't eaten any solids. Sometimes, I felt that having a day of riding in the Hollywood Hills with Nancy wasn't worth the amount of work I'd have to do when I got back.

In the early days of my job, I had felt I was a friend, a partner in raising Jade. But as time went on, the atmosphere changed. I felt a bit taken for granted. There were bad moods – not mine – and tempers could be frayed. I wasn't getting enough time off and, sometimes, I felt like everyone was blaming me for everything. Even Wendle, the new driver, went mad, shouting that I hadn't let him in, when I didn't even know he was there. Then Mick asked why I *had* let some people in – when I didn't even open the door!

One highlight was Genevieve and John Phillips' Buddhist wedding ceremony, held in LA's Chinatown where a local Chinese restaurant was filled with the sounds of chanting monks. I don't think this was a normal, orthodox Buddhist wedding. Just an idea they thought was cool. I was grateful to the giggling bride – who was either nervous, stoned, or both – for letting me have Jack as my guest.

In February, I wrote a long letter to my parents, telling them all about various discussions I'd been having with Mick about health insurance and hospital bills. The American system was very different to ours and I did worry about how hospital bills would be paid if I was ever ill. In the end, I needn't have worried as I could sense my time with the Jaggers was coming to an end. I was young and I wanted proper time off and regular pay, not to mention proper insurance. I think any nurse would have asked for that.

Mick's driver and right-hand man, Alan Dunn, came back. His arrival was accompanied by a lighter, more relaxed atmosphere, like things were at the beginning. While I was showing him around, he mentioned that Mick and Bianca were behaving a bit strangely towards him. It was comforting to know it wasn't just me.

The band were all there one day for a photographic session for the cover of their album *Exile on Main Street*, and the secretary had brought some jewellery over for everybody – some specially-made small red and gold Rolling Stones lips logos on gold chains. Just a few for the band members and staff. Mick made sure I got one, which was really nice of him.

Then Bianca said she would be going to New York...*again*. She left on 7th February, after missing her plane every day for nearly a week.

Thankfully, we found a temporary nanny. Mrs Weld was the mother of movie star Tuesday Weld, and she was such a sweet person. Jade was well taken care of by her on the rare occasions I had some time off.

"Have you ever seen Elvis live? I have two free tickets, want to go?" Nancy asked.

Did I? Of course I did! So Mrs Weld came by early on the evening of 17th February.

After stopping by Nancy's, we made a quick detour to the Troubadour club, but Las Vegas was our destination. After a journey of just over four hours, we finally arrived at the Hilton International Hotel, where Elvis stayed on the 30th floor in the penthouse suite.

Elvis performed fifty-eight consecutive sold-out shows in 1969, breaking every attendance record in Las Vegas. He even continued breaking his records throughout the early 1970s, and I was privileged to witness his greatness in person on Saturday 19th February 1972.

It was finally time to see 'The King' and I was itching with anticipation. A roaring crowd clapped and cheered as the music started. Elvis took the stage, wearing black and looking very professional like the true showman he was! From 'CC Rider' to 'Closing Vamp', the whole night was fantastic (there were a few off-key moments, but the backing singers drowned them out). I'm forever grateful for Mrs Weld watching Jade; I wouldn't have missed that for the world.

After lunch and a brief tour of Vegas, we drove back through the desert to Los Angeles. A dense wall of smog that began seventy-five miles outside LA let you know you were approaching the city.

Letter to my parents, 21st February:

> I keep thinking about you with all those power cuts. It sounds really bad this time. I'm still hoping to get home soon. There are two possibilities – firstly that Bianca, me and Jade will go to Paris. Or that Mick and Bianca will go on holiday to Indonesia, and Jade and I might stay with you or with Mick's parents in Dartford.

I came home to find the house hectic with people rushing in and out of business meetings organising the Stones' next tour, which was just around the corner. Little did I know that I would be doing exactly that myself just a few years down the road. In the evenings everyone went out, and Bianca didn't come back for about a week. So once again, I found myself alone in the big, creepy mansion. Only, this time, my imagination wasn't running wild.

The phone rang.

A man on the other end of the line said he had stolen pictures from the car outside. He claimed somebody let him into the house and that's when he took the phone number. I thought it could be quite worrying, so I called Mick at the studio, but he said not to worry. Even Alan said that I was being silly. It's annoying when you feel you're not being taken seriously! Nobody seemed to realise how creepy it was here all alone in this weird mansion. Especially as the Charles Manson murders happened only a couple of years ago, and not too far away from Bel Air.

Many times I had to bite my tongue. In fact, Michael Caine once said that Bianca would argue about anything until you felt you were going mad. This is just what I experienced too. Eventually, crunch time came, and I knew I had to leave. At Norland, we had always been taught that we should leave if the children became too attached to us. This was beginning to happen. It was natural, because any child becomes attached to the person they spend the most time with. I could see how hurtful this was to Bianca, as it would be to any mother.

However, I couldn't just leave the Jaggers without a nanny, so I offered to stay until they hired somebody else. During the next few days, I interviewed candidates until I found the right one, a girl named Donna who accepted the job.

My last day with the Jaggers was Thursday 2nd March 1972. I had mixed feelings and was emotional about leaving. In all honesty, I felt a bit sorry for Bianca. She seemed quite lonely sometimes, especially as Mick was always so busy. And it can't have been much fun for her hanging out with the nanny when Mick was out.

Of all the rock and roll wives I met over the years, I was the most impressed by Bianca's future charitable work and her Bianca Jagger's Human Rights Foundation – good for her. I only saw her a few times in the following years, but we always got along well with a hello kiss.

Throughout my time with the Jaggers, Nancy remained a good friend and even invited me to stay at her apartment when I left them, and she even let me use her car (what a chum!).

While I was staying with her, we went to a concert by the prog rock group Yes. We didn't have tickets, so we decided to blag our way in! Back in the early days of my college years in London, the bass player, Chris Squire, and I dated for the whole summer. I thought I'd use that to my advantage when we arrived at the venue. In my most impeccable English accent, I approached security. "Excuse me, gentlemen. My husband's the bass player, Chris Squire, and I've misplaced my pass. Would you mind getting me through?" Quite hilariously, they believed me.

I managed to find Chris among the melee and confessed that I lied and said I was his wife. He laughed, "Well, you nearly were once!" We spent the night together – for old times' sake.

At twenty-two, I was having the time of my life, and I wanted to continue having fun with my friends in LA. Who could blame me? But, as much as I was enjoying myself, I knew real life had to kick in at some point.

I had an interview scheduled for another nannying position with a Mrs Rosenberg – you may know her as Joan Rivers. The house was very ornate and had gilt everywhere, and the sofas and easy chairs were covered with plastic, which struck me as odd, as it was the first time I'd seen anything like that. Her daughter, Melissa, was a toddler, but in the end, I decided against the job. I knew living in LA full-time was not for me. England was where I belonged, so I would go back and find a job.

Looking back, no matter how many opportunities I had to live in LA throughout my life, I could never do it. I've often wondered why I never wanted to stay. As great fun as it was, especially if one had an English accent, on reflection, I realised it all came down to missing my family too much.

An addendum to Jean-Pierre Rassam. I never did get to join him at the Cannes Film Festival again as I really had to work. However, we stayed in touch for years, regularly meeting up in Paris or London. The last time I saw him was in Paris on the Stones tour in 1976. His mother and sister asked me to try and help as JP was now addicted to heroin. I went to the weird, empty apartment where he was staying, and saw the ravages his heroin addiction were causing. I shouted and screamed that he was wasting his wonderful talent. But I couldn't help him. Nor could his mother or sister.

I left, never to see him again. In 1982 he was living with the film star Carole Bouquet and they had a son, Dmitri, who is now married into the Monaco royal family. JP would have loved that!

Sadly, JP died of an overdose in 1985 at only forty-three, in the Hôtel Plaza Athénée.

Chapter 6

New Horizons

In May of 1972, I returned from LA and never expected to see Mick and Bianca Jagger again...or so I thought.

After returning from LA, I bought a small flat in London, which turned out to be one of the best things I've ever done. Thanks to the inheritance I received from my grandfather I was able to get on the property ladder and, even though Chelsea was the place to be, I simply couldn't afford it; but I did manage to find a one-bedroomed flat with a small balcony in Hurlingham Road in Fulham.

My old friends Terry Harrison and Jasper Parrott, who ran Harrison/ Parrott, a management agency for classical musicians, asked me to do PR for them. It was on quite loose terms and part-time. Terry and Jasper are two of the best men I've ever known, being decent, honest and highly ethical. They looked after musicians like André Previn, Vladimir Ashkenazy, Radu Lupu, Kyung Wha Chung, Sheila Armstrong, Tom Allen, and Cristina Ortiz.

I used a small electric typewriter in my sitting room – not even one that was self-correcting! In the age of computers and instant everything, people have no idea how tedious even the slightest bit of typing was then, especially if you made a mistake. There was no liquid Tippex available to make corrections, only Tippex paper.

During that time, I had only my typewriter and the telephone – and I'm not talking about a smartphone that gives you instant access to information. We had nothing like that back then. At the time there weren't even any fax or telex machines. Just good old-fashioned telephones to make and receive phone calls, and a typewriter for all documents and correspondence.

Then I was given the chance of a lifetime which I really couldn't turn down...

To China

In the following I have used spellings contemporary in 1973:
Peking, Mao Tse-tung, etc.

My childhood dream was to travel the world, and live a good, fulfilling life, and I was well on my way to achieving that dream.

An aunt of mine worked at the Foreign Office in the Far Eastern department (she even had to sign the Official Secrets Act). Through her, I met a woman who was going to work at the British embassy in Peking as the Second Secretary. She was allowed to invite a limited number of friends or relatives, but as none of them wanted to go, she invited me.

During Mao Tse-tung's era, China was largely closed to any visitors; people were rarely allowed in, unless they were diplomats, of course. Since 1949, the Chinese borders were closed to most of the world because of the Chinese Revolution and communist takeover. It wasn't until 1978 that China opened its doors to foreigners and tourists, so going in the early 1970s was an astonishing event, and very, very different from what it is now.

Visiting Communist China was a rare opportunity. On the other hand, I didn't want to go alone. The journey was a big undertaking and could be risky for a young woman by herself. The only reason I got a visa was that I had this official invitation from the British embassy in Peking. I had two choices: either go alone or not go at all. And I really wanted to go, so I plucked up the courage to do this massive journey alone. Even with an invitation, I had to go through a lot of red tape. Travelling by train was my only option as I couldn't afford to fly (train travel is much more expensive today than flying, but it was different then). To get to Peking on the Trans-Siberian Express I had to obtain the necessary visas. So I went to the Russian embassy in London to get a Russian visa. But, oh no! They couldn't grant me one until they had my Chinese visa.

At the Chinese embassy in London, I was faced with another catch-22. I couldn't get my Chinese visa until I had my Russian one. For days, I went back and forth between the two embassies, queuing outside for hours. Eventually the Chinese relented, because of my invitation from the British embassy in Peking. Most of the hotel and travel arrangements were handled by Intourist, but it wasn't until I was on the trip that I realised much of what I had been told was unreliable. There was misinformation about money, train schedules, and visas. Since I couldn't read or understand Chinese script, I had no idea my Chinese visa was wrong until I was in the middle of Siberia many weeks later.

I packed everything up, rented out my flat and on 7th May 1973 I left from Liverpool Street Station for Peking. The first leg of this epic journey was to the Hook of Holland where I changed trains for Moscow, via Rotterdam, Hanover, Helmstedt, Berlin, into Poland and through Warsaw

InTourist Moscow Ltd invoice, 1973

and Minsk, arriving in Moscow on the 9th. This part, first class, cost £60.70, plus £17.25 for two nights' accommodation.

I wrote copious notes on airmail paper and sent them to my parents, who luckily saved them all, but I won't include them all here – they would probably fill a whole other book!

From my 1973 diary:

> 7th May: The train between Holland and Russia seems very European, although it is actually Russian. Am on my own at the moment in a 2-bunk compartment. Nice warm blankets & the door even has 2 locks! It was stifling at first, then they put on the air conditioning, so it ended up being freezing! The guard (who reeked of garlic) took my passport & ticket, and then made my bed for me. He also offered me tea – I think – as he didn't speak a word of English or French, so I've now dug out my Russian dictionary.

I arrived in Moscow on the dot of 4pm on 10th May. The station seemed very unprepossessing, with only about four platforms – although each seemed miles long. I wandered around for about fifteen minutes but couldn't see the Intourist desk. I was starting to get worried. I asked some soldiers if they spoke English – "*Niet!*"

Feeling close to tears, I heard a voice behind me. "Excuse me. I'm from Intourist." I nearly wept with relief. The Intourist rep carted me off to a car and I was whisked away to the Hotel Russia where I stayed for two nights and took in a ballet and a three-hour sightseeing tour.

First impressions of Moscow? Very few cars; enormously wide streets; a few trams; thousands of people on foot. I think the cars must have been taxis. The buildings were very big and there were enormous pictures of Lenin everywhere. I saw a few palaces in rather bad shape – everything with red flags outside – and a few of those beautiful churches with the gold domes. I had a great time, wandering around Red Square, visiting St Basil's Church with its utterly astonishing domes. I knew Ivan the Terrible had commissioned St Basil's, and had demanded the architect be blinded afterwards so he could never again create anything as beautiful.

Back at my hotel, I was told strictly, "No wodka in room, no food in room," by the Russian female guard on my floor. There was one on each floor, sitting at a desk in the corridor. Mine had filthy fingernails and her head wrapped in a dirty scarf. She treated me with utter disdain. Of course, I couldn't speak Russian, but I gave it my best try with my phrase book… but she wouldn't even meet me halfway. She just demanded to go through all my belongings every single time I returned to my room.

I had no choice but to eat in the hotel's dining room, but the food was very unappetising, to say the least. And that was even for foreigners. I knew it was far worse for the locals.

On 11th May, I was able to pick up my passport from the hotel front desk, where I'd had to hand it in on arrival, and take a taxi to the station to take the Trans-Siberian Express to Peking. My telegram to Elizabeth in Peking simply said: *Leaving Moscow 11th May.*

The Trans-Siberian Express departed Moscow late in the evening of 11th May, and arrived in Peking on 20th at a cost of £55.66 for a first/'soft' class ticket. (I had no choice on which class I travelled.) I was rapidly learning that time was elastic and inefficiency was rife, as the information from Intourist was frequently wrong. I'd discovered that the journey to Peking

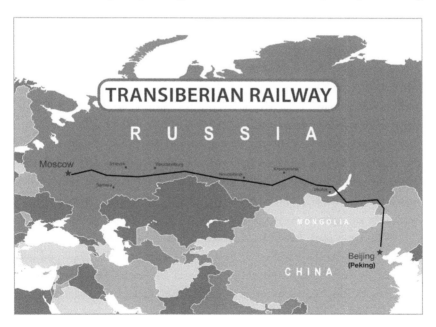

might take eight days, not six, and that the arrival time might be 8.12am, not 12.08pm as I'd been told in London.

Moscow station was just like you see in films, with steam gushing out from under the trains, all noise and smoke and barely lit, so everything was in a sort of yellowish haze. After walking the whole length of this very long train, I found Carriage 3 – my first class 'soft' compartment with four bunks. I was quite overwhelmed by it. Everything was so clean and the linen was obviously freshly washed and ironed. There were starched white tablecloths, clean curtains, and a little table light. I saw a long mirror on the door, and that the compartment was painted a pleasant pale green colour – altogether most pleasing and unexpected!

Thankfully the train was blissfully warm, so I thawed out. An extremely nice guard came and made up my couchette for me. He seemed to be a real gentleman. The toilet in the corridor was nothing to speak of, though – the floor permanently soaking wet, although they had decent loo paper. The worst thing was that the water for washing in was freezing and only dribbled out of the tap. I had to put up with this for nine days and nights!

The two guards (male *provodniks*') in my carriage were fantastic – making sure I was well looked after all the time. They were there for the whole journey. They showed me the samovar – a large hot water urn – in the corridor, which was on the go all the time. Every evening they would pull down my couchette, which was on the top level, and make it up with pristine clean white sheets and a nice pillow.

Occasionally local Russian farmers would share the compartment with me (when there was no room in 'hard' class) and some would kindly offer me some of their food. I would often wake up in the night only to look down on local Russian farmers playing cards – completely ignoring me! It was quite an experience – to say the least.

The train took me eastwards, day by day, via Novgorod, Omsk and Novosibirsk – which has one of the grandest stations in Russia – and onto Irkutsk. At every station the train driver and engineers would bang on the wheels with huge metal hammers to check for cracks in the metal, and to break up any ice that might collect when the train was stationary.

I am the first European to go through the Manchurian border since the Cultural Revolution

Everything changed at the border in Manchuria, northern China – literally. First, I noticed several very high and imposing lookout towers where uniformed Chinese and Russian guards stood with rifles. I had been made aware by my aunt that there were frequent 'wars' – more than skirmishes, from what I could ascertain – along this border, so it didn't overly surprise me. All passengers had to get off the train, as the carriages were jacked up – the original wheels wheeled out, and replaced with other wheels – as the railway-line gauge changed at this point. Fascinating. Obviously, I started taking photographs – until two officious Chinese soldiers rushed up to me, shouting, telling me to stop, and confiscated my camera.

They then hustled me off to some buildings, where I was put into a large, high room, with just one tiny window about 20 feet up the wall. No chance of seeing the outside at all. It was very frightening, and seemed to be some sort of prison cell… I soon discovered it was an interrogation room.

I waited for what seemed like hours, and it was really freezing. Eventually another Chinese man came and sat opposite me with my passport in his hand and said: "You are not allowed into China."

I was dumbstruck. What was he talking about?

"You have the wrong type of visa – one that says you are flying direct from London into Peking."

"But no," I said, "obviously I'm not. It was always the plan to take the train, as I did not have enough money to fly."

"You must go back to Moscow on another train," he said.

This went on and on, to and fro, neither of us willing to give in – especially not me. I was terrified at what would happen to me, stuck out in this remote, desolate outpost, which didn't even seem to have a town or village nearby, and nobody knowing where I was.

Impasse.

All I could do was plead and plead. Eventually, he relented, presumably because there wasn't another train for days. And anyway, what would he do with me in this place, which seemed to be home to about half a dozen soldiers? Also, I think he melted a little because I told him I couldn't afford the flight from London to Peking. Who knows?

He started chatting and said, "China is developing – England has already developed." He added that he hoped that China and England would become more friendly. One astonishing thing he told me was that I was the first European he had seen go through that particular border since the Cultural Revolution in 1966!

We ended up on quite good terms, and he wished me a good journey to Peking, praising Chairman Mao all the while. He also gave me a Chairman Mao badge, and Mao's Little Red Book, which I still have. And I even got my camera back, with the film intact of the photographs of the lookout towers.

Eventually, ten days after leaving Moscow, I arrived in Peking and the Min-Zu Hotel. There was a big wall inside the front door of the hotel which guests had to walk round, either to the left or right, to get to the lobby – this is to keep out the evil spirits.

The first thing I noticed about Peking was the hundreds of people on bicycles. The city was a sea of bicycles! The second thing I noticed was the absolute absence of cars. I saw hardly any traffic at all, only a very occasional taxi or official car. Everything was austere, clean, quiet…strange and other-worldly. And, of course, they were all, except a few soldiers in uniform, wearing the ubiquitous grey or blue Mao suits, which consist of a pair of shapeless, baggy trousers, a white shirt and a blue or grey jacket.

The only televisions I ever saw were in the hotel lobby, and all they ever showed were repeats of the various Communist May Day celebrations – absolutely nothing else – just these things repeated interminably. But I really didn't mind. I hadn't gone there for comfort, but to see this unique country at first hand. The only way I could phone home was to book it about five days in advance and, even then, the call could only last for about five minutes.

I cycled to the Forbidden City, the Temple of Heaven and many other sights around Peking, where I was continually stared at because of my blonde hair and brown eyes. Children would often pluck up the courage to touch my hair, which was so sweet! I also went on a champagne picnic to the Ming Tombs with the embassy staff.

The Great Wall was a surprise as it was so much bigger than I'd ever imagined. Not in length, which one can't tell from a visit, but in height and depth – it's massive. I soon realised that this was necessary, as hordes of Chinese would use it to gallop along on horseback, usually in warfare. Many millions of tourists have been there now, but in 1973 very few had ever visited it.

Meeting Chou En-lai, Premier of China

On 1st June I was invited to the Official Queen's Birthday Party at the Ambassador's Residence in Peking. The invitation had the Queen's coat of arms on the front, and was written in both Chinese script and in English. Inside it said:

> On the occasion of the Birthday of Her Majesty Queen Elizabeth II, the British Charge d'Affaires and Mrs M H Morgan request the pleasure of your company at a Reception at No 1 Kuang Hua Lu on Friday 1st June 1973 from 6pm–7pm.

What an honour! I was very excited and incredibly pleased to have been invited.

I was told I would meet Chou En-lai, the first Premier of the People's Republic of China, so I should dress appropriately. Oh, goodness, now I was worried. I only had a few clothes with me because I was travelling light, so it was a toss-up between rather tight, scruffy jeans or a minidress. As it was in the days of a dress being smarter than jeans, I opted for the minidress. Consequently, all the Chinese stared at me non-stop.

Apparently Premier Chou was known for his shrewdness, charm, and erudition. It was he who opened the country up somewhat by hosting the US table tennis team in Peking in 1971. He served as Premier from 1949 until his death in January 1976.

From my 1973 diary:

> What a wonderful thing – little me being invited to this prestigious event. It was held in the garden of the Residence, with recordings of Mozart being played through the very tinny loud-speakers, which sounded horrendous

– like being in some strange old film. I was introduced to various Chinese dignitaries, including Premier Chou En-lai, who all stared and stared at my legs. A tad embarrassing, but what was I to do? Stupidly I didn't have my camera with me. Some magnificent ancient Chinese men there. Speeches to Mao first by one of the English staff, then to the Queen by a Chinese diplomat.

This experience taught me to take a smart dress on my future travels, as you never know where you might end up!

On to Shanghai and then Hong Kong

I left Peking on 6th June 1973 at 1.45pm, and had a first class four-berth compartment all to myself. I stopped off at Hangzhou and Suzhou on the way. Reading my diaries now, I can see that I thought Shanghai was not nearly as lovely as Peking, and I didn't see any interesting historical buildings, although the massive 1920s buildings were pretty amazing, especially the hotels and banks. But I observed that life was fascinating – all the little streets teeming with people of all ages, and the shops opening out onto the streets and selling the oddest things. People seemed friendlier and didn't stare at me quite so much. I stayed in a beautiful old hotel, very 1920s and clearly built by the English for the English. My room was very grand with a lovely marble bathroom, all for only £3 a night! From the window I could see the river with its floating traffic of junks, sampans and ships. I went walking every morning and saw hundreds of people doing exercises in the parks. They called it shadow boxing then, but now we know it as tai chi.

From Shanghai I travelled to Hong Kong by rail. To get into Hong Kong from Canton, passengers had to clamber over the railway lines to get to the ticket office. The train stopped a mile before the border, and we had to disembark and walk along the railway line to the Hong Kong border and the British authorities. Then, suddenly, I was in Hong Kong!

What a shock to the system – colours everywhere! Everything was different. It was like returning from another planet. There were ice creams, drinks, Coca-Cola, newspapers, and Chinese people dressed in Western clothes. I especially noticed the advertisements for Smarties and other Western goodies. So strange after a month of being in spartan, austere China.

I feel so very fortunate to have been able to visit China in 1973, at such an utterly unique point in its history. In the decades since, everything has changed. The cities are now much like other large international cosmopolitan cities anywhere in the world. You can now see obscenely wealthy young people driving around in Rolls Royces in Beijing.

I had a lovely week staying with friends in Hong Kong. I briefly considered going on to Japan, but eventually concluded that it was too expensive. Instead, I decided to get a cargo boat to Singapore, then I would go on to India, and back to England from there.

Cargo Boats

On 26th May, I got up very early to get the boat to Singapore. I watched a cargo of potatoes being loaded and thought how unsafe it looked. The boat was listing badly, but it was my only choice of transport so I took a deep breath and got on board. Four days later I arrived in Singapore where

*Travels through China (top) and India showing Caroline and Dwarko
at the Samanvoy School (Photos from author's personal collection)*

I walked for miles through the old streets and went to Raffles Hotel for an orange juice. It was an expensive glass of juice, costing about £4, but worth it just to be able to say I'd been there. Raffles was amazing, and just how I'd always imagined: very large and beautiful and colonial, with wooden shutters and uniformed waiters everywhere. The entire place had a hush about it, and was obviously only for the very rich.

My next cargo boat journey was to India, through the Andaman Sea and the Bay of Bengal, arriving at Madras in southern India. The cabin was okay, but very hot. Unfortunately, I became ill and missed seeing Kuala Lumpur…then the boat broke down and was blown off course to Ceylon (now Sri Lanka).

It took eight days to cross the very choppy Bay of Bengal to get to Madras, where I stayed at the Young Women's Christian Association (YWCA). Not far out of the city is Mahabalipuram Beach, famous for its temples and monuments. All along the beach there are massive semi-submerged stones, apparently from ancient ruined temples.

While I was there, I realised my clothes didn't seem respectful enough so I bought a cheap, cotton, wrap-around long skirt in a darkish lilac colour – pale colours are no good because there's dust and filth everywhere. This skirt became a treasured item for me, and lasted for many years and many trips to countries where one had to cover up to be respectful to local customs.

From Madras, I travelled on to Calcutta. No more cargo boats, but back to the railways. My arrival in Calcutta at 7am was a shock to the system – I hadn't been expecting the abject conditions at Howrah Station, although I had heard it described as 'infamous'. The loos were utterly disgusting.

Waiting for my connection to Delhi, I took refuge in the first class lounge and watched the comings and goings with fascination, amazed by the hundreds of people who seemed to be living in the middle of rail platforms with all their belongings in boxes. Some would put down a rug, or in some cases a piece of paper or cardboard, then undress and settle down on top of their clothes and go to sleep. Later, they'd wake up, cook and eat a meal, and this seemed to be their life.

I went for a brief walk across Hooghly Bridge and felt so helpless at the sight of all the beggars and the disabled. There was nothing I could do to help there and then, but within days I had a chance to work for a week in a school for 'untouchable' children. I stayed with an old school friend who was working at the school, out in the jungle near Bodh-Gaya. What a wonderful experience, and a relief to be able to do something practical, even if it was for a short time.

Bodh-Gaya is a place of pilgrimage for Buddhists because it's where Buddha, Gautama Sidhartha, found enlightenment under the Bodhi tree. I visited the temple there, and stood beneath the enormous Bodhi tree. Some Buddhists insist it is still the same tree, whereas others say it is a direct descendant of the original tree. The place certainly feels sacred, and is a strong link for Buddhists with their founder.

While I was in northern India, I found a doctor for a cholera jab that I needed to gain entry to Iran later on. But oh, what a situation. Needles kept in an envelope; a huge old-fashioned glass syringe, a bit like we use for cattle at home. The doctor proceeded to boil a pan of water for the needle, then took it out and wiped it with cotton wool... Oh shit, shit, shit, I thought in a panic. I knew that was wrong – what's the point of sterilising things then wiping them with unsterilised cotton wool? But I didn't say anything because I thought it would be rude... Oh how stupidly polite we English are sometimes! It taught me a big lesson. Don't keep quiet if your health or safety could be compromised. The ramifications of this would last for many months after I got home – as it gave me hepatitis A.

The Himalayas to Kathmandu

Next, I headed to Raxaul and then took a cart to the Nepalese border to catch the local bus. The bus journey was quite horrific once we got into the Himalayas. The road was very narrow and we were continually coming face to face, at great speed, with other vehicles. The road itself seemed to be rotting away in places – with a few landslides. There had been a terrible accident just the day before, when a bus went over the edge and we saw the remnants of suitcases, clothes etc, all strewn down the steep mountain side. Eventually, I arrived in Kathmandu at about 6pm, in the pouring rain. As soon as we stopped, I was surrounded by Nepalese guys with cards telling me how good their hotels were: "Only two rupees." Goodness – so cheap.

I took a taxi to the K Guest House where I had a room with a bathroom and freezing water for twenty-two rupees. This was less than £1. I was grateful to find a nice Tibetan restaurant attached, where the food was a lot better than I'd expected after hearing so many stories about it. I had previously been warned to beware of Nepalese food, but it all looked so good that I ignored that warning – to my cost.

During the early 1970s, at the time I was travelling, the serial killer and fraudster Charles Sobhraj was kidnapping and killing foreign tourists in the Far East. Watching the BBC series *The Serpent* makes me realise now how fortunate I was not to have any serious problems on my trip. It certainly makes me wonder how I would have reacted to someone like him… I like to think I'd have had the sense to see through his creepiness, but who knows. Maybe I was just very, very lucky. The TV series certainly showed the realities of India at that time, and I hope young people who travel there now are aware of the dangers. I was always as careful as I could be: I never looked directly at strange men, especially in the street; I would buy a local paper, and try not to look too much like a tourist; I tried not to look too 'lost', walking with a firm step. If I ever felt I was being followed I would pop into a shop or hotel and wait.

My travels took me by bus through Pakistan, Afghanistan, Iran, Turkey and on through into Europe. There are a few eventful things I remember of the journey – the worst one was nearly being attacked in the Khyber Pass. This is an extremely remote area, ruled by various tribes. It is part of the old Silk Road, now known as the Asian Highway, the only road from Peshawar in Pakistan to Kabul in Afghanistan. The bus had stopped with a puncture – luckily the driver was competent and quick, as he knew it was a dangerous area and, just as he had finished, we heard loud shouts and saw about six men rushing up the hills towards us with their faces covered with their ubiquitous scarves, and waving rifles and knives over their heads. In a total panic we all leapt back into the bus, and the driver took off like a crazy man. As we left, I looked through the back window to see these men – quite close by now and looking very angry indeed – shouting and waving their weapons and trying to catch up with us. We left them behind in a cloud of dust…but we were all terrified.

I wish I could recount all my adventures during this amazing trip, but they'd take up a book in themselves! Readers who want to know more can visit my website and blog at rocknrollnanny.co.uk.

Quarantine

On returning to England, I moved back into my flat in Hurlingham Road and took up where I'd left off, doing PR for classical musicians, but I soon started feeling extremely ill.

The doctor probed me with questions. "Are you a heavy drinker?" he asked. "Or is it possible you were infected with a dirty needle?"

"No," I replied, concerned. Though I saw some drugs when I nannied for the Jaggers, the most I did was take some mescaline with some chums on a trip to Disneyland.

I had hepatitis A. We calculated the likely time frame and it ended up being exactly the time I'd had the cholera jab in the jungle in India. Initially, the doctor told me that I would need to be hospitalised and kept in isolation since it was such an infectious disease. After swearing I would stay away from everyone, I begged to go home to my parents. I even had to promise that my cutlery, crockery, bed linen and towels would be cleaned and laundered separately.

So, that's what I did for about six months.

My parents had a bedroom and bathroom at the top of the house, where I could easily isolate myself. Not being able to see or speak to anyone was frustrating and lonely, but my mother was a saint. Mealtimes became a routine. My mum would leave meals outside the door, and I would put everything back when I was finished.

Since I knew I would be in bed for some time, I decided to use the time wisely and read all of Jane Austen.

PART TWO

ROCK N ROLL NANNY

Chapter 7

The Who

In 1974, after recovering from hepatitis, I had to knuckle down to some hard work. Fortunately, Harrison/Parrott asked me to carry on doing publicity for their classical artistes, who were then some of the most exciting, up-and-coming young classical musicians at the time. I even arranged for the soprano, Sheila Armstrong (now Dame Sheila), to be photographed by Patrick Lichfield. He was fascinated by my little 125cc Harley Davidson motorbike and came out into the street to look at it. I loved my job but – and there was a big but – I was only paid if and when the articles actually appeared in the newspaper or magazine. Very often, the interviews would not be published for months and, needless to say, I was struggling financially. I was also doing a lot of running around for many of these musicians, basically being a PA. I loved the work and enjoyed being useful to such talented people, but I simply could not afford to continue running errands for free. Sometimes I regret not staying in that world, but life throws us many different and weird challenges.

I had stayed in touch with Alan Dunn, Mick Jagger's assistant, and one day he told me there was a secretarial/assistant's job going at the touring office of the Stones, The Who and other groups. He said he and Mick thought I'd be good at it.

My initial response was: "Why me? I'm a nanny. I've never done anything like that."

Alan replied: "Because all the band like you – and the wives trust you."

That was that. My salary would be £14 a week – finally, a regular income! It really was an offer I couldn't refuse, especially after struggling for years to get paid fairly or on time. I immediately agreed to take the job.

At the time, I had no idea that this was one of the most sought-after jobs in the music business

Five One Productions

Five One Productions was set up and run by Pete Rudge and Bill Curbishley. The two had met while working as juniors at The Who's Track Records company. After becoming dissatisfied with Kit Lambert and Chris Stamp, who ran it and managed The Who, they took things into their own hands. They set up Five One Productions to organise the tours for the groups at Track, such as The Who, Golden Earring, Humble Pie, Marsha Hunt and others. Following Pete's successful tour management of the Stones' 1973 tour, he was moving to New York to set up a sister company, Sir Productions. Their UK assistant wanted to move to the States too – hence the need for an assistant for Bill in London. So I went to meet Bill and the then-assistant at their 69 New Bond Street office, where we all got along famously.

The following day, Alan and I had tea at Mick's Cheyne Walk house where I saw Jade – my baby – now a precocious four-year-old. Goodness knows how many nannies she'd had in those intervening years. As Alan and I were leaving, Jade clung to my legs and begged me not to leave. It broke my heart.

I started work with Bill at Five One Productions in March 1974. We shared the building with the management companies of Pink Floyd and Marc Bolan, of T Rex. Marc always had a large number of fans waiting outside, hoping to catch a glimpse of him, but I was used to this kind of thing from my days of working with the Jaggers.

In early May I had my very first experience of The Who, which was pretty unforgettable. Ironically, I had no interest in rock and roll, so I didn't pay attention to gossip or news about it. Even though Keith Moon's ways were well known to many, I was naive to them.

Bill and I went to their dressing room after a concert in Oxford – but, bloody hell, where was the loud banging coming from? My first sight of Keith Moon was when he – quite literally – burst out of a wardrobe, arms and legs flailing, wood panels, planks of wood, splinters everywhere, screaming and shouting, "Everybody fuck off out of my way!" But he became a charming, polite young man after Kit Lambert calmed him down and introduced me to him: "My dear girl," Keith said, "how very nice to meet you."

This was my first encounter with the maniac known as Keith Moon. Throughout the years, I had many strange, exciting, frightening and odd encounters with him, until he died in 1977. Little did I know that first night that I would have to deal with much worse in the future.

Another thing I remember from that evening was that Kit offered me a tipple of brandy contained within the silver handle of his walking stick. This was elegance and decadence at its best! I'd never seen anything like it. Kit's business partner, Chris Stamp, was the brother of the film star Terence Stamp, while Kit was the son of the eminent composer, Constant Lambert. Interestingly, I knew more about the Lambert family than anyone else there. This was thanks to my music teacher who knew Constant and his Spanish wife well. Fortunately, this prepared me for the family's eccentricities. (Both Roger Daltrey's and Pete Townshend's memoirs talk about their problems with Lambert and Stamp.)

While working with the classical musicians – and, later, the rock and roll musicians – I had continued with my private music lessons. In 1973 I auditioned for the London Symphony Orchestra Chorus (now known as the London Symphony Chorus). Since I didn't think I would get in, I'd kept my audition a secret. To my surprise, I did get in! Singing with the chorus through those twenty-odd years gave me a sense of sanity in a world of insanity, but I didn't realise it at the time. I was just getting started in the rock and roll world...

On 18th May 1974, I had my first taste of looking after The Who, and their personal and technical needs, while planning an open-air gig at Charlton football ground. All their roadies were so lovely and sweet to me, especially the wonderful Bob Pridden, the band's monitor mixer. One day, Bob had come to the office to collect a cheque.

"Make it out to Lady Pridden," he said.

"Oh, piss off," I replied. "Don't be so silly – who shall I really make it out to?"

"No, really – that's right," said Bob.

It turned out that he actually was married to the daughter of an earl!

He told me about their early courting days when his wife posed as the stable girl at the big house. She always met him by the back door, so he wouldn't be put off or intimidated. We all became firm friends, would meet up regularly for dinner, plus I would stay with them often at their beautiful lakeside home.

My first job with The Who was the Charlton gig, where I had to learn about how to suss out the backstage, the dressing rooms and so on. This concert was where John 'Wiggy' Wolff, the band's production manager, spearheaded the use of lasers. The local council were immensely worried about the dangers. They even cited the laser in the James Bond film *Dr No*. 'Would the lasers be properly cooled…?' and 'What if one shone into someone's eyes, blinding them…?' While it seems silly to think about it now, lasers were a new concept in the 1970s. To see my boss Bill Curbishley in action was all good training for me, as he calmed everybody with assurances that all safety measures were in place and no one's eyes would be burnt out.

It was at that concert that I first met and became good friends with Rolling Stone Bill Wyman and his girlfriend Astrid. Mick McKenna and Keith Harwood were also there to record the concert. They ran the Rolling Stones' Mobile, the Mighty Mobile, which was a truck that contained everything necessary to record outside concerts. I also met the radio DJ Nicky Horne, who would later become a huge fan of Lynyrd Skynyrd, and once even put out a message over Capital radio for me to please contact him about them!

Bill Curbishley was easily one of the best – and nicest – bosses I ever had. He was always calm and sensible. He very rarely raised his voice, if ever. I would learn a few years later that his demeanour was totally different to his partner, Pete Rudge's. I was very lucky to work so closely with Bill. He treated me, and everybody else, with respect and courtesy. This surprised me quite a bit, as he told me about his early years and what a terror he had been. Growing up in the East End of London, he had a reputation as a bad boy and knew various criminals, including the Kray brothers. He even ended up in prison for grievous bodily harm (GBH). He told me, however, that he had been stitched up and hadn't done what he'd been accused of. Mind you, he said: "If I hadn't gone in for something I didn't do, I'd have probably gone for something I *did* do."

As I understood it, Bill used the prison years sensibly by keeping his head down and studying. After he came out, Chris Stamp, his old East End chum, offered him a job at Track Records. This was where he met Pete Rudge, who'd been a social secretary at Cambridge University, where he used to book The Who and other bands to play.

Because Bill took me to pretty much every meeting with people – like the lawyer Paddy Grafton-Green, the accountant Bryan Walters, and the promoters John and Tony Smith, and Harvey Goldsmith – I became adept at understanding complex contractual details, all of which fascinated me. After six months, Bill made me a company director. In those days, it was quite unusual for a woman to be a company director at the age of twenty-four. This showed me how much he trusted and relied on me.

Over the years, however, his wife Jackie was to cause me considerable grief, accusing me of having an affair with him and of stealing other people's jobs. None of this was true, of course. The affair accusation came just two months after I started working for Bill when I was trying to arrange flights for their Spanish holiday. Bill asked me to book flights for him and his family – wife and two children – to Spain. Since it was the height of the summer season it was impossible for the agent to get four seats on one flight. They could only do three on one flight, and one on another. So it was decided to put Jackie and the children on the first flight, with Bill going two days later.

Little did I know Jackie would interpret this as Bill wanting to be with me during those two days without her being there. It was horrifying, and had nothing to do with Bill and me wanting to be together – that was utter nonsense. I suppose it's not surprising that Jackie took over my job some time later, but for some reason her mantra became: "Beware of that Sally Arnold. She steals other people's jobs." Classic projection. As Madeleine Albright once said, "There is a special place in hell for women who betray other women."

To a degree, I can understand a wife's fear of her husband's assistant. As Bill's assistant, I was privy to his every move. At any point in the day I knew where he was, who he was with, and what he was doing. This would be galling for any wife I imagine, but it certainly didn't mean I was having an affair with him. Although I admired him tremendously, I would never do such a thing. But I did know when he did things Jackie didn't like, and I was often sworn to secrecy. For example, when he met up with old prison chums including John McVicar, who often came to the office. I have to admit I found these people exciting and fascinating, like many a young middle-class girl would!

Bryan Walters was the company's accountant. Originally, sometime in 1973, he, Bill and Pete Rudge met for lunch and all got quite pissed! Bryan was asked to do the accounts for the Rolling Stones' Denmark tour. Lawyer Paddy Grafton-Green said they were the 'clearest set of accounts' he'd ever seen. I learned that Bryan helped set up some complex tax schemes for The Who and the Stones, and that the problems with Lambert and Stamp were near-unresolvable, which hampered the various deals The Who wanted to do with Rudge and Curbishley. During this time, Bryan shared a house with Tony Dimitriades, manager of the group Ace (who became famous for their wonderful song 'How Long?'). After moving to Los Angeles, Tony managed, among others, Tom Petty and the Heartbreakers, and Joni Mitchell.

Later in 1974 I had to organise everything for The Who and their UK roadies for the upcoming US tour. This included visas, itineraries, technical requirements, work exchanges and work permits, travel, hotels, and rider requirements. A rider is a list of all their requirements, mainly for their dressing rooms. This was all done in conjunction with Pete Rudge's new company, Sir Productions, in New York. This was also the first time I had a meeting at the American embassy, with Pete Townshend. Pete had an old drug conviction, which officially barred him from entering the States. Thanks to the embassy officials, we were able to sort everything out. We got the necessary paperwork he needed for his work permit and visa to get into the United States.

As I'd had no experience of this type of work, and no one had instructed me on anything, I used my common sense. For example, I gave copies of the itineraries to all the wives and girlfriends of the band and crew. Roger Daltrey's wife, Heather, thanked me profusely for this, as apparently nobody had ever done that for them before.

Chapter 8

Duties of a Tour Manager

My work would start long before the tour did. It was enjoyable and varied, but most of it was invisible. While Bill negotiated concert dates with the various promoters around the United Kingdom and Europe, it would take me months to plan and arrange everything, including travel and accommodation, booking flights/cars, paying invoices and ensuring all deadlines were met. Including my everyday work as a PA as well, ensuring birthdays were remembered, necessary letters sent, early morning/late-night calls made.

As part of my pre-tour duties, I checked maps of Europe and borders with the trucking guys, Edwin Shirley and Roy Lamb. I also helped organise rehearsal space, instruments, roadies, and technical stuff, as well as less technical things like briefing the artists who designed the artwork for posters and merchandise. Since there were no computers back then, it was a time-consuming process to prepare the itinerary with all the information we needed: dates, venues, hotels etc. (I believe I was the first person to put in details of local doctors in itineraries.) Not to mention ensuring that the rider requirements were sent to all promoters and fulfilled at each venue. Also, when necessary, I arranged for session musicians, extra instruments to be hired or purchased, a support band and their crew. Plus, meetings with the Department of Employment, Equity and obtaining any visas and work permits necessary.

The organisation of 'per diems' (daily subsistence money on top of their wages) for crew and band members was especially important as it remunerated them for being away from home. I didn't have a per diem since all my expenses were covered by the tour. I always had massive hotel phone bills because I contacted so many people due to changes and problems – from promoters in advance of our arrival, to lawyers, accountants, and travel agents.

The equipment was trucked ahead, and the crew had to arrive first at every venue and set up before the band's arrival in time for the soundcheck. On that subject, we also had to obtain the necessary legal and insurance requirements. In order to book the relevant technical equipment, I worked very closely with Brian Croft, who handled all the sound and lighting through his company ESP. Creating carnets was my least favourite job. These are import/export documents that list every item, including every cable and lead, to be shown at every border without having to pay taxes on this equipment. Sometimes pedantic border guards would insist on unpacking and checking everything.

The coordination of work exchanges is a regular task for American bands that come to tour Europe. An exchange was initiated months before by exchanging the number of man-hours of an American band coming here with an English band going to the United States. Everybody in the business – managers, agents, promoters – kept in touch and organised exchanges with each other's bands. Work permits are issued only after an exchange has been approved. It took a lot of time to fill out the paperwork, which I would then deliver to the necessary government departments by hand, as the post was too unreliable for such important documents. When the Lynyrd Skynyrd boys came over from the States, I would even have to go to the airport with the actual physical permits, wait at the immigration desk, and point out the boys to the immigration authorities, who would double-check everything and stamp their passports. The boys were then in my care.

During early mornings on the road, I would have made and received numerous phone calls, preparing for the next gig or next week. I would then wake up all the band and crew by phone, telling them to pack and be in the lobby by a certain time, calling them all again and again if necessary. In the lobby of the hotel, I'd also check that each person had paid for any extras they'd charged to their room, before ushering them out to the limos or tour bus. Plus, I kept track of on-the-road accounts/per diems/extras (often for drugs!).

Airports were a nightmare. The boys would be wandering off everywhere, and it was ridiculous trying to round them all up to board the plane. My inner nanny kicked in and I decided to hold on to their tickets and boarding passes for them, knowing that otherwise they'd lose them.

With the big bands, like The Who and the Stones, we often had our own planes, which was much easier, as the check-in was not in the public areas. I had piles of signed photographs to give to various airport personnel to speed our way through the checks. As soon as we boarded the plane, the shenanigans began. It was booze by the gallon, and sometimes coke on tap, then I had to manage these drunken, stoned guys on landing.

With the Stones, we had an advance man who met us at the hotels after arranging the rooms ahead of time, for which I was grateful. Otherwise, it would be down to me to check them all in and give them their room keys when we got there and, after check-in, I still had a lot of work to do. I'd hurriedly use a typewriter in the hotel's office to type out a rooming list, then copy it for everybody. On the Stones tour, I had my own portable electric typewriter in my 'office' trunk, an electric laminator so that I could make official backstage passes whenever any were needed, and a small transformer. I needed the transformer because the power was different in each country. For example, Paris had different voltages: it was 220 volts in some parts of the city, but 110 volts in other parts! Very confusing.

I always had to be a few steps ahead of everyone. As soon as we were settled in the hotel, I would dash off to the venue to check out the available dressing rooms and set up signs where necessary. It made life easier for me since I knew where the boys should go when they arrived. Then I'd race back to the hotel and would have to chivvy the boys out of their rooms (or the bar) for the trip to the venue for their soundcheck, usually held a few hours before the gig. After the soundcheck, we'd hang around the backstage area, eating whatever the local promoter had provided. These were usually the ubiquitous 'cold cuts'...never a nice thing to eat in the middle of a chilly winter. If the hotel was close by, we'd often go back there before having to head back to the venue again for the show. For me, this was always the worrying time, as often one or more of the boys would disappear to a local pub or drug dealer or suchlike. Rabbit (John Bundrick, keyboard player who went on to join The Who) was always doing this on the Crawler tour of America. I always knew I'd find him in the nearest bar. On one of the Skynyrd tours, Artimus just decided to disappear for the day in Paris. He hired a massive Harley Davidson motorbike and cruised around the city quite happily until the police arrested him for not wearing a helmet. Consequently, he didn't appear for the photo sessions with the press, so stage manager, Dean Kilpatrick, took his place. Nobody seemed to notice the difference between Arty and Dean! Luckily there wasn't a gig that night, so he only missed that press call, and eventually returned much chastened by the ordeal with the Paris police – and then me getting very angry with him because of his disappearance.

Sometimes, all I wanted was to be away from everybody, but those moments were few and far between. Since the only time I had any peace and quiet was during those two hours when the band was on stage, I would often hide in the ladies' loo with a book. Even so, that peace didn't last long since I had to tidy up the dressing rooms during the show. Often, I would walk around the auditorium among the audience and listen. The Skynyrd girl singers would always ask me how they sounded, so I'd offer feedback. I'd often

Sally with Artimus Pyle, Lynyrd Skynyrd tour bus, 1977
(© Kate Simon, with kind permission)

bump into the various venue staff and management, or the local promoter's people, and we'd have a chat and a giggle – sometimes with a drink and a line or two of coke. If the band played a song I liked, I'd rush backstage and stand at the side of the stage to listen.

After the concert we'd jump straight into the limos or bus waiting outside the backstage door and rush off to the hotel, where the parties would begin. I, however, would go to the hotel's office to plan for the following day, typing out schedules I called newsletters. When I was done, I would walk around the hotel pushing these under the door of everybody. Every night, I'd itemise the next day's activities: time of the wake-up call and baggage call; time to be in the lobby ready for transport; the name of next country/town; arrival time; soundcheck time; performance time; whether or not we'd be going through customs (and not to be carrying anything illegal). I often had to write coded messages warning about sniffer dogs at upcoming airports or borders.

I was frequently woken in the middle of the night by the hotel manager or the police because of some ruckus or other, which I had to sort out. One memorable experience was with Skynyrd in Bristol, where I was woken by the hotel manager and the police after someone had wrecked the hallway on our floor and then disappeared. I knew it was Leon (Wilkeson, the bass player), but didn't say anything. All the rooms were checked and everyone was present and correct – with the exception of Leon's room, where the window was wide open. I knew he'd climbed out, along the ledge (three storeys up!) and into truck driver Roy Lamb's room next door. The police demanded to be let into that room.

My response was a very firm 'No' with the reasoning that Roy was the main truck driver, and it was vital that he got his allotted hours of sleep. "We absolutely must not disturb him!"

The police and co eventually all left – so I went to Roy's room, and who should be in there but Leon. Of course. He was such a naughty boy!

The wrecking of the hotel floor had included breaking the safety glass in the hallway doors. The next morning, the hotel manager gave me a massive bill to replace it. I immediately phoned a glazier to find the true cost of this safety glass, which of course, was far less than I had been quoted. I wasn't going to have the wool pulled over my eyes!

Basically, I was an administrator, but a bloody good one, making sure that everything was dealt with so that the musicians could do their job: performing. I was always the first one up in the morning, usually because I had to make a number of phone calls to plan the days ahead. Then it would start all over again...

Chapter 9

The Who as People

In those days of working with The Who, I didn't know Pete Townshend very well. I got to know him much better in the 1980s when he entrusted me with the Double O Charity but, in 1974, he could sometimes come across as grumpy and irascible. There were times when he did things that shocked people. We had just hired a new guitar roadie, Alan Rogan (who also worked with Keith Richards and Eric Clapton, and who very sadly died of cancer not long ago). At the time, Alan was the new boy; all the other roadies had been with The Who for many years. He once had to rush onstage during a performance to sort out a cable and Pete – quite literally – kicked him off the stage and into the audience with a heavy foot on his backside. That poor boy. I felt really sorry for him. Pete was always very precious about 'his' stage and hated anybody else on it, even a working roadie.

Around this time, I got to know Roger Daltrey well. I had daily contact with him about his timetable, travel, and accommodation while he was filming Ken Russell's *Tommy*. When I visited him on the set in Marlborough, Wiltshire, for the hang-gliding sequence, he got annoyed that I wouldn't stay with him overnight…silly boy! He would try it on with a lot of young women, but I most certainly wasn't going to fall into the trap of having a fling with him. On tour, I would often stand in the wings when they performed 'Baba O'Riley', as Roger would hold out his hand to me when he sang the line, "Sally, take my hand." That was truly lovely. So endearing. I have a photo of Roger and me with the artist David Oxtoby taken at Shepperton Studios, where much of *Tommy* was filmed.

I stayed a few times at Roger's fabulous Elizabethan mansion in Sussex and found him and his wife, Heather, to be lovely people. At one point, they asked me to bid at Sotheby's for some stained-glass windows designed by Edward Burne-Jones, for their house. Bidding with other people's money – many thousands of pounds – while terrified of buying the wrong item, was quite a frightening experience! Roger and I also had our disagreements though. And I once got a card from him, sent with a massive plant, saying:

Thanks for everything, even the rows! Lots of love, Roger.

Roger and John were very different people to Pete, who was somewhat enigmatic. He's quoted as saying, "Offstage I'm a mouse, albeit a mouse with mood swings." Interestingly I didn't see him with many girls on the road, and it seems that most of the infidelity came later. In an interview in *The Sunday Times*, Roger said, "Pete can be tricky. It can be like walking through a minefield with a blindfold..." This was exactly how I found him to be. You just never knew what mood he would be in.

John Entwistle was married to his childhood sweetheart, Alison. Both of them were always really nice to me. Their London home was an unassuming house in an unassuming street in Ealing, but John had tried to make it like an old English mansion inside, with suits of armour everywhere. Totally out of place – and not even ironic! They also had an amazingly weird, huge Gothic-style mansion in Gloucestershire, where I stayed a few times; it had a massive hallway and ballroom where John had hung loads of beautiful marlin he had caught in the Caribbean – again not ironic, just totally horrendous and inappropriate. Of course, John wasn't faithful to Alison, and he even tried a drunken snog on me – but I soon told him to get lost, saying that Alison was my friend. She ended up happily living with their driver after she and John split up.

I think Keith Moon's quick wit was less down to education than to having a blotting-paper mind. He picked up things extremely quickly from better-educated people like Peter Sellers, Peter Cook and Kit Lambert, his mentor for many years. Keith was an enigma. I don't think many people really got to know him. When he was drunk, which was most of the time, he was a bit difficult to handle, but still wonderful fun. In fact, when sober, he was a sweet and kind man. I learned how to manage him, although I'm not quite sure why he obeyed me. Fear of a bossy woman, maybe?

Around this time, Keith met a new girlfriend, Annette Walter-Lax. We formed a wonderful friendship, and I stayed with them when they lived in Los Angeles. I honestly don't know how she kept up the pace with him. I certainly couldn't. I remember going with him to some local 'British' pub in Malibu, and we were in there for hours! I couldn't get away, being reliant on him for transport. Later on, he lent me his limo, which I drove to Disneyland

Sally with Roger Daltrey and David Oxtoby, 1979
(Photo from author's personal collection)

with some of my LA girlfriends. Imagine three young women turning up in a massive black American limo. Great fun, and such extravagant things were the norm when working with rock stars. Especially Keith.

When he died in 1977, Annette came to live with me at my flat in Fulham for about six months. It was a time which brought us extremely close. I had been with Keith and Annette the night before he died, at Tramp, the nightclub. They had gone home to their West End flat, and Annette told me Keith snored so loudly that she slept on the sofa. The next morning she couldn't wake him…

In an attempt to stop his massive alcohol consumption, Keith had been prescribed Heminevrin by the infamous Dr Dymond. Apparently, Heminevrin is supposed to be given only under medical supervision, but Dr D gave Keith bottles of the pills. Annette described to me how Keith took them – by tipping a pile of pills into the palm of his hand, and swigging them back with a glass of brandy, whisky, or whatever alcohol was to hand. One is not supposed to take any alcohol with this medication. That's how Keith accidentally killed himself. Annette had probably saved his life many times before, as she told me she had often found him comatose and had had to push her fingers down his throat to make him puke and breathe again.

Later, Annette married actor Gareth Hunt and they had a son, Oliver. I often stayed with them in their lovely house in the Hampshire countryside. After Gareth's early death, Annette and Oliver moved back to her home in Sweden. We are still in touch to this day.

During those first couple of years with Bill Curbishley and Five One Productions, The Who were busy with various projects apart from *Tommy*. John had recorded his solo album *Mad Dog* and formed his band Ox (I organised the tours in the United Kingdom and United States). Pete Townshend was a misery at this time, and out of it on coke, heroin, and booze. Roger was doing well with his acting, not only in *Tommy* but also in Ken Russell's *Lisztomania* – a spoof on the life of Franz Liszt. Throughout the years, I often bumped into Ken Russell, and we'd always reminisce and share a lot of fun memories from those days.

I don't think I appreciated it at the time, but Bill would take me for lunches and dinners with some extraordinary people, like David Puttnam,

Kit Lambert, Chris Stamp and his brother Terence Stamp, the film star. One day in October my diary notes:

> Went to pick up Baron Fredrick Von Pallandt. Saw a screening of *Tommy* at Pinewood Studios with Bill, Chris (Stamp), Roger and Heather (Daltrey), Pete Townshend and Ken Russell.

While on my first European Who tour, I was astonished by the craziness. It was the first time I experienced their madness on stage – Pete smashing his beautiful, expensive guitars, and Keith wrecking his drum kit. The crew spent many hours cleaning up the mess, while I took the band to our hotel, where they continued their craziness, drinking and taking drugs. I usually tried to miss these parties, as I had to work very early the next day, phoning the next town or country's promoters or the office back in London. Plus,

Left: Keith Moon, and right: Annette Walter-Lax
(Photos from author's personal collection)

I knew I would be woken by the hotel management or the police if necessary. I often wondered how much all their wreckage cost in total, but I assumed they were so wealthy they just didn't worry about it. Keith was notorious for letting off cherry bombs in hotel toilets, then trying dynamite for goodness' sake!

There were so many things going on. It was such a busy time for everyone. Keith was in the film *Stardust*, which was in production, so I had to arrange his travels to and from filming. Pete performed a solo charity concert at the Roundhouse in north London, plus he played a one-off gig in Portsmouth to thank the *Tommy* crew. Keith and Annette then jetted off to LA for a break. However, everything regarding Keith Moon turned into a nightmare. He would wreck hotel rooms and apartments, so I always had to pay for damage or move them – again. I was fortunate to have a great deal of help from Dougal, his assistant. Luckily, we worked well together to sort things out.

The first time I met Eric and Pattie Clapton was at dinner with Bob and Mia Pridden, and we became good friends. Though I never worked with Eric, I used to visit them in Sussex, driving down with friends, like actor Oliver Tobias. Eric once tried to make a half-hearted pass at me, but I quickly put him in his place by laughing and saying, "Don't be so silly, Pattie's my friend." Thankfully he never tried again. As I would always say about sleeping with rock stars, I'd prefer to be the one who didn't, than one of the hundreds who did. It was all too easy to sleep with them, and, of course, there's always been a differentiation between men and women who sleep around: for men, it's simply a matter of being another notch on the bedpost and "Well done, mate", whereas for women – well, they're just 'sluts', aren't they?

Some years later, in 1977, Eric wrote and recorded 'Lay Down Sally', which became a popular hit. A journalist friend and I were chatting one day when she said, "You know 'Lay Down Sally' is you, don't you?"

I laughed. "Don't be silly!"

But I asked Eric about it the next time I spoke with him, and he replied, "Of course it's you! Can't you tell? It's all upbeat and bubbly – just like you."

Others have approached him and said, "We're friends of Sally Arnold, who says she's 'Lay Down Sally'," and he agreed.

It must be true, I guess!

Many of the people I knew at the time were getting treatment for heroin addiction and alcoholism, such as Pete Townshend and Eric Clapton, so I got to know Dr Meg Patterson and her family. Meg was a Scottish doctor who treated various addictions. Her treatment involved attaching tiny electrodes to the ears to stimulate the production of endorphins. Meg's theory was that, when a person is trying to come off a drug or alcohol, the drug has replaced the body's natural endorphins, which causes withdrawal symptoms. The electrical stimulation she used to create more natural endorphins was supposed to ease the worst of these withdrawal symptoms. I think this was the precursor to the TENS machine.

Around this time I met Pete Meaden for the first time. Pete had been The Who's first manager, when they were the High Numbers, and he had really discovered them before Kit Lambert and Chris Stamp got involved. Pete invited some of us to Dingwalls in Camden to see his new group, the Steve Gibbons Band. Bill Curbishley then took over their day-to-day management, along with Pete M, with me doing all the necessary administration. They were a great bunch of lads. This was an extremely busy time, with John and Roger doing solo albums, Keith working and playing hard in LA with people like Ringo Starr, and John's band Ox touring again.

During that time, I was also singing with the LSO Chorus at various concerts. The most memorable concert that summer was a live TV broadcast of *Carmina Burana* with André Previn at the Royal Albert Hall on BBC One for the Proms. The tenor, Tom Allen (now Sir Thomas), fainted in the middle of this live broadcast, crashing right into the lead cellist. It was really very dramatic. The look on Previn's face as Tom fell was a picture – an 'oh shit, what the hell shall we do?' look of shock and horror. A young man came up from the auditorium who knew the tenor part, and we continued. Other excitements were singing under the ever-energetic Leonard Bernstein, the deep-thinking Rumanian Buddhist Sergiu Celibedache, and Leopold Stokowski who, at rehearsals, poked all us young sopranos' bums with his walking stick saying: "Oooh, what lovely young ladies!"

My two worlds overlapped sometimes. When we were recording at

Abbey Road Studios, which was of course made world-famous by the Beatles' sessions there in the 1960s, I was chatting to one of the members of the LSO, who told me a story about Paul and Linda McCartney. This man had been making a phone call from one of the booths in the lobby when a young woman rushed by and begged him to hide her in the booth – Linda McCartney was after her because, apparently, she was having an affair with Paul...

Chapter 10

Lynyrd Skynyrd

My destiny. My greatest happiness and my greatest despair. My undoing. That summer of 1974 I had been given a pile of records by a chum at MCA Records, including *(Pronounced 'Lĕh-'nérd 'Skin-'nérd)* by Lynyrd Skynyrd. Even though I usually didn't like rock music, I found that album to be captivating – I felt their music connected with something in me, that it resonated. In short, I loved it. *I loved, loved, loved it!*

Then, one day in the office, Bill told me that Pete (Rudge), who was now in New York permanently, had just started managing a new group and wanted us to organise a European tour for them.

"They've got a really weird name," Bill said. He showed me the telex Pete had sent, which had the name Lynyrd Skynyrd on it.

I shrieked. "Don't worry! I'll do it. I'll take over and organise everything. I think they're amazing!"

When Lynyrd Skynyrd first came to England in November of 1974 as support for Golden Earring, they had never even been outside the United States. After just two days, they christened me their Den Mother. They were often like lost little boys in strange countries, so they needed safety, comfort, and the security of knowing someone would always look out for them – me.

On their first night in London, I took them to the Speakeasy Club, which was madness! I had no idea how much they could – or would – drink. Who paid for it? Me, of course! That taught me to make sure I always had enough cash on me. They were impressed because so many rock stars hung out there, and I introduced them to old friends like Chris Squire of Yes. Bob Pridden, The Who's monitor mixer, came with us too. He was always up for a party, so the drinking lasted for hours. To avoid the expense of bringing an additional roadie from the States, I asked Bob to do the same job for Skynyrd, and from then on Bob was their monitor mixer too. He and the band got along like a house on fire.

Initially, Skynyrd's rider requirements were quite normal: a few bottles of Jack Daniels, or as they called it, 'jet fuel'. Only later did they demand Dom Pérignon champagne, which they drank with ice (totally ruining it, to my mind!). When it came to their per diems, some people would spend every penny right away – usually on drugs or booze. Others would be miserly and would even try to put extras on their room tab, which I had to get them to pay themselves at check-out or deduct from them later; and others would save as much as they could, eating only at the venue where food was provided for everybody. Just like kids with their pocket money!

All of them immediately made me feel comfortable. Over the years, I got to know each of them individually and even stayed with their families at their homes in Jacksonville, Florida. We all loved one another like brothers and sisters – it wasn't sexual (well, not for me, anyway!).

Gary Rossington was like a puppy with his long, glossy hair, dark eyes, and his sweet nature. (When I went through cancer and chemotherapy later in life, he helped me financially when I was broke and unable to work. As did Pete Townshend.) During the band's first tour, he was engaged to Martha, so he couldn't wait to get back to her. Unfortunately, their relationship didn't last. He's now married to Dale Krantz, the singer we hired for the Rossington Collins Band (after the Skynyrd plane crash). Dale has given him and their daughters an extremely happy and stable life, which is wonderful after all that he has been through.

The most fun was Leon Wilkeson, the bass player, who was always humorous and kind. I still have one of his bonkers drawings – a cartoon of all the band members titled with the most absurd names Leon could think of. He became one of my closest friends and would often stay with me at my flat in London, just as I did at his house in Jacksonville. Sadly, he never really found a wife who was good enough for him, at least that was my opinion. He deserved a truly loving relationship, but it always eluded him.

The pianist, Billy Powell, was a quiet fellow until he got drunk, then he made up for lost time. The story of how Billy became a member of the band is quite amazing. He'd originally been a roadie, until Ronnie Van Zant realised he was an excellent piano player. When I say he was excellent, I mean Billy had classical training and could play fantastically. From classical to jazz to boogie woogie and heavy rock, he could play it all – truly an amazing pianist. Though, like Leon, he had a rather sad private life and was unable to find lasting love.

In those days, Allen Collins was unpredictable, always larking around, but he was still a sweetheart. He was like a lanky giant spider with long legs and arms! I liked him and even comforted him when he was heartbroken about missing the birth of his first child, Allison, on that debut tour. Yet, I could always tell that there was a darkness about him, which was later truly revealed after the plane crash, and you didn't want to get on his bad side.

I didn't know guitarist Ed King or drummer Bob Burns very well, as both left the band soon after that first European tour. Although Bob seemed quiet and meek, I soon realised there was a darker side to him as well.

My first few days with the Skynyrd boys on that first tour were dramatic, to say the least. I had arranged for them to stay at the fabulous Portobello Hotel in Notting Hill Gate. On their first night, Bob had some sort of mental 'episode' (I believe he later ended up in some kind of institution). In the middle of the night, I got a phone call to say that 'one of them had strangled the hotel's cat, thrown it out of a window, and run off' and that I must 'fix it immediately or they will call the police'. What to do? This was worse than any of Keith Moon's antics. I was horrified. I leapt into my Mini, raced to the hotel to pick up Ronnie Van Zant, and we drove around Notting Hill for hours trying to find Bob. Around 9am the next morning, we found him wandering around Hyde Park, stoned out of his mind – or maybe just mentally unbalanced. I realised I would have my work cut out for me with these boys.

Artimus Pyle, who went on to replace Bob Burns as drummer, was an enigma. He could be brooding, difficult, unpredictable and unreliable. As I said in the beginning, he missed the bus one day, so I left him behind as I had threatened to do. When an important rule is broken, consequences are inevitable. Plus, Artimus was frequently stoned on acid, which certainly didn't help my job. Nevertheless, he was also very deep-thinking, which

I learned to appreciate later when we had a brief fling.

As soon as Lynyrd Skynyrd took the stage, the magic would begin, and what magic it was. Words aren't enough to describe it. I feel that their leader, Ronnie Van Zant, has never really been recognised enough. The man was a fine wordsmith, a poet. His songs told stories. They were heartbreaking stories, political stories, love stories and stories of street fighting. He was a genius and will always be a hero to me. Ronnie and I had a special bond and I miss him terribly. He was a charismatic and wonderful person, not your average rock star, but his charisma shone through. Ronnie was rather short and tubby and performed without shoes – an oddity, but not even his mama could get him to wear them. The world was a better place with him in it. When sober, he was the archetypal Southern gentleman, but when drunk, he could become very dark and vicious, and he would fight with anyone who pissed him off. In fact, Skynyrd usually had an almighty fight after a gig, arguing about some mistake, a bum note, or something else only they noticed. I never did, and I'm sure neither did anyone else in the audience.

Left to right: Gary Rossington, Allen Collins and Artimus Pyle of Lynyrd Skynard
(© Kate Simon, with kind permission)

Just like young boys, the fun and games began after the fighting was over. Everything you could imagine – women, drugs, rock and roll – would happen at the hotel. As usual, I stayed away from the partying, knowing I would have to deal with the hotel manager who was bound to appear at some point. I had to keep a clear head at all times, and be able to 'snap to it' in case of emergency, or in case of police arrival – which also frequently happened.

I was tour manager for all of Skynryd's European tours throughout the United Kingdom and Europe up until the plane crash in 1977. If there's one thing I discovered about these Southern boys, it's the fact that they have an ambivalent attitude towards women – a sort of 'madonna/whore' mentality. Fortunately, they put me on the madonna/mother side and respected me, listened to everything I told them, and always obeyed me. People have often asked if it was difficult to work with these 'ignorant rednecks'. My impression was that they preferred being bossed around by a woman they respected rather than another man. Maybe it was some sort of macho, ego thing?

Rather than treating them as adults, I often treated them like small boys. I remember Leon once saying, "Please don't give me the evil eye. You terrify me when you do that!" I remember thinking, what 'evil eye'?! I probably got so fed up with him one day that I chastised and glared at him. My nanny instincts must have kicked in! For some reason I felt a deep abiding love and affection for these boys. It was as if we'd all known each other in a previous life. That's the only way I can describe the bond between us. It was as if 'they' were an amorphous 'one'. Obviously, that doesn't make sense, since they were each unique and wonderful individuals, but their destiny seemed to be intertwined with mine. When they realised I truly loved their music, and was totally trustworthy, they started to include me in their 'group hug' and prayers before they went on stage. This was the most massive honour for me.

Lynyrd Skynyrd on The Old Grey Whistle Test, 1975

A YouTube must-see

When they came back for their 1975 tour, Skynyrd were asked to appear on The Old Grey Whistle Test (OGWT). I explained to the boys the importance of this show. There was no other TV show in England that played proper rock and roll. Their appearance on it was an honour, especially at such an early stage in their career. They – and I – were thrilled to be invited to play on such a prestigious programme.

I drove to their hotel on my Harley Davidson motorbike to check that the crew had already left with the instruments and gone to set up. Then I joined the boys as we travelled in two limos to the BBC at Shepherd's Bush. We went four in a car: me with Ronnie, Gary and Allen, and Bob, Leon, Ed and Billy followed (there were no girl singers at this point). What a laugh I had with those boys as they were all overwhelmed by London's sights and sounds – the traffic on the wrong side of the road, the small cars. I particularly remember Allen commenting on how scary our police looked with their massive helmets. At that time, the IRA was frequently setting off bombs, so the police were probably wearing some sort of protective gear. Isn't it funny how we Brits are so in awe of the American policemen on TV and film, yet these Americans were impressed by the English coppers on our streets?

As we walked through the lobby area, all the BBC staff stared in amazement at these guys with long hair and cowboy hats. I was glad to be met by my wonderful friend, Mike Appleton, the producer of the OGWT, who immediately put the boys at their ease, as they were very nervous. Good old Mike was always the most friendly and cheerful man.

The boys performed an amazing set that consisted of:
'Double Trouble'
'I ain't the One'
'Call Me the Breeze'
'Same Old Blues'
'Every Mother's Son'
'Sweet Home Alabama'
'Free Bird'

Watching it on YouTube, they all look so young and fresh-faced – as if butter wouldn't melt in their mouths. Ronnie had a famous snarl, with just a slight curl at the top of his lip, that could look quite menacing. Gary and Allen took turns playing lead guitar, and they managed without Ed King, their usual third guitarist, who had left the band not long before. By then, Artimus Pyle had replaced Bob Burns on drums. There are some wonderful close-ups of Gary and Allen's hands, and especially of Billy's on keyboards. My boys did well! When Ronnie thanked their UK management, Trinifold, he meant *me*, as I was the one who looked after them 24 hours a day, seven days a week.

Since the OGWT show, Mike Appleton has told me that Skynyrd's 'Free Bird' was the most requested song ever on the Whistle Test – over and above all the big bands: even Led Zeppelin, the Rolling Stones, The Who, and so forth. I truly believe 'Free Bird' is the best song ever written, and to be there, at the centre of it all, was magical for me. After the plane crash, all of this changed. I couldn't listen to their music without sobbing my heart out. Even when I was with them again in the wings (the newly formed Skynyrd, years after the plane crash, with Ronnie's brother Johnny singing) I had to leave during 'Free Bird' as I would always be so distraught that I would be on the floor in total despair of what I – we – had all lost…

Sally with Mike Appleton, producer of BBC's Old Grey Whistle Test
(© Michael Putland, with kind permission)

For me, the main magic was Ronnie's voice. If a voice can be charismatic, then Ronnie's certainly was. I was in heaven listening to these boys every time they performed, and I will never forget those wonderful, precious years when I was with them on every single European tour they ever did, as well as many concerts in America. Unfortunately, Ronnie's voice sounded especially rough the day they appeared on the OGWT because of a terrible cold he had. It's clear in all the other YouTube films that Ronnie's voice was usually so much better than on that show. Skynyrd's tours of Europe were always in the winter, since Pete Rudge, their manager in New York, wanted them back in America for summer concerts in the big stadiums. Rudge always looked at the financial side of things. It's no surprise all the boys got ill with colds and flu whenever they came to the United Kingdom and Europe. I was forever taking them for Vitamin B12 injections (that was the legal 'drug of choice' then). Although, they didn't relish the massive needle being stuck into their bums! We had a list of helpful, sympathetic and unshockable doctors who were great when we needed strong medication for some 'unspecified' illness, usually brought on by too much alcohol, grass and cocaine. Goodness – they could snort mountains of the stuff. During the drive back to the hotel after the recording of the OGWT, everyone was happy and in good spirits. After they arrived, the party ensued with all the usual accompaniments, so it was no wonder that their colds never got any better! The boys partied and enjoyed London life, as did I, seeing it afresh through their eyes.

The 'in' place for lunch and dinner at this time was Mortons and Tramp was the main nightclub. According to its owner, Johnny Gold, I was the first female member to join. Can that really be true? I still have my old membership card, which cost me the grand sum of £45. That was a lot back then, but nothing compared to what it is today. By this time, I had moved from my small one-bedroomed flat in Hurlingham Road to a much larger one off Fulham Palace Road, with two bedrooms and a lovely conservatory and roof terrace. Great for parties.

It was at that flat that Kenny Pedan, a lovely Skynyrd roadie I'd had a lovely quick fling with, tried to climb up the drainpipe to my flat. I rushed downstairs when my doorbell rang, and there he was, a long-haired Kenny standing between two London cops. The woman downstairs thought he was a burglar and called the police.

"Would you like to press charges?" the police asked me.

"Of course not," I said. "He's not dangerous or a criminal. Just silly!"

During dinner at Julie's restaurant in Notting Hill, I discovered that he'd had a 'sexual encounter' with a supposed friend of mine. I chucked a glass of red wine over him, walked out, and drove straight back to my flat. Twenty minutes later, who should be chucking stones up at my windows? Kenny. Despite everything, we remain in touch today, which is fabulous. He was one of the few survivors of the Skynyrd plane crash and the manic years.

Chapter 11

The Love of my Life

Following the success of the 1974 tour, Lynyrd Skynyrd returned to Europe in early 1975. With them was a young man, Dean Kilpatrick, who hadn't been with them previously. He was Ronnie Van Zant's closest and best friend, the person who did everything for them. Someone who knew them all so well that he could almost read their minds and sort out any problem. I didn't know it at the time, but this man would eventually become the love of my life.

Another thing I didn't know was that, after we met, he phoned his parents in Florida to tell them he had met the girl he was going to marry. I never would have dreamt that he would be interested in me, since he was so beautiful, but Dean flirted with me non-stop. I was living with a boyfriend at the time and I wasn't remotely interested in him. Many of the New York staff looked down on him, but they hadn't taken the time to find out anything about him. Dean was highly intelligent, smart as a whip – and *very* naughty! He wasn't a Southerner like the others, having been born and raised in Connecticut until his family moved to Florida when he was a teenager. Then he met Ronnie, Allen Collins and Gary Rossington, and they all became firm friends. Initially, he shared an apartment with some friends, including Judy, who later married Ronnie.

I would like to share some quotes about Dean that really put into words what type of person he was. In Marley Brant's book, *Freebirds: The Lynyrd Skynyrd Story*, Judy Van Zant says:

> Dean was a really flashy dude…he introduced me to Gary and then I met Ronnie and Allen and the rest of the guys.

And:

Dean is part of Lynyrd Skynyrd history because he goes back to day one.

In the same book, Ronnie is quoted as saying:

Dean will be with us to the end.

Little did we know how prescient that would be. In an interview for the book, Dean's mother commented:

He made quite an impression, especially with the girls, with his good looks, beautiful hair, and tall, thin body. Sometimes he looked like a Jesuit priest or a shepherd leading his flock through the airports with the band.

Brant writes:

With his tall stature and Celtic good looks, Dean was a magnet for the opposite sex. A little jealousy would sometimes erupt within the band, as Dean always had women hanging around him. However, the band soon realised that they could work their friend's magnetism to their advantage. Skynyrd was delighted when Dean decided to sign on as a full-time roadie.

Brant also quotes bass player Leon talking about Dean:

He was nothing but A-1 class, first class. Dean easily fit into the band's family as a loyal and trusted brother.

[From *Freebirds: The Lynyrd Skynyrd Story* by Marley Brant. ISBN: 0-8230-8321-7. The above is produced with permission from the publisher Backbeat Books, Rowman and Little Publishing Group. All rights reserved.]

Incidentally, this is the best book I've ever read about Skynyrd.

Also in the book *Lynyrd Skynyrd: An Oral History* by Lee Ballinger, who quotes Cameron Crowe, now a famous film producer/director, then a writer for *Rolling Stone* magazine:

Dean was an important guy. He was a great guy, a skinny, lively guy. He was like a spark plug and he would kind of dance around in between the other characters and really kind of set them off in a great way. It was a nice kind of chemical that was in the mix.

Bands tend to have that one guy that's kind of a link to the beginning – trustworthy, entertaining, quick with a joke, keep things up, keep things moving [...] these guys are the unsung heroes of a road tour. He was part of it. These are the guys who keep rock alive, real important parts of the spirit of a band, and ultimately, the music of a band. It's sad when you see a guy like that disappear from the history books (1998).

[From *Lynyrd Skynyrd: An Oral History* by Lee Ballinger. ISBN: 0-9720446-3-9. Publisher: XT377 Publishing. All rights reserved.]

True enough, that's what Dean was: their shepherd. On the road, he took care of all their needs, such as finding a laundrette nearby or a place to eat, organising all their backstage requirements, their clothes, and their onstage drinks and cigarettes. This made many people think he was just a gofer, a loyal runabout, their factotum, but there was much more. He planned to become an actor and was a very talented artist.

Dean studied art in Florence. When in Italy with the Committee for the Restoration of Italian Art (CRIA), he spent many months restoring damaged works of art in a monastery. He prevailed upon his parents to

Left: Dean Kilpatrick, and right: Sally and Dean, September 1977
(Photos from author's personal collection)

116

support and embarked on this adventure straight from high school. Dean and his fellow workers from other countries would take side trips to Venice, Milan, and Pisa on weekends. When returning home, he went through Paris since he was determined to see the Louvre. Dean was a brilliant artist and the centrefold of the Skynyrd Gold and Platinum album features a sketch he drew on the wall of the band's practice studio in Jacksonville. I saw it many times on my visits there, and it has some hidden gems and jokes which only those on the inside would understand!

Still, he was no saint. He and Allen got up to the most outrageous things – off into the night to clubs and bars, getting up to who-knew-what. Yet, Dean could always be counted on to do whatever was needed for the band the next day.

Artimus describes Dean as:

> …playing a vital role in the band. He was the No 1 go-to-guy at home and on the road. Any problems needed solving, he was our man. His dedication and efficiency were second to none. If Ronnie was the band's general, Dean was our aide-de-camp.

Artimus also said:

> I think Ronnie had a little hair loss one time when somebody threw a candle and the wax immediately dried all over the top of his head and it took weeks to get it out. He had Dean sitting there for weeks with a fine-tooth comb getting stuff out!

Dean never gave up on me over the years. I remember vividly how he reacted when he found out I'd split up with my boyfriend. It was one night in 1975 at the Hammersmith Odeon (as it was then). Dean and I were standing on the side of the stage as the band played, when one of my office staff told him that I was now single. I had never seen such a reaction! The man went into near-ecstasy when he realised that I was now available.

The next day he arrived at the office with a really huge bunch of flowers and a beautiful antique silver heart necklace for me. His ability to pull all this together in just a few hours amazed me. I couldn't help but wonder, did he already have the necklace, just waiting for the right moment? Being that the shops had just opened, he must have been pretty quick off the mark buying the flowers too.

The formation of management company Trinifold Ltd, and Trinifold Travel

Bryan Walters, our accountant, suggested we start our own travel company, since we spent a fortune on hotels and travel for the bands. I recommended Mike Hawksworth from a travel company we'd been using – and so Trinifold Travel was born. We started out as just me and Bill in the New Bond Street office, but when Mike joined us we had to move to a larger office in Kingly Street, behind Regent Street in the West End. Along with Bill and Bryan, Tony Smith, who by then was the manager of Genesis, and promoter Harvey Goldsmith became directors. I was offered a directorship by Bill but, unfortunately, I couldn't afford the £5,000 the others had each contributed to get the company going. It's a shame, as it became an extremely successful company and there were lots of perks, like weekends away in flash hotels! The majority of UK bands, managers, agents and promoters used Trinifold Travel for many years.

There were big dramas in 1975 when Bill Curbishley and Pete Rudge had some massive rows. These led to their split as partners, with Bill keeping The Who, and Rudge keeping the Stones and Lynyrd Skynyrd. Five One Productions closed down, so Bryan Walters came up with a list of company names, and Trinifold just came from a list of available names at Companies House (it wasn't started up by Bill and his wife Jackie, as Wikipedia incorrectly indicates). Bill asked me to be a director as well, and I still have a sheet of the original notepaper, which states: *Directors: W G Curbishley, S R Arnold and B Walters*, with our new address, 12 Kingly Street, a phone number and the telex number. No internet or emails then, of course.

There were so many arguments between Pete Rudge, Bill, Kit, and Chris around this time. I somehow ended up in the middle of a never-ending argument between them all. It wasn't about this one or that one; it was a culmination of things. With so many hands in the pot, I suppose these things are bound to happen. It got to a point where Kit began suing all and sundry, including Robert Stigwood (who produced *Tommy*), Bill, and even his old business partner, Chris Stamp.

In March of '75, the film *Tommy* had been released and was a huge success, but The Who remained at daggers drawn for much of the time. Pete and Roger didn't see eye to eye on anything. Pete was, seemingly, disillusioned with the whole business, not to mention he was almost always drunk or stoned. Roger (who I never saw drinking or using drugs) was filming and got fed up with Pete's attitude. There was an awful lot of animosity at this time, but of the band, John was pretty quiet during most of this. And Keith? Well, he was in the States a lot of the time, flying back and forth when needed, and one event is etched in my memory forever. We were in Scotland on a tour that October. While stuck at Prestwick Airport due to fog, Keith got into one of his hysterical moods. Fed up with being stuck for so long, the poor woman at the British Airways counter suffered an unrestrained Keith shouting, "What the fuck is going on? I want to leave now! Why can't we leave?" Not satisfied with the fog explanation he was given, Keith being Keith, kicked the computer, causing the entire airport system to crash. Not surprisingly, he was arrested and thrown into prison. Of course, it was my job to get him out in time for the next gig. I immediately called our lawyer at Theodore Goddard, Paddy Grafton-Green. As you can imagine, Paddy and I had numerous late-night telephone conversations about this and had

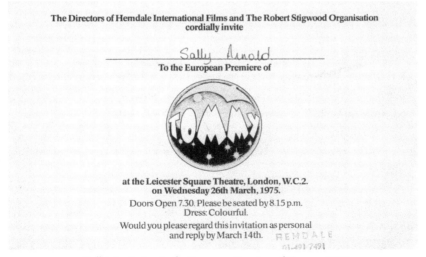

Sally's invitation to the European Premiere of Tommy, 1975

to enlist the procurator fiscal to release Keith from custody. In the end, we managed to get it done. Basically, this was my job – to get the band on that stage the next night come hell or high water.

A certain level of drama always surrounded Keith – whether it was as serious as getting arrested or as 'innocent' as pulling a prank. At another airport (or maybe it was a hotel lobby) Keith came up to me in a total panic, with blood pouring from his mouth.

"Oh my God, Keith. Are you alright?! What happened!?" I gasped. "I must get you to a doctor!"

I immediately jumped up to go to the lobby phone, when Keith burst out laughing. He'd been to a joke shop and it was fake blood. That was classic Keith – always playing jokes on everybody. I was always quite gullible. I believed everything – to my detriment at times.

One day, a man with a very foreign-sounding accent called my office and said, "Hello, it's Dr Buky here."

He sounded similar to Dr Buky, our German doctor, but he had never called the office...ever. I thought it was a prank call; in truth, I thought it was my boss Bill teasing me, so I said, "Oh fuck off, Bill. I know it's you..."

To my dismay, it really was dear, sweet Dr Buky. I'd used such foul language, and he was such a polite gentleman – I felt terrible and have never forgotten it.

I have to leave The Who

In February 1976 I was forced to leave Bill Curbishley and The Who. It started with Bill saying to me one day that his wife, Jackie, wanted to come and work in the office 'as my assistant'.

"Well, Bill," I said, "you know that won't work, but I totally understand that you've got to give it a go. Obviously your wife comes before your assistant."

So my boss's wife ostensibly came to work as my assistant.

Before this, everybody who wanted to speak to Bill came through me, his PA. I was the 'gatekeeper', but as soon as they knew his wife was there, they all wanted to speak to her. She had his ear more than I did, so I was very quickly edged out. Even though I understood that Bill had to bring his wife into the office to keep her happy, it broke my heart. I loved working with The Who and their crew. They were all wonderful people. I missed them terribly after I left although, thankfully, some of us stayed in touch for many years.

When I called the States to tell Pete Rudge and the Skynyrd boys that I was leaving Bill, Ronnie Van Zant's touching response was: "If Sally's leaving Curbishley, then we're leaving Curbishley."

True to his word, the band did just that and all their future European tours were handled solely by me.

Chapter 12

The Rolling Stones

In 1976, I met up with Pete Rudge on his next visit to London, and he asked me to run and head up his new company and office in London. We resurrected Five One Productions, initially for the Stones' European tour. From that point on, I was to organise the Stones' and Lynyrd Skynyrd's – as well as Pete's other bands' – European tours. Again, I was put in a position of authority as company secretary, with Pete and his then-wife, Frankie, as directors. (Later, Frankie went on to marry famous film director Elia Kazan.) I had to find and furnish premises for an office for the upcoming '76 Rolling Stones tour of Europe. This was quite an undertaking, as I had no one to help me at this point. The New York accountant and his assistant were also coming from the United States, so I had to find junior staff for the office *and* for them. The accountant turned out to be the wonderful Bill Zysblat (we always called him Bill Zee). He went on to be David Bowie's financial manager and made him a fortune with complex internet deals. I recently read that Bowie had *'the most impeccable estate planning on his death'* – all handled by Bill Zee.

The office I found was in a basement in Mount Street, Mayfair. Since I was in charge of purchasing all the office furniture and equipment, including telephone and telex lines, I bribed the post office guy with free albums to put the lines in quickly. Telex machines were the most technologically advanced equipment, which we thought were totally brilliant – revolutionary at the time. The written word could be transmitted without having to go through a laborious telegram process. The telex was a massive piece of machinery with a Qwerty keyboard and numbers. You had to type out (or rather, heavily bash out) your message, which punched holes into a thin strip of plastic.

To transmit the message, you would then feed the tape back into the machine and send it off to the recipient's number. Even though it was quite fiddly and time-consuming, at least it was something in writing, which was often necessary when it came to agreements and contracts. Plus, it was useful since long-distance calls to the States were expensive. Along with finding and furnishing the office, I also helped Pete find a nearby house to rent before, during and after the tour. The house was in Hays Mews in Mayfair and belonged to Joan Collins. It was literally just around the corner from the office, so Pete could walk to work. It was a beautiful old house, done up in flamboyant style, with huge ruched and flouncy curtains that trailed onto the floor – a luxurious and fashionable home at the time.

During the early stages of planning and organising this Stones 1976 'Tour of Europe' (nicknamed TOE), I remember being there late one evening with Pete. He was on the phone to Mick Jagger in Mustique. He passed the phone over to me, saying Mick wanted to speak to me.

"So, Mick," I asked, "do you mind if your old nanny is the assistant tour manager?"

He sweetly replied, "Of course not. We can have cups of tea together and talk about Jade."

Considering we hadn't seen each other for four years, and my departure from him and Bianca in 1972 hadn't been exactly happy, I thought that was a lovely thing for him to say. If my memory serves me well, there was also a peculiar thing going on for him at the time. Pete was worried about Mick's health and whether he'd be able to make the tour, since he was reportedly taking heroin. But all was well in the end.

In February we started meeting with the various European promoters: Fritz Rau and Mike Schiller from Germany, Norbert Gamsohn and Albert Koski from France, Claude Nobs from Switzerland, David Zard from Italy, Guy Merceder from Spain, and Mel Bush, Fred Bannister and Harvey Goldsmith here in the United Kingdom. Pete always drove a hard bargain with them, which was easy because they all wanted the Stones. This was also a time before big money was being made from touring, because there were no sponsors then – only the record company picking up the tab for some things, and the proceeds of the tours themselves. Even the promoters kept the interest from the advance ticket sales. That's all changed now as bands and managers have become much more savvy. We also met up with various technical guys such as Brian Croft for sound and lighting, Edwin Shirley and Roy Lamb for trucking, and Jim Callaghan for security.

Billy Preston, keyboard player and long-time associate of the Stones, had his own 40-foot trailer for his gear and at least one truck for the canopy roof. The local promoters provided the actual stages in those days, so there were no 'steel' trucks. Although, Brian told me we had four trucks hauling 30 tonnes of equipment. Apparently, for their 1989 Steel Wheels tour, there were ten semi-trucks worth of scaffolding to support the stage alone! The 30 tonnes of equipment seems so small in comparison.

On that 1976 tour, the vast stage cost £150,000 and took a team of fourteen to build at each venue. A bank of 300 lights weighing 16 tons was suspended 30 feet above the stage, and a mirror – 25 feet by 6 feet – was turned at an angle towards the stage, hovering some 20 feet away. It took eight hours to get the set down!

> The lighting was spectacular and so were some of the special effects. Jagger being swung from a rope far out across the audience was exciting, though it was clearly disappointing for him that the enormous inflated phallus that emerged during Starfucker was quite so limp. He's still unique.
> – *The Guardian*

Brian Croft was the stage and production manager, and the most important person on all these tours. He organised all the sound, lighting and crews (and for all my later charity events). I asked him to fill in some of the details, but he admits his memory is a little faded these days:

> As for memories – loads of them but none fit to print on account of incriminating those still living, for financial skulduggery, illegal drug use or things too vulgar to mention!

Those interested in the history of rock and roll's technical side can find a whole section on Brian Croft in the Appendix. He was involved from the beginning at the Institute of Contemporary Art (ICA) in The Mall in London in 1968. During those early days, there was no rock and roll business in the United Kingdom, and most of the crew came from the theatre world.

Today there are probably hundreds of such companies, but there were few technical providers at the time. One trucking company, Edwin Shirley Trucking; one lighting company, ESP; and one sound company, Marshall Equipment Hire.

My nannying experience was apt for working with rock stars. I sent out the following 'Nanny's Rules' memo to everyone on that Stones tour in 1976:

Springtime in Germany (inspiration by Mel Brooks)

1   All personnel, except the band, are allowed two pieces of baggage and everybody will be responsible for their own bags.

2   When anybody is out for dinner with any members of the band, it does not necessarily mean that the tour is paying, and they may have money deducted from their per diems.

3   Payment of 100 Deutsche Marks will be paid by everybody if they lose their photo pass.

4   Jim Callaghan is in total charge of security, and at the first sign of any trouble, whether it be at the hall or in the hotel, he is to be informed immediately. He is also in charge of 4 walkie-talkies.

5   The remaining security people are only employed for security, and are not to be used in any other capacity whatsoever.

6   All staff must pay all personal charges made to their rooms one hour before checking out, to avoid a 10% charge. Per diems will be paid every other Wednesday, beginning April 28th, for two weeks in advance. Salaries are available if required. Any enquiries: go to Bill Zysblat.

7   BAND: At the moment very little in the way of food has been requested from promoters in the dressing rooms, so please look in your books and anticipate your need for hot food. Inform Sally Arnold what you will need.

8   NO cars are to be taken by anybody from the hotel or anywhere

else without first clearing it with Alan Dunn. If a car is used without his knowledge, it will be charged to the individual.

9   No-one is to talk to any of the press whatsoever without first clearing it. Careless talk means lives…!

10   Baggage calls will be on each night's newsletters, as always, and on this tour especially MUST be adhered to.

11   The crew will not speak until spoken to!

12   NEWCOMERS: A newsletter will be distributed by Sally to everyone's room immediately after the show each night, informing everyone of the next day's arrangement. If in doubt about how to leave the show, speak to Alan before the performance and he will coordinate this.

13   Don't argue with foreign-speaking uniform-wearing gentlemen…however wrong they appear to be!

14   Once again, just to be boring, WEAR YOUR PASSES AT ALL TIMES.

15   Lights out at 9pm each evening and no noise…bed check at 10pm…

I would type the newsletters late at night on my portable typewriter, then go down to the hotel's office, where I could use their photocopier. I'd push a newsletter under everyone's bedroom doors so that they knew the plans for the next day: what time I'd be giving them all a wake-up call…what time their baggage must be outside their doors…what time they needed to check out of the hotel and pay their extras…what time the bus/limos were leaving…where we were going and how (plane, cars or bus)…name of the next hotel and venue…time of buses or limos for soundcheck…and, finally, time of the gig. We used pseudonyms for the band at check-in: Mick was Arthur Ashe (and sometimes Mr Mercedes Benz or Michael Philips, his middle name being Philip; our nickname for him was MPJ). Keith was Percy Thrower. Woody was Patrick Moore. Charlie Watts was Peter West. Bill Wyman was Robin Day. Billy Preston was James Burke. The percussionist Ollie Brown used his own name.

On this tour there were covered amps on the stage behind the band. The amps were hidden by drapes, and this was where the boys would put their coke and heroin. One side of the stage for coke, the other for smack. Keith and Woody also smoked DCs – dirty cigarettes. They would empty out some of the tobacco, replace it with whatever, and to all intents and purposes they looked just like normal cigarettes.

On 28ᵗʰ April 1976, the tour began in Germany, then went onto Belgium. Then to the United Kingdom, ending that leg at Earls Court on 27ᵗʰ May. After that, it was back to Germany, Holland, France, Spain, Switzerland, Yugoslavia and ending in Vienna. With forty-one shows in twenty-two cities in nine countries, this tour played to 554,000 people, easily eclipsing previous tours. It was also the first time the Stones performed in Yugoslavia and Spain. It was exhausting for us all, but we were young and enjoying ourselves.

By this time all the European promoters knew of my preference for classical music, so they would arrange for me to have tickets for, say, the

Ronnie Wood of The Rolling Stones, Paris, 1976
(Photo from author's personal collection)

Berlin Philharmonic or the Paris Opera. I usually went alone to these perfor-mances on my nights off, as it was my only peace and quiet away from the eternal noise and requests of the boys, although Charlie came with me to the Berlin Phil, where we had a whole box to ourselves.

The support band was The Meters from New Orleans, who were, on the whole, lovely guys. One of the band members even wrote me a letter at the end of the tour saying:

> You were the sunshine of this tour. You and you alone saw me through this shit. Thank you for being you and you will always be in my mind.

Then a letter arrived from their tour manager who said:

> Thank you so much for all you did for us, which was above and beyond the call of duty – I could never have done it without your help.

How truly lovely. It was heart-warming to feel so appreciated by these boys.

I did, however, have a nasty encounter with one of their roadies in a hotel. I was heading back to my room when this guy suddenly jumped into the lift with me. He shoved me to the back of the lift, pushed the button so that it came to a standstill between floors and started to try to get my clothes off while shoving his tongue down my throat.

"I want you to sit on my face..." he growled.

What is wrong with men who fail to realise this is *not* the way to try and seduce a woman? Better and more effective tactics exist. Luckily, I kicked and wriggled enough that I managed to reach the necessary button with my foot...and the lift continued going up to my floor, where I leapt out.

"Fuck right off and leave me alone!" I yelled – which, thankfully, he did.

This was the only time I've come close to being raped and, even though it probably only lasted no more than three or four minutes, I vividly remem-ber every second.

As the tour manager, many people were terrified of Pete Rudge, but I thought he was a silly little boy who had massive temper tantrums. He was a very different type of boss to Bill Curbishley. Bill was always calm, decent, and respectful. He was everything a boss should be. Pete, on the other hand, was the opposite. He had an explosive temper, was utterly controlling and dominated with an obsessive zeal. One minute he could be nice and charming, and the next a monster screaming and shouting at everyone around him. One member of staff even likened him to Hitler! At one point, I even threatened to walk off the tour after one particular row with him in Spain, but Bill Zee begged me to stay, saying the tour couldn't manage without me.

Working for someone like that is exhausting. However, I was wary of him and kept my distance when he was in one of his moods. An interesting biblical quote from Proverbs 18:2 states:

A fool hath no delight in understanding...

Most people didn't realise how much work I had to do as assistant tour manager. The work was never-ending. It was a 24-hour job dealing with a thousand and one problems at each show, hotel, airport, resulting in massive amounts of stress. I was constantly on the go, had to stay alert and be prepared for anything that came along, including when I encountered eccentric, extravagant, and well-known public figures.

At the Stones' Earl's Court show in London on Sunday 23rd May, I crossed paths with Princess Margaret. "Ah, cocaine," I heard her say. "Such an amusing drug, don't you think?" Later, the Atlantic label boss Ahmet Ertegun threw a party at Sotheby's where many famous people, including Van Morrison, were among the attendees. I also met Leni Riefenstahl at the Berlin concert on that tour. I had to look after her by showing her from backstage to her seat, and backstage again to see Mick. A fascinating woman, but her connection with Hitler always left one with a bad taste. In fact, when I first met the German promoter, Fritz Rau, I wondered if he had fought against us in WW2. I was immensely glad to find out he'd been part of the resistance.

One of the UK venues was near Bob Pridden's house, where some of us – including Mick – stayed. Bob lent me a car to get to and from the gig, but when I was leaving the venue after soundcheck, Mick suddenly decided he wanted to drive. He drove so badly, pushing the poor little car beyond its limits, that the engine died. There we were, me and Mick Jagger stranded at the side of the road, waiting for help. I kept wondering, how long was I going to be stuck like this with a very nervous Mick? Not long, I hoped. He must have been nervous about being recognised, which is understandable, but luckily Bob drove by a little later and rescued us. Getting stuck on the side of the road with Mick Jagger was the least of my worries during that tour. One of my main problems was with the keyboard player, Billy Preston, and his numerous boyfriends. There were always big arguments and breakups. Whenever he decided he'd had enough of one, I would have to arrange for cars and flights to get rid of him, only to arrange for another young man to fly in – it would then start all over again! I saw six boys come and go in total, maybe more.

All the way up to the last concert, there was always something happening. On the last day in Vienna, I was in the hotel lift with Keith Richards and his son, Marlon.

A woman got in and questioned, "Shouldn't that child be in school?"

Keith's response to her question was to lash out and shout, "It's none of your fucking business!"

I don't know what she was thinking, but the words running through my head were, oh shit.

Thankfully, the woman just left.

A few days earlier, I had asked Keith about Marlon going to school, but I'd received a less abrupt reply. "He doesn't want to. He says he won't like it."

"Well, how can he know he won't like it if he's never been?" I asked. "Why don't you let him try it and then decide?"

That's precisely what he did, and Marlon thrived at school. He even grew up to become an architect. Like most kids, he loved learning and is quoted in Keith's book saying that he just wanted to go to school.

Keith says in his memoir, *Life*, that he was unpredictable in those days. He would often have to be pushed on stage by a couple of roadies, and as he staggered on, he would start playing the wrong chords (no urban legend there, it's true!). He said there were times when his blood would boil. He would get irate, and a red mist would descend. It could be horrendous sometimes. He was also known as 'blood-change' on the road, because of the supposed treatments he would receive in Swiss clinics before a tour.

All of us assumed Keith had blood transfusions to rid his body of heroin. He says in his book that nobody will ever know for sure.

Marlon's mum, Anita Pallenberg, arrived just a few days after the Paris gigs in early June, just a few weeks after the death of their newborn son, Tara. Keith and Anita were devastated by the death of this baby. Anita had been addicted to heroin for a long time. She brought Dandy, their toddler, with her. One evening, Bianca (with whom I maintained friendly relations) and Astrid Wyman came to me to ask my professional opinion as a Norland Nurse. They had found out that Anita wasn't treating Dandy very well. My immediate reaction was to say we should report this to the police. Fortunately, there was no need for such drastic action. Not long after this, Dandy went and lived the rest of her life with Keith's parents and, under the circumstances, I think that was a good decision. She changed her name to Angela (her real name on her birth certificate).

Many years later, Anita and I found ourselves on the same botanical painting course at the Chelsea Physic Garden in London. We would chat for

Sally with Mick Jagger, Phil Carson and Marlon Richards (Keith's son)
(© Michael Putland, with kind permission)

hours about Keith, the children, and the tours. She was particularly proud of her allotment, which she tended daily, cycling to and from her flat in Chelsea. Brave girl!

Following the Stafford gig in May, Keith was involved in a car accident on the M1. The first I heard about it was when one of the roadies banged on my hotel door in London with poor little Marlon in tow. I was told what had happened while Marlon was in floods of tears, asking where 'Dada' was. Keith had been driving his Bentley back to London with a bunch of people in the car, including Freddy Sessler, his drug dealer. When Keith saw the police car behind him, he chucked a load of coke out of the window. Even so, the police found a big chunky silver necklace in the car with several ornaments on it – including a silver tube for snorting coke and heroin. Naturally, the police found traces of drugs in it and Keith ended up in prison at Newport Pagnell. Since we didn't know when he would be released, I was responsible for Marlon for the next day or so. He knew me well enough and we had fun together, playing with his dinosaurs and learning how to read.

At one point, Marlon asked me, "Will the birds be alright? Will they be able to get to sleep?"

Puzzled by the question, I asked what he meant by that. Marlon explained that Dada threw the 'stuff' out of the window, and he was worried that it would keep the birds awake since it always kept Dada awake.

When it came to the court case, Keith's lawyer asked me to be one of the people who would attest to Keith's good character. This would have been fine, but then he asked me to say I'd never seen the silver necklace. Which of course, I couldn't do. Not only had I seen it, but I had also even used the silver straw on it with Keith, Anita, Mick, Woody and others on various occasions. In fact, there were even publicity photographs of Keith wearing the necklace, which I'm surprised the police didn't discover. The lawyer threatened to subpoena me when I said I wouldn't say I had never seen it.

"Fine," I said. "Subpoena me, and I'll tell the truth about the necklace. I refuse to perjure myself."

I didn't appear in court, but others did, and I suspect they committed perjury. However, I did attend the court case in Aylesbury in October. I'm so glad I didn't have to appear, as it would have been terrifying to lie in front of so many barristers and the judge – all in their robes and wigs. This was the first time I'd ever attended anything like that, and it was all pretty intimidating even without having to take the stand.

At this time, a journalist friend had been nagging me to introduce her to Keith, as she wanted to write a book about him. Eventually, I gave in and asked Keith, who said okay. She proceeded to write the book, but I never got the promised credit, and she then just dropped me as a friend. How nice. Having got what she wanted, I guess I was no longer any use to her. Sadly, this was not the only instance of published interviews gone awry. In 1990 or thereabouts, the writer A E Hotchner asked me if he could interview me for his upcoming book about the Stones. Stupidly, I agreed, but not before writing to the band, asking if they objected. None of them did, so I carried on. It was a mishmash of misquotes and exaggerations, and I even threatened to sue Hotchner at the time. With the benefit of hindsight, I realise that he was just being 'creative' by misquoting me and probably others, to make it sound more outrageous (no doubt to sell more books). Around this time, Simon and Schuster, the publishers of Hotchner's books, contacted me to see if I would help them on a problem with their *Andy Warhol Diaries*.

Andy Warhol wrote in his diaries about Bianca taking cocaine. Bianca threatened to sue Simon and Schuster for damages, claiming that she'd never taken the drug. And the publishers wanted me to say I'd seen her taking coke. I refused to get involved. Bianca prefers to forget those days, but Andy Warhol wrote many times about her being at Studio 54 with him. Someone once said the club was like Rome before the fall.

During the years between 1974 and 1980 I frequently visited New York, and went to Studio 54 a few times with various people, sometimes Bill and Astrid Wyman, and Lorna Luft and her sister, Liza Minnelli (Judy Garland's daughters). It was totally bonkers. There was even a large model of a popper (an amyl nitrite capsule) floating above the dance floor, going backwards and forwards on wires! Due to who I was with, I was privileged to enter the VIP areas.

When it comes to the Stones, I'm often asked what they are *really* like. I can readily say that Keith was great. He's a good guy when he knows and trusts you. The other question is how come he's still alive after taking so many drugs for so long? Well, as he has said himself, he only used high-quality drugs and was meticulous about how much he took. The same thing is asked of Mick. When I was nannying Jade in 1971–72, he was fine. So much so that I testified on his behalf in the divorce from Bianca, and stated that he was the better parent. On the tour, however, he tended to be defensive and offhand. Even though he would often say, "Come on, nanny, let's have a cup of tea," and we would sit and chat about Jade and how she was doing, he could also be very disdainful. Keith even wrote in his book that Mick would slowly begin to behave defensively and if he wasn't making things difficult, you'd think he was ill!

During one of our long train journeys, Mick and Keith asked if they could come into my compartment where I'd gone to read and for some peace and quiet. "Of course," I said. Then they sat down and wrote a song together, each singing and strumming their guitars. At the time, I didn't realise how privileged I was to be in such a position. Sadly, my memory fails me, and I can't remember which song it was, or which album it was on.

There was also never any drama with Charlie. And Woody was always sweet and easy to deal with. Although, he once left his passport at the hotel in Berlin, which was only discovered upon arrival at the airport. Someone had to race back to get it (again, that's why I always tried to carry everyone's passports on the road). On that flight out of Berlin, I was sitting between Woody and Keith. There was a very great deal of heavy turbulence and I was terrified, as the plane couldn't divert out of the 'flight corridor' it had to stay in while flying over East Germany. I don't remember which one of them gave me a pill, but thankfully it put me straight to sleep. The next thing I remembered was being woken up and taken through the next airport by them. This wasn't the only time Keith and Woody came to my rescue. The two of them helped me out in another situation that was much more critical. I was in my hotel room in London with Woody, Keith, and others. While sitting at the desk doing my accounts, the coke (or so I thought) was passed around on a picture taken off the wall. It was white, so I took a rather large line, assuming it was coke but, after a few minutes, I began to feel... odd. Very odd.

Luckily, Woody and Keith realised what had happened. "Oh no, Sal! You didn't think that was coke, did you?"

I'd never seen white heroin before, so had just assumed it was coke. A lesson learned. Needless to say, I became very ill, but they looked after me for hours and were both so kind to me.

During one of the last nights of the tour, I was exhausted, but still needed to do some paperwork. I didn't want to take any coke or speed. I just needed something to keep me awake for a little while. To my surprise, one of the roadies told me to ask Charlie. What!? I had no idea Charlie had anything like that. So I knocked on his door and he beckoned me into his room. I managed to pluck up the courage to ask him if he had something that would help me stay awake for a couple of hours so I could finish my work. He opened his suitcase where he had a variety of pills. It was like a private doctor showing me his wares!

Pointing at different bottles he said, "These will keep you awake for two hours, these for six hours, these for longer. Which would you like?"

I opted for a two-hour pill. Having known him since I was a nanny for Jade in 1971–72, I was very surprised to find out about this side of Charlie. Although, some years later when I was running The Who's Double O Charity, Pete Townshend told me that Charlie had also had problems with heroin. Keith also notes in his book about the 1984–85 period that Charlie was having his own wobbles. This was a surprise at the time, but it's well known now. He was always kind and thoughtful, quiet and unassuming. His clothes were always immaculate – he wore gorgeously cut three-piece suits. Quite the dandy in an unobtrusive way. He was completely cool and collected. Even when we went baby shopping together in LA all those years ago, no one noticed him. One time, my parents bumped into Charlie when they visited me at the office in London, and he was extremely polite and courteous, which absolutely floored my father. Initially, he didn't believe Charlie was a Rolling Stone. He thought the band were all long-haired louts!

A couple of times Woody came knocking on my hotel bedroom door late at night, but I always told him not to be silly and to go back to his room. Especially as I knew and liked Krissy, his then-wife. I once had an especially amusing experience with Woody and Mick trying to seduce me when I had to take something to Mick at Cheyne Walk. He and Woody were already quite pissed and stoned when they tried to get me into the bedroom.

I'll never forget Mick saying, "C'mon, baby girl, you know you want to."

How many times had I heard him use that phrase when trying to pull some female or other? As always, I quipped, "Don't be silly, it's me! Nanny."

At the risk of repeating myself: I never wanted to sleep with any of these guys as it was all too easy. I would prefer to be the one who didn't, rather than one of the hundreds who did. Although many young women were hanging around (I hate the word groupies), Charlie and Keith were never interested in them. I shared Keith's quoted feeling that it was all a bit of a cliché, and *'all too easy'*, as he wrote in his memoirs. He knew he would be judged too, of course. Bianca was well aware of Mick's antics though. *The Sunday Times* quoted her as saying they were 'nobodies trying to become somebodies'.

The 1976 tour was followed by a one-off gig at Knebworth on 21st August. The other bands playing were the Don Harrison Band, Hot Tuna, Todd Rundgren's Utopia, 10cc, and my boys, Lynyrd Skynyrd. Fred Bannister promoted it in conjunction with Five One Productions (it's now available on YouTube). The crowd was enormous, obviously eager to see the Stones. Many of them didn't know much about Skynyrd, but then quickly went from indifference to adulation…my boys had done good again! I'd flown them in by helicopter and they were quite overawed to be at the pre-show champagne party with Jack Nicholson, Dave Gilmour of Pink Floyd, Jim Capaldi, John Paul Getty III, John Philips of the Mamas and Papas, Ian McLagen, Van Morrison, Judy Garland's daughter Lorna Luft, and Paul and Linda McCartney. The Stones finally took the stage at 11.30pm and played until after 2am. This late ending had a massive knock-on effect on numerous people – not least my choir.

Thanks to a conversation I'd previously had with Mick, I arranged for members of the London Symphony Orchestra Chorus to perform that night. Mick and I had been sitting next to each other on a flight when we were listening to, and singing along to, 'You Can't Always Get What You Want', reaching those lovely high notes. Originally it was sung by the Bach Choir on the recording. Mick knew I sang with the LSO Chorus, and asked if

I could arrange for them to sing 'Land of Hope and Glory' at the Knebworth gig. I agreed, even though it blew my cover. The choir had no idea what I really did for a living. Since I got tired of people asking me "What is Mick Jagger like?", I just said I was a secretary. Most of my workmates didn't know I sang in the choir, either. It was like living a double life. With a choir of about fifty people now in the set, I would not only be responsible for the Stones, but also for Lynyrd Skynyrd, and the LSO Chorus. I even had to hunt out Bob Dylan, as a mutual friend had asked me to tell him she was there. I rushed around backstage trying to find the man among the milling throngs of famous musicians who were hanging out there! The whole event was extremely hard work, to say the least.

Drama ensued afterwards as it seemed the promoter, Fred Bannister, lied about ticket sales and allegedly ran off with some of the money. It even reached the point where the band demanded that aerial photographs be used to count the audience. Bill Wyman mentions this in his book.

That September, we lost a member of our touring family. Mick McKenna and Keith Harwood were travelling on the M4 after leaving Mick's country house, Stargroves, when they were involved in a car accident. Though Mick was very badly injured, he managed to continue running the Stones' Mobile. Tragically, Keith was killed. He was a sweet, friendly man and his death was devastating to all of us. This was the first time I had lost someone I considered a friend so young. Little did I know I would lose many more the following year.

After the tour, Stu (Ian Stewart, the sixth Stone, who was the original pianist and then their production manager) asked me to work in the Stones' office. In the end, I decided not to, as I didn't want to continue living a life of sycophancy – nor did I want to spend my days running around doing errands for Bianca and Astrid. Some years later, the Stones' PR guy at Rogers and Cowan asked me if I'd be interested in working for him on a Stones tour, but I declined. Somebody once said there is nothing healthy about fame. Celebrities often have short fuses, are insecure, arrogant, and egotistical. I didn't need to live vicariously through my work to boost my ego. And anyway, Skynyrd was the only band my heart was really into, so I would continue working with them.

I stayed with Bill and Astrid Wyman in the south of France quite a few times after that tour. They introduced me to some amazing people – we had lunch at the artist Marc Chagall's house, and also with the American writer James Baldwin. Bill had become good friends with them both over the years, and it was thrilling for me to meet such wonderful creative people. Another time we went out for pizza with Princess Caroline of Monaco. I'll never forget being in her limo on the way to a nightclub, driving along the Croisette in Cannes. She told us how keen her mother, Princess Grace, was on wildflowers and taking her children for walks in the hills above Monte Carlo. The famous song 'If they could see me now' came to my mind then. There was little old me hanging out with famous artists, writers, rock stars – even princesses!

Bill and Astrid were the best hosts, but I wasn't fond of Bill's habit of asking all the women to 'show their boobs'! I'm in no way prudish; I just found it childish and distasteful. There's a time and place for nudity, and the dinner table is not it. On another occasion, Bill showed the film *Deep Throat* in his private cinema to a few friends – well, I fell asleep! The film was quite ridiculous, in my opinion. How many times can you watch a blow job without getting bored!? Even when I witnessed it in real time, I fell asleep! On the Stones' private plane from Barcelona to Nice, a member of the Spanish crew offered some of us a few pills to help us stay awake. By mistake, he gave us sleeping pills! After getting on the plane, I fell asleep and woke up periodically in a daze and saw Anita giving Keith a blow job on the other side of the aisle. This was just the sort of thing you'd see on rock and roll tours on private planes. I was so bored and uninterested in what was happening, I just went back to sleep!

Finally, as well as the lovely thank you letters from The Meters boys, I had another one from our advance man, Mike Crowley, who said:

> I can't even begin to tell you how much I've enjoyed working with you. You've made it all much easier. If there is anything I can do for you – ever – please don't hesitate to call [...] Please stay with us in Washington if you need a place. And don't forget that you will have a private lane and a fat pilot at your disposal!

Top: Author James Baldwin and Rolling Stone Bill Wyman
Bottom Left: Artist Marc Chagall, Bill Wyman, Astrid Wyman
Bottom Right: Sally with Astrid Wyman and Marc Chagall
(Photos by Sally Arnold, South of France, 1981)

Chapter 13

Lynyrd Skynyrd Again

After that Stones tour, I needed to find a new office. Since I would only be working on Lynyrd Skynyrd's European tours in the near future, my Mount Street office was too big. Harvey Goldsmith offered me space in his offices in Welbeck Street. (Harvey split from John and Tony Smith and became an independent promoter. Tony Smith went on to manage Genesis.) My small office was next door to Paul Loasby, Harvey's number one man at the time, and we became very good friends. I admired his brilliant mathematical mind, which made him invaluable to Harvey in negotiating deals with the various bands they were promoting. Plus, he was the only one I knew in the UK music industry who liked the same things I did – classical music, particularly Wagner, literature, and the theatre. It was nice to have that like-mindedness, which was rare in that world.

From that office, I organised the next Lynyrd Skynyrd tour of Europe. Pete Rudge was still in New York and Bill Curbishley was no longer there to help me or take charge. I was on my own. It was challenging but rewarding – I felt in my element. I was good at the job and enjoyed being so busy.

During the early part of 1976, as I was also organising the Stones European tour, the Skynyrd boys arrived to headline their next tour. On the first night of their tour, Leon Wilkeson, the bassist, decided to throw a table out the window of the Holiday Inn in honour of his good chum Keith Moon. Leon was such a wonderful guy despite, or perhaps because of, his very naughty nature. Whenever he had the chance, Leon would play all sorts of pranks. He even persuaded a London policeman to give him his helmet, which he proudly wore on stage many times.

After the table incident, I received a letter from the Holiday Inn Group banning Lynyrd Skynyrd from all their hotels. I saw this letter being sold online and I wondered who was selling it. I'd had a bad experience with a guy who I'd asked to help me sell my rock and roll memorabilia, so maybe it was him. He actually tried to rip me off, so I took him to the small claims court and won. Lesson learned: be careful who you trust.

During this tour we all stayed at the farm of a friend of mine in the Cotswolds, Gloucestershire. It was midwinter, with snow everywhere – especially cold for these boys from sunny Florida. Not surprisingly, Ronnie ended up with a sore throat, so a totally mad chum of mine rubbed a mustard pack on his chest. It seemed to do the trick though! While at the farm, Simon Kirke, from the band Bad Company, showed up and they all jammed, the sound of their music wafting through the house. The next morning after a huge breakfast, I took Gary and Artimus riding at Steve and Nicole Winwood's house, where I stabled my horse. The three of us went riding in the freshly fallen snow. Eric and Pattie Clapton were visiting Steve and Nicole at the time, so I arranged for them all to come to the Skynyrd gig in Bristol. To my embarrassment, the Skynyrd boys kept bowing and genuflect-

Allen Collins and Ronnie Van Zant of Lynyrd Skynyrd, Knebworth, 1976
(© Michael Putland, with kind permission)

Lynyrd Skynyrd at Knebworth, 1976
(© Michael Putland, with kind permission)

ing to Eric, calling him 'God'. I was rather embarrassed as I knew he hated it.

I continued to keep Dean Kilpatrick at arm's length during this tour. I didn't honestly think he would be good boyfriend material. With girlfriends all over the world, he was a player, a naughty boy. He usually dated models or actresses and I couldn't help but think, how could I possibly compete? Still, he continued to chase me. He would phone me nearly every day from wherever he was in the world with the band. He even saw me through my short-lived crush on Artimus, the drummer.

Dean was very clever. He knew Artimus and I had had a quick fling, but of course it could go nowhere as Arty had a wife and family. I had joined the band in San Francisco early in 1977, and Dean took me to Arty's hotel room, where his wife and family were staying too. Dean instinctively knew that once I'd seen this family set-up, I would give up my passion for Artimus. How right he was. I had no desire to break up a family. But it was all just that little bit too obvious for me, and I didn't give in to Dean. That night, he chased me down the hotel corridors, drunk and stoned, declaring his undying love for me. I certainly didn't want to deal with him in that state. So I hid from him in Ronnie's room. That's where I learned how

'Southern men took their cocaine' as Ronnie would tell me!

We sat up until very late, drinking Jack Daniels and taking coke. Ronnie laid out massive lines along the edge of the tabletop, about three feet long! There was no way I could do that amount. I was always a light-weight when it came to drugs. Ronnie proceeded to tell me that he wanted to get into country music at some point, and mentioned that he'd like me to manage them. He also told me how much Dean was in love with me and had been from the minute we met. When I told Ronnie about my doubts, how Dean always had such beautiful girlfriends, and that I feared that I wasn't good enough for him, he quickly put my mind at rest. In fact, all three girl singers also told me Dean really loved me, and it wasn't just a passing infatuation. Hearing this, and considering the fact that he'd chased me for two years already, I decided to give him more of a chance.

That night, I ended up sleeping in Ronnie's bed. He woke up the next morning with an erection (naturally!). When he tried to screw me, I just said, "Don't be so silly. All boys wake with an erection. It means nothing. We don't want to ruin our precious friendship."

I'm so glad we didn't have sex. I didn't want to ever change or ruin the deep friendship we had. It was far too important to be ruined by a quick fuck. One of the women in the New York office had slept with Ronnie (and other members of the band), and I didn't want to be like that. I knew how the band and crew spoke about her – with disdain and a total lack of respect. This woman had tried to sabotage me behind my back, spreading rumours about me because she disliked me intensely. The most ludicrous one was that I had slept with Jimmy Page of Led Zeppelin, and Peter Grant, the band's manager. Not only was this utterly untrue, it was borderline ridiculous since I'd never even met either of them! She never knew who I had actually slept with: I managed to keep that a secret from pretty much everybody.

Rumours are one thing, but she went so far as to remove my name from the list of people Ronnie Van Zant wanted to give silver, gold and platinum record awards to. The other girls in the office would put my name back on the list, only to find it erased, again and again. I often wondered why she hated me so much. It wasn't until thirty years later that I found out that Pete Rudge used to scream and shout at her: "Why can't you run the office like Sally does in London?" No wonder. I wish I'd known that before, then many things would have made more sense to me. Throughout my career, it was always men who supported me and gave me opportunities. While I always tried to help other women, I was usually bitten in return.

The first time I really got to know Dean was in San Francisco. I had a blast walking around the city with him. We went over to Fisherman's Wharf, wandered around the weird and wonderful stalls, and he bought me a lot of crazy gifts. It was great to spend three days eating, drinking, and getting to know each other better, without the usual band nonsense that usually surrounded us. During this trip, I realised that maybe I could love him, but I didn't tell him this until our next meeting in Jacksonville, in September 1977, for the wedding of Gary Rossington and Martha.

Their wedding was rather unusual. Dean and Allen Collins were the best men, and one of the crew members, Dave Evans, officiated. He had recently been ordained as a spiritual priest and performed a wonderful ceremony. I'm still in touch with Dave who recently retired from working at a scientific laboratory in San Francisco and is still a spiritual priest. (I love the mix of science and spirituality that he has.)

During the time of the wedding, I stayed with Dean in his wonderfully stylish apartment overlooking a tributary of the St Johns River. At the time, I was so worried about him because he had just been released from the hospital after a terrible car accident and had his spleen removed. He was so pale and wan. In the photographs of us at that time, he truly doesn't look like his normal, smiley self. I didn't realise what a big deal this surgery was until my mother underwent it after a car accident. I remember Dean sobbing at one point. Looking back, I now think it was probably because of the pain, though he never mentioned that to me. Instead, he ploughed on through the agony.

It was on this trip that I gave in to Dean's wiles. He was fascinated by beautiful people generally and interested in sexuality not just being straightforward; we recognised that in each other. But not everything was wonderful. He was often in considerable pain from his operation. It was such bad timing for us, but neither of us worried too much about it because, by this time, I realised that I really could love this man and that we had a future together. Even though I'd been proposed to before, I'd never actually agreed to marry anyone, apart from Jean-Pierre, as I'd never really wanted to get married before. Suddenly, everything changed. Dean suggested we have a double wedding with Gary and Martha.

"You're crazy!" I said, "It's their day. We mustn't spoil it. We don't need to rush into getting married immediately. There's no hurry. We've got our whole lives ahead of us."

We chatted about our future together. I would manage the band and Dean wanted to study acting and art. So we thought about where to live, and decided on Atlanta. We wanted to be somewhere we could get some culture, with good art galleries, restaurants and classical music. We had it all worked out. The only people we told were Ronnie and Judy, Allen and Gary, and both sets of parents. Little did we know that our plans would come to nothing. It sounds like something out of a film, doesn't it – we've got our whole lives ahead of us…then a love lost…

Also on this visit for Gary's wedding, I spent many hours with Ronnie,

Gary and Martha Rossington, 1977 (Left: Billy, and right: Artimus and Ronnie)
(Photo from author's personal collection)

145

Judy and their baby daughter Melody. While I was there, an alligator got into their swimming pool and frightened the life out of me. Ronnie just grabbed his rifle and scared it off – apparently that was quite common. I had never seen anything like it before: a 'gator in the garden! Ronnie also took me to visit his parents. I'd met his father, Lacey, when he came over for one of the tours, but never his mama – or 'sister' as she was known to them all. They said anyone Ronnie trusted as much as me must be a good person, so they welcomed me into their home.

Once again, Ronnie asked me to manage the band. We were sitting outside having a drink in the early evening, with the sun setting over the St Johns River in front of us – me, Ronnie and Judy.

Ronnie said, "I hope you realise I was serious when I asked you to manage the band? Our management deal with Rudge is up in November, so we want you to move over here and manage us from then on. We've been having doubts about Rudge for some time now. Join us on the upcoming tour, which will give us time to sort out all the details, and at the end of the

Left to right: Allen, Ronnie, Artimus and Billy of Lynyrd Skynyrd, 1975
(Photo from author's personal collection)

146

tour in Hawaii we can all celebrate. We can give you and Dean a fantastic engagement party!"

Having lost The Who previously to Bill Curbishley, Rudge needed Skynyrd badly since he was only tour managing the Stones at the time, not their manager, as some mistakenly thought.

"But Ronnie," I said, "you know that Rudge will never let you go that easily. He'll shoot my kneecaps off if I take over your worldwide management, since you're his only money-making band."

"Nah, it'll be fine," Ronnie said. "Besides it's what we want – it's what the whole band wants. And don't worry about Rudge. We'll look after you...!"

I don't want to repeat his exact words, although I recall them vividly, but he was hinting at reciprocal violence.

So it seemed my future with these wonderful boys, and married to Dean, was all set. What's that phrase: God changes things while you're busy making plans...or something similar? I knew that Ronnie had sounded out a couple of other people about managing the band so we'll never know what would have happened; but it was me who Gary and Allen chose to manage the survivors' band, the Rossington Collins Band, and Judy Van Zant always reiterated that Ronnie had wanted me as the manager of Skynyrd.

Then I had to return to London. I'll never forget the drive to Jacksonville Airport. A friend was driving, and I was sitting on Dean's lap in the passenger seat. We were happy and in love. Large, dark storm clouds gathered overhead, and I was terrified of flying in such bad weather. Dean calmed me down, saying pilots and planes were used to flying through these storms and not to worry, everything would be fine. As it was, of course.

My last sight of Dean was of him waiting behind the final security desk waving me goodbye. I had no idea that this would be my last sighting of him. I happily waved back, and flew off to New York to meet up with various people to discuss managing the band. I was so excited for the future. A whole new life lay ahead of me. I couldn't wait to get back and hunt for an apartment or house in Atlanta for us to start our new life together.

Chapter 14

The Lynyrd Skynyrd Plane Crash

What happened next… How do I even begin? How do I write about the plane crash? How do people cope with tragedies like this?

To begin with, that phrase 'time heals' is rubbish. I believe the quote from the Queen Mother describes it well: "It doesn't get any better, but you get better at it." Yes, I have the benefit of time gone by – over forty years now – and I have been through the classic stages of grief: denial, anger, bargaining, depression and acceptance. Yet sometimes it still feels like it happened yesterday. I don't think I could have written about it before.

I had organised things in London, rented out my flat, and I was all packed and ready to join Skynyrd on their upcoming tour of the States. I was supposed to join them on Thursday 20th October. Their first Madison Square Gardens concert was to be on 10th November, and we were all excited. Their friends and families would be there, and it really was a big deal for all of us. Plus, I was looking forward to the big party the next night, when Dean and I would officially announce our engagement. We'd then have a proper engagement party in Hawaii at the end of the tour in early 1978 with all the band and crew.

On the evening of Tuesday 18th October, Dean phoned, as he did every evening.

"Hey, baby doll. How ya doin? We've got a big problem with the fucking plane and pilots. The plane's falling to pieces and the pilots are always drunk. Ronnie's furious, especially with Rudge for hiring such a cheap plane, so he demanded a new plane. So, change your flight, baby doll, and come out on Saturday instead, as we're getting the new plane on Friday."

That conversation saved my life.

Evening Standard, October 1977

On the evening of Thursday 20th October 1977, Lynyrd Skynyrd's private plane crashed. This was the last flight on that plane, but the pilots hadn't put in enough fuel. Well, they put enough in for a *normal* flight, but one of the magnetos failed. The unexpected malfunction used up more fuel than anticipated, which led to the plane running out of fuel just ten minutes and a few miles from the airport in Baton Rouge. They crash-landed in the swamps and the people at the front of the plane were all killed – both my beloved Dean and wonderful, wonderful Ronnie Van Zant, as well as sweet, darling Cassie Gaines and her brother Steve, and the two pilots. If I had been there with them I would have been sitting up front with Ronnie and Dean, so he did, quite literally, save my life.

The first I knew about it was just after midnight in London. I was asleep in my flat when the phone rang. It was another English tour manager friend who was in the States. He told me he'd heard on the radio that Lynyrd Skynyrd's plane had crashed and they didn't know if there were any survivors.

I spent the following hours in turmoil, trying desperately to phone Dean's parents. It took me hours to get through and I was in despair. Was he alive? How badly was he injured? What about all the others – my wonderful friends who I loved so dearly? How could this have happened? When I eventually spoke to Mr Kilpatrick all he said was, "We've lost him."

I don't remember much about what happened in the days that followed. At that moment, my life fell apart. The plans we had made for our future were gone – all of them. My beautiful, beloved boy was gone. How could he do this to me? How could he leave me? What was I going to do now? His poor parents, oh my goodness. What they must be going through…it doesn't bear thinking about.

I eventually managed to contact my dear friend, Ginny, at the office in New York. She told me that Ronnie, Steve and Cassie Gaines had also died. There were so many lives totally and utterly destroyed by incompetent pilots. Cassie – dear sweet Cassie who shouldn't have been on the plane anyway. She was supposed to have been in one of the trucks with her boyfriend. Poor Carina, Steve's wife, and their little girl. Oh God – no – poor Judy and Melody, to lose their beloved Ronnie.

A nasty incident at this time was about the woman at the New York office who seemed to really hate me. One of the worst lies she told about me was to Dean's parents after he had died. She told them I wouldn't be able to go to his funeral as I couldn't get into the States because I had a drug conviction. How horrible and unkind can one person be? Apart from being totally untrue, what about the shocking effect this lie could have had on Dean's parents when they were told this about their soon-to-be daughter-in-law? That lie was wicked in the extreme. Many years later, when I was being given a lunch party in New York by mutual friends, this woman asked to come. "No," I said. "I never, ever want to have anything to do with her ever again."

It's all common knowledge now, but the plane had nosedived into the ground, with the nose breaking off. The six people at the front had died on impact – the two pilots, Ronnie, Dean, Cassie and her brother Steve. A few years ago, Kenny Pedan (the Skynyrd roadie who climbed up the drain-pipe at my Fulham flat) tracked me down. He's one of the few survivors of the plane crash. In his email, he told me that they'd done the rehearsals in Georgia with the new music for the album *Street Survivors*.

"That's the best stuff I've heard since I've known you," he said to Ronnie.

To which Ronnie replied, "It's just some ideas Steve and I came up with."

Kenny thought it was brilliant. It just goes to show how well Steve Gaines had blended into the band as the new guitarist and songwriter. Kenny carries on in his email:

> We went on to do 6 shows before the plane crashed. I think I was hurt least of all, with a broken nose and a few cuts and fractures. Artimus, his drum tech, Mark, and I were the only ones able to walk. We made our way through the swamp to a farmhouse. There are so many stories I've heard over the years, some from Billy, some from Artimus and all seem to have a different version of what happened. In Billy's version he was the hero, in Artimus's version he was the hero. I heard Artimus claim, on Howard Stern's show, that he was shot in the shoulder by the farmer. That's not true. He just fired a shotgun in the air because he was scared that we were escaped criminals from the nearby jail.
>
> I had nightmares for years. Cassie and I were watching the sunset when the engines failed. She got up to go up front, but then she came back, and we switched seats so she could get seated more quickly. It bothered me for years

that she died and I lived. But I guess it just wasn't my time. It didn't ruin my life, but it put one hell of a hole in it. You're one of the few people in the world I can talk to about it and who knew the band well.'

The people in the middle of the plane survived, but they suffered terrible injuries; the people in the back were not hurt as badly. Over thirty doctors attended to all of them in various hospitals in McComb. It took four hours to remove all of the passengers and pilots from the plane.

Leon Wilkeson, the band's bassist, later told me what it was like. Just a few minutes before the planned landing at Jackson, the pilots warned them that both engines had cut out and that they would have to make a crash landing. Leon was sitting in the middle of the plane, and took the crash position, as everybody else did – except Ronnie, who was asleep on the floor at the front of the plane. Obviously there was panic and fear, but Leon couldn't face telling me about it.

He described the last few minutes:

The plane was going down, I could see the sun setting out of the window, there was a noise that sounded like gunfire – pop, pop, pop – the tops of the trees were being sliced off by the plane. It landed nose first into the swamps. The next thing I remember is lights and noise and wind above me from the helicopters. They managed to get us out and took us all to hospital.

I still have the *London Evening Standard* article dated Friday 21st October 1977 with the front page headline: ROCK STARS KILLED IN AIR CRASH. The report from Gillsburg, Mississippi continues:

Ronnie Van Zant and five other people died when a chartered aeroplane carrying the Lynyrd Skynyrd rock band ran out of fuel and ploughed into a thicket in Mississippi.

The dead included guitarist Steve Gaines, his sister, singer Cassie Gaines and the plane's pilot and co-pilot. Twenty other people are in hospital, some in critical condition.

Identification was hampered because the passengers were playing poker and had their wallets with identification paper out when the plane crashed. A federal aviation spokesman said, "It's a miracle anyone walked out." The plane was a chartered twin-engine, propellor-driven Convair 240.

The hospital said at least six survivors of the band had been admitted. They were Gary Rossington, guitarist; Allen Collins, guitarist; Billy Powell, keyboards; Leon Wilkeson, bass; Artimus Pyle, drummer and Leslie Hawkins, back-up singer.

The aeroplane, en route from Greenville, South Carolina to a concert tonight at Louisiana State University in Baton Rouge, ran out of fuel and began a death glide. It clipped the tops off tall pine trees for 100 yards and then slammed into the thicket. It almost made it to an open field.

A member of the Gillsburg volunteer fire department said when he reached the crash, three members of the band had scrambled out of the aeroplane and gone to a house a quarter of a mile away for help. "They were in pretty bad shape, one of them had some ribs sticking out and the other two had blood all over them," he said.

The official report from the National Transportation Safety Board stated that 'the probable cause of this accident was fuel exhaustion and total loss of power from both engines due to crew inattention to fuel supply'. Contributing to the fuel exhaustion were inadequate flight planning and an engine malfunction of undetermined nature in the right engine which resulted in higher than normal fuel consumption.

The ever-wonderful Brian Croft was one of the many people who contacted me. I still have the handwritten letter he wrote to me:

Oh Sally, what can I say that could possibly help at a time like this. I was deeply shocked when I heard the news about the terrible accident. If you need someone to talk to, please don't hesitate to call me. It must be like losing family for you, love. You have our deepest sympathy, Brian.

I have never forgotten the kindness he showed during the most terrible time of my life. He and his wife are true friends indeed.

Instead of going to our engagement celebration, I changed my flight to the 23rd and flew out for my fiancé's funeral. Dean's friends met me at the airport and I was so distraught they gave me some Valium to calm me down. I don't remember much of the following days, but I vividly recall seeing Dean's body in the casket at the chapel of rest. I'd never seen a dead body before and I wasn't ready to see my darling Dean's. Initially, I was too emotional to look at him but once I overcame that, I managed to touch his lovely hair and kiss him goodbye. He looked serene and peaceful, but not quite 'Dean'. With his friends by my side, we decided to put a joint into the casket with him, knowing it would amuse him. I told his mother about this many years later, and she wasn't at all upset, thankfully. And then came the funerals...

Ronnie's private funeral was held at Rivermead Funeral Home in Orange Park. Billy was the only band member well enough to attend. Dave Evans, the roadie and spiritual priest, officiated just as he had a few weeks earlier at Gary and Martha's wedding. Our hearts were broken beyond words – especially when we saw Ronnie's casket with the black cowboy hat on it, being carried down the aisle by his brothers and friends.

Dean was buried at the Arlington Cemetery after a beautiful service, where I sent him roses for many years afterwards. I have visited his grave many times since, as I did Ronnie's vault at the Memorial Gardens in Jacksonville.

In 2000, Dean's mother emailed me to tell me that the graves of Ronnie, Cassie and Steve had been vandalised and there was a reward for the culprits. Ronnie's grave even had to be moved though, because fans tried to dig it up.

Dean's mother died at the end of 2021 at the grand old age of ninety-eight, and we enjoyed emailing regularly. Her emails provided a semblance of comfort:

> When Dean told me he'd met the girl he was going to marry, he didn't have to say anything else. I knew he had found his soul mate, his true love who would fulfil him with her love always, his Sally.

> He told me that you were sweet and beautiful and very, very intelligent and came from a really nice family, etc. It was easy to see he was head over heels in love with you. I knew he would never settle for anything less, Sally. You were 'all of the above and then some'.

Recently, one of his cousins wrote to me as well:

> You are such a special person and it makes us even prouder of Dean to think

that he chose someone like you, Sally, to share his life, and that you could feel the same about him.

Dean's mother has given me permission to repeat this eulogy from his funeral:

> During his many years of working with Lynyrd Skynyrd, Dean Kilpatrick was well known for his peerless professionalism and impeccable personal ethics. Dean was there from the beginning, jumping in to do whatever he could to help the band become the superstars he felt they were destined to become. He was very much a member of the Skynyrd family and the members of the band quickly embraced him as one of their own.
>
> Dean was the quintessential Renaissance man. He was a truly gifted artist and participated at the age of eighteen in the restoration of fine art in Italy as part of Jacqueline Kennedy's assistance to that country following a devastating season of floods. Throughout his time with Skynyrd, his artwork graced everything from sketchpads to the wall of a recording studio. A natural extension of his art and talent was his trend-setting fashion sense. The man knew how to wear clothes. And the ladies loved him.
>
> Dean had a keen mind and the ability to master whatever may come his way. Whether it was complicated mechanics, custom building or the intricacies of touring, his work reflected only the highest levels of accomplishment. Dean's wit was legendary, and he had an outrageous sense of adventure and fun.
>
> But far and away the overwhelming consensus of those who knew Dean was that he was the consummate friend. Dean was extremely loyal and was someone who could be counted upon in the best and worst of circumstances. He displayed a gentle, generous side, always silently watching for those who might need his help. He was always there with a welcoming heart, and he remains a very bright light in the lives of all those who were blessed to call him a friend.

From Skynyrd's first tour in 1974 to the last one in 1977, I had been with these wonderful guys through every minute of every single one of their eight European tours. For me, they were a huge part of my life. I shall never, ever forget the ones we lost in the plane crash: Dean, Ronnie, Cassie and Steve. Then later Leon and Billy, and Allen of course, despite the grief he would cause me.

I stayed with Martha Rossington (Gary's wife of just a few weeks) and went to the hospital with her and Kathy Collins (Allen's wife) where the survivors were being treated. Although their husbands were still alive, their physical injuries would take many years of treatment, and they had all lost their closest friends. We were all in a state of shock. Every one of us had been changed forever. Chuck Flowers, an original roadie and very old friend of Ronnie's who hadn't been on the plane, felt he should have died with them. He was so overwrought that he shot himself with a gun Ronnie had given him. The trauma of losing so many friends, especially Ronnie Van Zant, was too much for him.

By 1st November, I was in Atlanta staying with Dave Evans and hanging out with guys from the Southern bands Wet Willie, Little Feat, and the Atlanta Rhythm Section, all of whom knew and loved the Skynyrd boys. We were all mourning together.

A couple of years later, I stayed with Leslie Hawkins, one of Skynyrd's backing singers. She was in a terrible state, both physically and mentally. She was only able to leave her house for short periods of time, and one of those times was to take me to a rodeo – a real, proper rodeo. Her friend was competing in the national rodeo championship. It was thrilling! They displayed amazing horsemanship and physical skill. The unfortunate thing is that they don't stay in this for very long since they are always getting hurt. Leslie told me in a 1978 letter that neither the band nor the management helped her out:

> I only have workman's compensation coming in now, which is not very much. Nothing from the band. Not even insurance. The guys all have that, which helps them. I didn't find out I didn't have it until too late. I guess you can tell I still have a little trouble writing, but my arm is gradually improving.

After Skynyrd's plane crashed, I'm not sure what Pete Rudge did. I heard he opened a sportswear shop in Madison Square Gardens. I think he did two more Stones tours and managed various bands. I only saw him once many years later at the Chrysalis party in 1998 in London. He had to be pointed out to me, as he looked so unrecognisable. A facelift perhaps? But he did say that I'd been the best assistant he'd ever had!

Chapter 15

Crawler

In 1977, following the funerals in Jacksonville, I tour-managed Crawler in the United States. Previously they had been Backstreet Crawler, before band member Paul Kossoff died. Their manager, an old friend, told me that it would be good for me to get back to work immediately. This was a lifesaver. The job was hard at times, but I threw myself into it. The infamous Rabbit (John Bundrick) was the keyboard player in the band, and his drinking and drug taking were legendary. He once kicked in a glass door in a hotel, in a drunken rage, resulting in a horrible gash in his leg that I had to clean and bandage for the next few weeks. Even so, he was a sweetheart and a true Southern gentleman when he wasn't drunk. We became firm friends. He frequently stayed in my room on the road so I could look after him and keep him company. Holiday Inns always have two double beds, thankfully!

My diary is blank for most of the tour during November and December, except for a few days in the South for gigs in Dallas and Houston. From there I flew to Jacksonville to see my friends from Skynyrd. I visited Judy Van Zant, Teresa Gaines, Gary and Martha Rossington, Billy and Stella Powell, and spoke to Allen and Kathy Collins. Then I visited Dean's parents. This was such a sad and difficult time for us all. We had lost our beloved boy and nothing would ever be the same again.

Throughout the years, I have travelled to see Dean's mother several times. She also lost her daughter to breast cancer, and her husband died just after Dean. For so many years she had only me to talk to about Dean, until her death at ninety-eight in 2021.

Following my time with my Skynyrd friends and family, I flew with Crawler from the humidity of the South to Portland, Maine, where it was cold with deep snow. Then to New York for a few days, where I managed to see my friends from Pete Rudge's office. In the New York hotel, a strange thing happened.

The receptionist called my room one day and said: "Are you sometimes known as Sally Kilpatrick?"

I stuttered something like, "Well, yes, why?"

"We have a call for you."

I waited, wondering who was going to be calling me at my New York hotel referring to me as Sally Kilpatrick.

Then I heard a woman's voice: "Hi Sally, my name's Linda Blair."

Yes, it was the actress from *The Exorcist*.

"I found out you were staying there," she said, "and decided to call you to say how sad I was about the Skynyrd plane crash. Dean and I were good friends, and he told me all about you, and about how much he adored and respected you, and that he couldn't wait to marry you. That's why I asked for the English woman, maybe called Sally Kilpatrick – as I don't know your proper name!"

This was strange. We had all thought Dean had had an affair with Linda Blair, yet there she was telling me that all he did was talk about me when he was with her.

The tour with Crawler was my final tour in the States. I was seemingly living the dream, flying out to America regularly, mixing with celebrities, travelling first class, and staying in fabulous hotels – but I'd had enough. My heart wasn't in it any longer. On my return to England, I decided to set up my own company and approached a colleague, Gillie Prudence, who was working for the promoter Harvey Goldsmith. We set up Tours Unlimited with an office in Brian Croft's TFA Electrosound warehouse and offices. An article in *Billboard* magazine, dated 10th June 1978, stated that we could '…be just the answer to the multitude of problems encountered by promoters and tour managers'.

The London Evening News reported how well we were doing, and I was quoted as saying, "Basically it's like nannying them all. Super-nannying. One has to be tactful, diplomatic, and make an effort to get through to the toughest nuts."

We organised a few gigs for different bands, including some early shows at the Hammersmith Odeon for the Boomtown Rats, and for the American Blues guitarist Albert King, who told me I was the best tour manager he'd ever had.

My friends, Steve and Nicole Winwood, told me that their neighbour, Mike Oldfield, was planning his first tour during the early months of 1979. Although Steve knew me mostly on a personal level, he recommended me as a tour manager to Mike. I was surprised by this, but I could only assume he observed me working with the Skynyrd boys a few years back.

Steve and Nicole were my regular weekend hosts, as I kept my horse there and went out with the Cotswold Hunt. Prince Charles hunted with us occasionally, and he and Camilla Parker Bowles even joined us for a Hunt Breakfast at a friend's house. It was widely known that they were dating then. Steve taught me a great deal about the history of hymns and their composition in the Victorian era, especially by such composers as Ralph Vaughan Williams, Gustav Holst, and Hubert Parry. I even met Viv Stanshall (of the Bonzo Dog Doo-Dah Band) at the Winwoods' and what an astonishing man he was! During one of my weekends with Nicole and Steve, we all went to Mike Oldfield's house for a party. A lot of their musician friends were there, and they started jamming together. Nicole then got me to sing with her and Steve in 'Gimme Some Loving'. Imagine, little old me singing with the wonderful Steve Winwood! That was a very big high.

There was considerable gossip about this upcoming tour of Mike Oldfield as he had never toured before, even after his earlier success with *Tubular Bells*. I was the only female tour manager pitching for the job against three men, two of whom I knew well, Richard Ames and Rick French. I'm still in touch with Richard, and it's great reminiscing with him. Funnily enough, after he lost the Oldfield tour to me, he toured with Kate Bush. A quick aside here – Bernard Sheridan, a well-known music business solicitor, had left me a few messages for me to call him. Since I owed him some money, I didn't do it right away. Unfortunately, this was a big mistake on my part since Bernard had recommended me to Kate Bush as her manager. I don't have many regrets in life, but not calling Bernard then is one of them.

I still have a copy of my job pitch for Mike Oldfield, which I typed on a very old-fashioned typewriter:

Mike Oldfield Tour 1979

With reference to my meeting with Steve Lewis of yesterday (24th October 1979) I would like to present you with the following proposal for the above tour.

I am prepared to act as Tour Manager to advise on such things as:

The itinerary, routing and local promoters.

Recommend and/or help in finding various musicians and in the hire of instruments. I suggest that with such a large personnel of 46 musicians that there is a Head of Section with regard to the choir and orchestra.

Venues: I will liaise and coordinate on behalf of Mike Oldfield with all venues and promoters, taking care of all staging and rider requirements.

Rehearsals: I will help in coordinating rehearsal time and space if required.

Equipment: I understand that Tom Newman is the sound mixer and Pete Edmonds is the stage manager, so I will liaise with them as to any technical requirements and with East Lake Monitors regarding any construction.

Trucking: I visualise the need for 2 trucks. A 40' artic for all the P.A equipment and a 26' truck for the staging, band gear and lighting truss. Although I understand that High Life is quoting for this, I can if necessary help in obtaining other quotes.

Lighting: Again, if required, I can obtain quotes on the rig consisting of one overhead truss.

Crew: If, as I understand it, the tour is to carry its own risers a crew of 5 men will be needed for stage set-up (plus of course the local stage hands). PA crew should be 3 men and lighting 1 or 2.

Cash flow: The Tour Manager is to pick up monies at venues, pay our per diems and wages and keep thorough tour accounts, and of course take into account the possibility of any local tax problems.

Rider: To be compiled with the assistance of Tom Newman, Pete Edmonds, Mike Oldfield and Virgin, and to be made clear, understandable and correct.

Insurance: To be considered. I can recommend an insurance agent who is fully aware of all touring aspects.

Travel and Hotels: Scheduled flights would present many problems with such a large touring party, but I can arrange all this through Trinifold Travel who I have used on all my previous tours. They would also be happy to put in a quote on a 50-seater private plane. I can also get prices on different quality hotels from which you can choose. Booking would need to be done as soon as possible, but I would be happy to prepare a budget and logistics for this. A coach (small) would be needed for the crew. A specialised coach could also be considered for the band and/or crew depending on routing and timing. I must mention at this point that the travel agent would require money up-front for any pre-paid hotels and all air fares.

Baggage Man: Very necessary with this amount of people checking into hotels and going through continental airports.

Work Permits: Required for Spain, which I can arrange for you.

Purchase and/or hire of such things as: Music stands, amps, mics and mic stands. Again I can help with all this.

Should you consider using the company Tours Unlimited to liaise all aspects of the tour using myself as Tour Manager then may we suggest using our office as a central base? Otherwise I think the Tour Manager is definitely going to need an office with access to telephones, a telex and photo copying machine.

This was in addition to the extra-large line-up of musicians. Thanks to my previous experiences with large touring parties, such as the Stones in '76, I knew about the necessity of having a luggage man, the size of trucks, and so on. I also created a budget for this tour and I was told by Virgin's accountant that mine was by far the most accurate – even better than his! At last, my father could no longer say I was useless at maths. As long as you know what's necessary, which requires experience, creating a tour budget is really just common sense.

As part of the interviewing process, Mike Oldfield accompanied each potential tour manager to a few venues in Europe. I travelled with him to Barcelona, Spain, where I knew the promoter, Guy Merceder, and his crew very well. On our flight back to the United Kingdom, Mike offered me the job there and then. Amazing! During that same flight, he proceeded to tell me a bit about his history and why he had never toured before. It seems he had always been extremely shy and didn't want to perform, especially on a big stage for a tour. Nevertheless, he had great success with the 'cult', Exegesis, and was able to overcome his pervasive shyness because of their teachings. My knowledge of this cult was limited and mostly negative. Though, my interest was piqued when I discovered how much the Exegesis seminars had really helped Mike come out of his shell. This gave him the confidence to live a more normal life and take on this tour. I remember him saying I didn't need to attend the seminar because I seemed confident and unafraid of the world. I'd heard so many stories about how Exegesis destroyed people's lives, but when I came across them again a few years later, I experienced their manipulative ways first-hand.

Mike had ordered a massive eight-and-a-half-ton bell to be cast at the Whitechapel Foundry, with his specific harmonics incorporated in its casting. I remember collecting it from the foundry in my little Mini! My carpenter brother then made an especially sturdy stand and flight case for it.

The core band rehearsed on a barge on the Thames in Chelsea. This was where I first met Nico Ramsden, the lead guitarist, with whom I would later fall in love. Initially, though, he thought I was too bossy (that's what a tour manager needs to be sometimes!). To me, it was all about being efficient. In short, we hated each other.

Not long after I met Mike, he asked me to help him with his teeth. His two top incisors were rather prominent, so I sent him to my dentist who quickly sorted this out by filing them down. Mike then had a lovely set of teeth.

As well as being tour manager, I was also the official chaperone for the teenage choir girls on this tour, as I was a qualified Norland Nurse. Yes – Mike's choir were all underage girls! I doubt that would be allowed these days. They came from Queen's College in Harley Street in London. While the crew and musicians enjoyed having all these young girls around, it gave me some terrible headaches. I often had girls sobbing on my shoulders because they were 'in love' with one of the roadies. Each country we visited also required that I report to British embassies or consulates. They wanted to make sure these 'children' were being properly cared for and not exploited. We once had officials try to stop a concert midway through because it was past the 'children's bedtime'. Of course, there was no way these officials could get past security without my say-so. Rather than risking a possible riot if the concert had to be stopped midway through, I told the security guys to say they 'couldn't find me'.

Mike's antics on this tour were quite strange. I employed some of my London Symphony Orchestra chums for this tour, since 'Tubular Bells' needed an orchestra. There was an awkward moment when Mike tried to secretly record a concert – without telling any of the musicians. All sorts of ructions ensued, with many of the musicians threatening to leave immediately. He had not even told me what he was doing, and if he had, I would never have allowed it. There's one thing you simply do not do, and that's record musicians without their permission. There was fury among both the band and orchestra members, and I did not blame them one bit. It took a great deal of diplomacy on my part to keep them from walking out. Mike has written about this in his memoirs, too. This escapade caused him to fall in all our estimations, and it wasn't the only one. The night before a concert was to start, he crept around the stage removing all the printed music from the orchestral musicians' music stands. When they found out, they were enraged since they were used to always having the music in front of them, but like true professionals, they all played fine without it.

Having said that, classical musicians weren't all sweetness and light. I thought I'd seen it all with The Who and Lynyrd Skynyrd, but these classical musicians were something else altogether – rowdy and drunk practically all the time. They were very difficult to control, causing terrible problems in hotels, airports, and venues. Again, it took every ounce of diplomacy I could muster to communicate with the police and hotel managers. In fact, I even had to sack one of the violinists because of his drunken behaviour. Since he is now famous and well respected in the classical world, I won't mention his name. When I was interviewed at that time for the Old Grey Whistle Test,

I remember saying: "I thought rock musicians were difficult, but they're not a patch on the classical guys! Come back rock 'n' roll, all is forgiven!" I believe this interview is still available with Mike Oldfield's album from that *Incantations* tour. Strangely, most online information about this tour is inaccurate.

The tour was a great success, and when we returned to the United Kingdom Mike asked me to be his manager. We even planned to establish a brand new recording studio and a company to rent equipment, which I would run. I agreed, somewhat cautiously, since I wasn't entirely sure I wanted to work long term with Mike, but I thought I'd give it a go. Then Nico and I went on holiday to France. We borrowed Mike's Range Rover, in exchange for me letting him stay at my flat in Fulham. Nico and I had a wonderful holiday. He was the first person I had fallen in love with after Dean had died in the Skynyrd plane crash.

On our return to London, Mike had disappeared – and, bizarrely, I never heard from him again. I feel he missed a good opportunity with me, as I had been in touch with my contacts at the British embassy in Peking.

Mike Oldfield Tour, 1979
(Photo from author's personal collection)

The plan was almost in place for Mike to perform in China – years before anyone else was able to accomplish this. Although… I think I had a lucky escape, as working with Mike was never going to be easy.

That year, I had a massive New Year's Eve party at my flat in Fulham – even Keith Richards and Ronnie Wood came. Great fun was had by all! One of my friends asked Keith about the Open G guitar tuning he uses, and about Nanker Phelge, credited on various albums – and he was so chuffed to get the truth from the horse's mouth! If I remember correctly, it's from when Brian Jones, Mick and Keith had shared a flat in Edith Grove in London with a guy called Jimmy Phelge, who would make a stupid face with his fingers in his mouth, which they called 'doing a Nanker'. So, when the band's Glimmer Twins Productions started up, they would credit Nanker Phelge.

Chapter 16

The Rossington Collins Band

Despite being in the midst of a lovely affair with Nico, who is still a good friend, when I was contacted by Gary Rossington and Allen Collins of Skynyrd in October 1979 – with them pleading with me to move over there and manage their new band – I couldn't resist the lure, the siren's call of Skynyrd. So, I left Nico and moved to Florida to manage the Lynyrd Skynyrd survivors, the Rossington Collins Band. I rented out my Fulham apartment, and I also left my small company Tours Unlimited, which was sad, but I simply couldn't resist the plea from the Skynyrd survivors. The line-up, all previously with Skynyrd, was: Gary Rossington and Allen Collins – guitarists and writers; Leon Wilkeson – bass guitarist; Billy Powell – keyboardist; plus a new drummer, as Artimus had injured his foot in a motorbike accident; and a new female singer, Dale Krantz, who was supposed to be the lead, upfront singer, but they ended up with Barry Harwood instead.

When Gary and Allen met me at the airport, they were like little puppies – excited to have me as their manager and help them with their future. They told me this was exactly what Ronnie had wanted, and they wanted me, too. It's interesting they didn't ask anyone else to manage them at this time, not even Pete Rudge – probably because they still blamed him for the plane crash.

The situation looked promising. For the first few weeks, I lived with Gary and Martha at their beautiful home on the banks of the St Johns River with their horses and dogs. After a few weeks, I moved into my own apartment at Club Continental in Orange Park, a beautiful private housing estate set around a lovely Spanish-style mansion on the river. My boyfriend, Nico, came over to celebrate Christmas with me there. It was around this time that I became aware of just how badly hurt the Skynyrd boys had been – physically, mentally, and psychologically – by the plane crash and the loss of their leader in Ronnie, their best friend in Dean, and their dear friends Steve and Cassie Gaines.

Gary and Leon seemed to have the worst physical injuries and spent many hours in physiotherapy. Allen wasn't as damaged physically – but, by God, he was a changed man. Normally, he was naughty, like a kid, although rather reckless when driving stoned, but now he was nasty and vicious. He would take drugs from the minute he woke up until the minute he managed to drop off for a few hours' sleep. His wife, Kathy, died some years later as a direct result of this horrendous lifestyle. She had to keep up with him, or else he'd go mad, shouting and screaming at her. So, Kathy would start her day at the normal time, feed the children and take them to school after just three or four hours of sleep. She would then try to organise her house, the shopping and so on. Allen would wake sometime in the afternoon and demand food, booze, grass, and cocaine, and Kathy had to partake with him. He demanded that she take the same – and keep up with him until the small hours of the morning. All the while she was trying to be a good mother and wife. During her third pregnancy (after already having two daughters) she suffered a haemorrhage while in the cinema with friends and died instantly. It was heartbreaking. Allen's instability and recklessness were evident from the beginning. Some years earlier, he had put his toddler daughter on the back of his motorbike without strapping her in. Of course, he drove so badly that she fell off...she survived – just.

Even though the Rossington Collins group featured four original band members, it wasn't Skynyrd any more. They knew it, I knew it, and the fans knew it. For some reason they weren't allowed to use the name Lynyrd Skynyrd. (I think Judy Van Zant owned the name, but many years later she relented, so they continued to tour as Lynyrd Skynyrd with Ronnie's younger brother, Johnny, as the singer.)

While living with them, I realised that without Ronnie's strong leadership, they were like lost little boys. Although I tried my best, I couldn't take Ronnie's place or even manage them properly. I just wasn't strong enough to deal with all the darkness, their internal pain, and the awful angst that was just beneath the surface of us all. We had all lost our hero, our leader, the only one who could have saved them from themselves.

There was also something odd going on behind my back. My intuition kicked in and I started feeling very uncomfortable, and I wasn't being paranoid. There was a concerted effort to get rid of me. As early as 1980 there were personal tensions between Gary and Martha Rossington, Dale Krantz and her boyfriend – one of our roadies. My main issue, however, was with the band's new lawyer and accountant. Although they've both passed away now, I won't name them; I'll use AA and BB instead. Both AA and BB did not like me. They intentionally made things difficult, unpleasant, and ignored me on many issues. For example, in letters to MCA Records they would say I was '*just the tour manager*', so I insisted they correct the record.

I tried looking at things from their perspective. The information they had about me was probably minimal since I arrived without much notice. (I'm sure the most they got from the boys was that I was their 'European tour manager'.) Nevertheless, the situation was a battle right from the start.

Gary and Allen first asked me about the percentage these two men were getting, which I of course queried. AA and BB demanded 15%. 15% of *what*, I thought. Touring, recording and from when? Lawyers and accountants are usually paid for work done and on proper invoicing. All of this was most unprofessional. I agreed not to take a percentage, even though I was ostensibly their manager. I could have insisted on something similar for myself to ensure some sort of security. Especially since my whole life was devoted to them. All I did was eat, sleep, and breathe around the Rossington Collins Band. For what? A paltry $300 a week. I couldn't understand why they didn't use our old colleagues in New York: the lawyer Ina Meibach and our accountants Aaron Schechter and Bill Zysblat. Maybe it was because they were connected with Pete Rudge, and the boys didn't want any connection. Given their emotional wounds, that's my best guess, anyway.

On 9th January 1980, I met up with Dave Evans, Skynyrd's engineer, and we drove together to a rehearsal place in Batcave, North Carolina, where we met up with the rest of the band. As usual, Billy Powell found some complaints the night before departure. He decided he would need his Steinway piano, and my first thought was, why didn't he think of that a week ago?! And so it began…

The plan was to rehearse for the Charlie Daniels Jam in Nashville on 12th January. Gary told me that Artimus's leg was not getting better after a motorbike crash, and he couldn't keep a steady beat. I had a long conversation with Artimus, and despite being told many times that he would be waited for, he was paranoid about not being wanted. Having no one talk to or listen to him made him angry and frustrated. I'm not surprised though, since he was generally belligerent and pig-headed. Let's put it this way – his opinion was always the right one and he refused to listen to other opinions. When I went off to play Scrabble with some of the others, I discovered that Artimus had suddenly resigned! In reality, he was his own worst enemy and was miserable all day the following day. I told Artimus his job would be there when he was ready.

As January turned to February, not much changed. All of them were arguing with each other, their wives, and the roadies. It was non-stop and I seemed to be in the middle of it all, trying to calm everybody down. They couldn't even agree on the length of their set – should it be forty minutes or fifty? Wait! Or fifty-five!? It went on and on and on. When a film crew from *PM Magazine* visited New Orleans, it seemed to go well, but it had interrupted the band's rehearsals…again. There was always something – if it wasn't the film crew, it was stopping to have a few more lines of coke.

Eventually, the honeymoon ended, as I thought it would. Allen was becoming more and more paranoid and increasingly difficult to deal with. He was stoned out of his mind all the time and turned into a nasty person. After him being my staunchest ally, Allen suddenly turned against me. He even shouted at me for 'letting journalists ask about the plane crash'. Whatever next? Though he was never the brightest person, becoming the band's 'leader' had totally gone to his head. Without Ronnie to keep things in check, there was no way Gary could control him. I knew the writing was on the wall, and I probably wouldn't hang around much longer, especially as the trust and respect had gone. I wished Ronnie and Dean were still around. We would have managed the band together so well. I had no life of my own and felt so taken for granted. I was slogging my guts out booking gigs, travelling, hotels, preparing itineraries and riders, hiring extra instruments, dealing with each of them daily with their personal, band and drug problems.

The first gig for the Rossington Collins Band was on 11th February 1980. At last! I finally got them on that stage after two and a half years. They were totally and utterly fantastic, which reminded me of why I wanted to work with them. They were the only band/musicians that gave me that special buzz. In the beginning, there were only a few minor issues, which was to be expected. Halfway through the show, disaster struck when the amps suddenly cut out. Although it was an easy fix (a plug had come unplugged) the crew took a long time to figure out the problem. After that, things got worse. Gary's amp went next, and he kicked it over, his leg tangled in the guitar lead. Afterwards, Gary and Allen told me to lash out at the crew to make sure that it wouldn't happen again.

During the second show, the strobe guitar tuner didn't work. Goodness, whatever next? I almost felt that we were jinxed. The next day, we had a meeting at the hotel with a lot of shouting, which never got us anywhere. It only caused more stress, tension, and bitter resentment. Although, it didn't seem like Allen had any other way of communicating. He'd shout in gabbling incoherent phrases, with mad, bulging eyes and spittle everywhere – like a man possessed, which I suppose he was. The demons never seemed to leave him.

Many so-called friends and hangers-on tried to get backstage after the concerts. I had to get quite heavy, which I hated, but I had to obey the band. They didn't like having other people backstage because they were always tense and wired after a gig. It really wasn't a pleasant experience to be around them, especially after things went wrong. ('Twas ever thus, even in the old days with Ronnie in charge. The physical fights they had then were legendary.) Gary and Allen had two groupies hanging around them, which caused Allen to get even more uptight because they wouldn't leave him alone. This showed me the big change in him, since he usually loved having women around him.

We were all emotional and tearful afterwards. Not because of the problems, but because we actually got back on the road. As soon as we got back to Jacksonville, Allen got worse. During an argument about some stupid equipment list, he went off the deep end, calling me a liar. I tried to explain the facts to him, but he was ranting and raving. He would not listen, so I decided to leave. I would not be called a liar, especially by the most untruthful person I have ever met. It made me wonder if he was seriously insane.

So, I left. I couldn't stay with all this doubt and suspicion about me. While trying to decide what to do, I spent a few days with Dean's parents, Mr and Mrs Kilpatrick. Both Allen and Gary's wives were stunned and shocked by all this. They didn't blame me for leaving, but they did try to convince me to stay, as did all the crew.

After a few days, I called Gary, who begged me not to leave. He said he needed me, and the band needed me – that he would almost rather Allen leave than me. He also suggested that Allen start his own band. However, I told him how disappointed and humiliated I felt, that nobody deserved to be treated the way Allen had treated me. I felt extremely let down. After all, I had given up everything in my life for them. We talked about how difficult it was to do all that they asked me to do, especially when they changed their minds so frequently. Moreover, they expected everyone to automatically know that they were Lynyrd Skynyrd when they refused to engage in interviews or speak about it. The fact that they wouldn't do the interviews which they'd asked me to fix, made me look stupid. Despite my title as an 'advisory manager', they refused to let me advise them. Gary begged me to stay and told me how much he loved me. They were always, always using the word 'love' but didn't really mean it, not in the true sense of the word. They said it so often it was like saying 'hello'. It's a very Southern trait I've discovered.

Dale Krantz phoned me and begged me not to go, and I talked for hours with Leon and Dave (Evans). Allen was so irrational that all of us questioned our sanity for staying around such a selfish, mad man. Kathy, Allen's wife, called me and told me she'd lied to him about something, and when he discovered it, he took it out on me. One by one, the rest of the band and crew came to me and begged me to stay. There had been so many kind people that I couldn't let them all down. Although it may sound conceited, they had all been sweet enough to ask me to stay when they didn't have to. In the end, it was really Gary's request that convinced me to give them another chance. He could always get to me, that Gary!

We spent 17th February at the Hyatt Regency in New Orleans. We were in town for some gigs when Allen got up to his old tricks again.

He came into my room and told me to leave, saying, "You don't like America."

I thought that was a strange thing to say, but I didn't take the bait. "Allen, I would have gone to Timbuktu to work with you boys. I'm doing the accounts, and I have to get back to work."

The next thing he said revealed a lot about his cryptic message and strange behaviour. "BB (the accountant) handles that side of things. You don't need to."

I thought to myself, now we're getting to it. Once again, AA and BB seemed to be at the root of all this. Allen was so unhinged and paranoid, he'd believe anything they said. My intuition told me something definitely wasn't right – and that was evident when I noticed that Gary could not look me in the eye.

AA & BB were lording it over everyone at the gigs when I noticed that AA had lumps of cocaine dropping out of his nostrils. He was a lawyer, for goodness' sake. No wonder everything was so upside down and back to front. They were *all* taking coke, which was making them all paranoid and nasty beyond belief.

The shows went well, except for when one of our new roadies decided to kick people off stage even though they needed to be there. In retaliation, the promoter warned that if the band went one minute over, he would pull the plug!

In both Atlanta and New Orleans, Gary and Allen continued to fight. When someone came up to Allen and asked him if he was in Molly Hatchet's band, Allen punched them in the face.

Then came the final straw for me. Allen had been firing his rifle outside (stoned as usual, of course) and had aimed it at Craig, one of the roadies who had been with them from the start. The only reason Allen missed was because he was so stoned. That was it for me. I was out of there while guns were being fired at people at random. It was just total madness. I'd had enough. So, I packed everything up, finished filing all the paperwork and accounts, and left them neatly on the table in my apartment.

I booked a flight home. After staying with Leon for a couple of days, he took me to the airport. On the night I left my apartment, Allen and Gary broke in. In a hugely drunk, stoned, and angry temper tantrum, Allen trashed the place. He threw all my carefully prepared accounts and paperwork everywhere. Gary apologised for everything to me years later, but he couldn't stop Allen. Nobody could.

After I left and Kathy had died, Dale left her boyfriend, moved in with Allen, then ended up with Gary. At least she stayed with him and made him happy. They got married, had two beautiful daughters, and she helped him get off coke by getting him away from Jacksonville and all its temptations. Martha ended up getting married again and moved to Miami where I stayed with her and her new family a few times when we would mull over the madness of those far-gone days.

Allen's final chapter was that he had another car accident, stoned as usual, in which his girlfriend died. The accident left him paralysed from the waist down and wheelchair-bound. Then his wheelchair fell off the ramp of a vehicle, with him in it, which weakened his body so much that he died of pneumonia. As of 2022, all the original Skynyrd band members have died except Gary Rossington and Artimus Pyle.

I think I had a lucky escape. Very few of those people were normal. Especially after becoming so rich and so famous when they were still mere children, utterly naive and not very well educated. Not one of them was able to handle it and they became monsters no one could deal with. And what about the figures they'd challenged? Well, I stayed in New York for a few days with Bill Zysblat, and had meetings with the band's accountant, BB. Of course, all my figures were spot on. Despite the accountant's numerous complaints to the boys, everything tallied, as I knew it would.

One final nice touch was a fantastic letter I got from the promoter in Florida, Sidney Drashin, who said:

> I can never forget your tireless efforts on behalf of the Rossington Collins
> Band and they've become the big stars you thought they would.

I've kept in touch with everyone in Jacksonville, though it took me many years to be able to listen to Lynyrd Skynyrd's music without sobbing. If

I was driving when they came on the radio I had to switch off, as I couldn't see through all the tears. Billy and Leon died a few years ago – Billy died of a heart attack, and Leon was left alone in a hotel room.

In August 2001 I had an email from Martha about Leon:

> I need to tell you something. I hate to tell you this way, but I'm just afraid that I won't be able to 'talk' to you... Leon died recently. I'm so sorry. I know how close you two were. They haven't figured it out completely except that he died in his sleep at 4 in the afternoon in a hotel room in Ponte Vedra beach. The preliminary autopsy showed chronic lung and liver disease, but no immediate cause of death.

> I didn't go to Jax, but they had a private ceremony one day and a public one the next. It's my understanding that the band replaced him almost immediately as they had dates to play. But I have felt very badly for Billy and Gary. Teresa (Gaines) was completely beside herself as she had seen Leon just a couple of days before and he seemed just fine and they had a very good time, went out to dinner and really enjoyed themselves. She couldn't understand it and from everything I've heard they still don't know exactly what happened.

Then Dean's mother emailed me:

> It is really so sad about Leon. Dean was so fond of him. The papers say they found chronic lung and liver problems. They had a nice public service at the cemetery and when the band played at the Jaguar game in the Jacksonville Stadium, they had a few minutes' silence in memory of Leon. Usually the commentaries on TV and in the papers look for derogatory remarks to make about the band and their behaviour. The band has gotten some good press recently for a change. Things seem to have changed for the better.

Of all the survivors of the plane crash, I miss Leon the most. Our friendship grew so close. He came to stay with me in London several times, and we spoke often on the phone.

Another close friend from those days is Dave Evans, the legendary guitar maker and Skynyrd's engineer. We still talk about our memories now. Not forgetting roadie Kenny Pedan of course, who survived the crash and who still emails me regularly.

Even when Lynyrd Skynyrd started up again with Ronnie's brother, Johnny, singing, I didn't want to work with them any more. I'd moved on workwise. But I always meet up with them in London and go to the gig, despite sobbing my way through it.

Except for a Peter Gabriel tour, I more or less left rock and roll. My years of servile sycophancy were over. No more 'yes sir, no sir' to spoilt, entitled rock stars. And my attachment to Skynyrd was over too – but not the memories. Never would I forget the wonderful early days with Ronnie, Dean and co.

I also helped out the Penguin Cafe Orchestra. I knew their founder, Simon Jeffes, quite well, and the ukulele player was my old friend Neil Rennie. They needed a tour manager for a small tour of Europe at one point, so I stepped in. Simon then died tragically young, so his son Arthur has now taken over, and Penguin Cafe continues.

There were other things in my life that nourished me, so no more rock and roll. I didn't need to live vicariously through my work, like others who seem to thrive on the egotism of this type of work.

Sally with some of the boys at Judy Van Zant's Free Bird Bar
(Photo from author's personal collection)

PART THREE

GIVING BACK

Chapter 17

Festivals and Charities

On my return to England, Peter Gabriel's manager contacted me saying Peter wanted a female tour manager for his upcoming European tour. Thank goodness – back to normality – and far away from the madness of Allen Collins!

There's really nothing much I can say about Peter other than he is probably the most 'normal' rock star I have ever met or worked with. He's just a really nice guy. No dramas, no ridiculous demands, just a very lovely, sensible man. In fact, in a review of Mike Rutherford's 2014 book, *The Living Years*, Peter is described as kindly, a benevolent and slightly scatty dreamer, and very far from the rock star archetype – with which I totally concur.

The tour with Peter was great. He wanted us all to stay in the best hotels, and to travel by first class train all across Europe. Simple Minds were the support group on that tour (some years before they became famous). Nice guys, too, as I remember. And I had a fun quick fling with their tour manager!

I still have a lovely letter from Norbert Gamsohn, a French promoter well known for producing many of the biggest and best jazz festivals in France. He said:

> First of all I would like to repeat what great personal and professional pleasure it was to work together on Peter's tour. Thanks again, darling, for your friendship and help. I hope you will have a good rest and some time to enjoy the music you prefer!

As always, all the local promoters knew of my preference for classical music.

I only ever had one weird moment with Peter on that tour, in Italy, when he got the wrong end of the stick and accused me of shouting at the drummer. Here is my letter to him explaining the reality of the situation:

> You have remembered the Gerry M. incident quite wrongly. The facts were that, as your Tour Manager, the local promoter had provided me with a car for work, and when we were in Florence Gerry wanted to take the car to score drugs, when I needed it to meet with the police, the promoter David Zard, and the security guys because of a threatened riot... When I told Gerry he couldn't have the car, he freaked and struck out AT ME, but missed and hit the car – he then proceeded to hit and thump the car in a temper tantrum, which is when you looked out of the hotel window and assumed I had 'upset' Gerry... I leave you to draw your own conclusions as to who was in the right or wrong now you know the facts.

Gerry had become chums with some visiting dancers from the New York City Ballet, and he brought them back to the hotel where they all drank a lot and took coke together. Who'd have thought it – ballet dancers taking cocaine!

Many years later, I introduced Peter to Larry Adler, the American harmonica player. Larry and I became firm friends after a big charity event where we originally met. He had played on a CD of Gershwin music with Peter and others, but he and Peter had never met, and wanted to. So, I drove Larry down to Peter's studio just outside Bath, where he gave us a lovely lunch. We did vaguely discuss putting on a concert with them both, but sadly nothing ever came of it.

I'm offered a job as General Manager with Peter Gabriel's World of Music, Arts and Dance (WOMAD)

Some years later, Thomas Brooman, the director of Peter's WOMAD festival, asked me to join his team. I was keen, and Thomas and Peter were keen, but a female staff member was not.

Well, that was quite a story...

First of all, Thomas asked if I would go down to their offices at Peter's studio near Bath, as they were looking for someone to help run WOMAD. The meeting was only supposed to last an hour, but we got on so well that we ended up chatting for over three hours. Thomas wanted me to meet up with Peter, but I couldn't make the date he suggested. "That's okay," he said. "Peter likes and trusts you."

I was then offered the post of General Manager from the end of February, on two conditions: one was a six-month trial basis – no problem; the other was I had to meet another member of staff. I won't give her name other than to call her MM, but suffice to say I could tell immediately that she didn't like me. She was antagonistic from the start, and I felt there seemed to be some resentment that she hadn't been involved in the initial meeting/ interview process. Then she slandered me very badly – by saying that she had been 'told' that I was an alcoholic and had been having treatment during the 'missing' months in my CV. Actually, I had been on my nine-month round-the-world trip in 1990–91. But it seemed she didn't believe me.

I told her that, even if I was a recovering alcoholic, I would be proud of having treatment for it, as I admired so many others who had gone through detox treatments and faced up to their addictions. This was true, because I had helped so many of them in the past, first at the Double O Charity, then at The CORE Trust. But it was obvious she was determined not to accept this, and nothing I said could persuade her. So, this was the third woman in my life who sabotaged me and my work.

The situation caused all sorts of ructions. I had been formally offered the job, and then it was pretty much taken away from me because of one woman. So, when Thomas asked me to 'hold on' for a while, I suggested that he speak to Pete Townshend of The Who, Mike Appleton from the BBC/Old Grey Whistle Test, Jackie Leven who was founder of The CORE Trust, and Jane Tewson of Charity Projects/Comic Relief – who would all recommend me highly. I told him he shouldn't listen to ancient gossip, innuendoes, half-truths and total un-truths, and that this woman's questioning had been utterly inappropriate and ill-informed.

I admit – I was furious and even wrote to Thomas and Peter saying that if this woman ever repeated such lies, I would take legal action and sue for slander. Part of my letter to Thomas said:

I feel I must point out a number of questionable facts – firstly how unpro-fessional and unsatisfactory that last interview was with MM. If that is the insulting way that professional, experienced and highly qualified people

Sally with Peter Gabriel
(Photo from author's personal collection)

are treated in interviews, it is probably indicative of any future treatment within the organisation. This invalidation of colleagues is something I find to be totally negative and counter-productive. I feel that people should pull together for the future success of a company – not pull apart because of personal aims or desires.

I should also like to point out that the statement made by MM about her having 'heard' I was a recovering alcoholic is slanderous – and as such, if it is repeated, I shall not hesitate to take legal action. I would also have a case, if pursued, on the post of General Manager being offered to me, a starting date and salary agreed and written in a draft contract – only to have it all cancelled at a moment's notice. I am copying this letter to my solicitor, to MM and to Peter (Gabriel) as I feel they should know of her totally false allegations.

My letter to Peter said:

I was asked by Thomas if I would be interested in the post of General Manager of WOMAD, which I agreed to. But because of all the negativity and spreading of slanderous gossip, I have decided to withdraw from the fray. I feel truly sorry for Thomas as he has invested a great deal of time and effort in the search for a General Manager, and obviously desperately needs help, but seemingly he does not have the brief to make a final decision based on deeply held beliefs. Hence the now rather protracted indecision based on the misplaced suspicions of another member of your staff. It has all been rather a waste of time hasn't it – when many hours of interviews with the people directly involved can be negated by a twenty-minute talk?

But karma has a strange way of working out, as this particular woman came into my life again some years later – when she needed my help, so I felt somewhat vindicated. But before my own company, there was Comic Relief…

Jane Tewson is the amazing person who originally founded Comic Relief, now also known as Red Nose Day. It was her idea, and she brought on board people like Richard Curtis, John Lloyd and Lenny Henry, who now run it. Jane, now MBE, has moved to Australia.

In 1980 I was recommended by a mutual friend to Jane, who was working at the charity Mencap at that time. She was looking for someone to help with a fundraising event. We met up, got on really well and proceeded to produce four events, the three later ones for her new company,

Charity Projects, which is now Comic Relief, and involved many of the same comedians.

Another person who should be credited with co-founding Comic Relief is the journalist Stephen Pile, who initially came up with the idea of the first International Nether Wallop Arts Festival. He approached Jane, and she got me on board. So, in reality we three were the first people to organise the initial large comic festivals for charity. However, once the BBC took over, I was no longer involved due to union requirements – but I am extremely proud that my work with Jane in the early 1980s created something so successful that raised millions of pounds for local and international charities. When Jane was awarded her well-deserved MBE she told me it was also for me and the others who had been involved from the beginning. A very proud moment for us all.

The first event took place on 1st June 1981: Fundamental Frolics at the Apollo Theatre. This was filmed by the BBC and it can be found on YouTube titled 'Fundamental Frolics Mix'. I am eternally grateful to the comedian Mel Smith, who taught me how to stage-manage for theatre people. I had only ever worked on and behind rock and roll stages, so had no idea of how the theatrical side of things worked. Mel taught me a great deal and it was a joy to learn from him. We also worked together on the next few events for Mencap, and then Charity Projects.

I still have the programme and the list of celebrities who took part. This included Griff Rhys-Jones, Mel Smith, Ian Dury, Alexei Sayle, Chas & Dave, Rik Mayall, Alan Price, Rowan Atkinson, Stewart Copeland and Andy Summers of The Police, Joan Collins, Chris Langham, Jon Anderson of Yes, Stephane Grappelli, Neil Innes, Hot Gossip, Elvis Costello, Pamela Stephenson and SFX.

Then there were the writers who supplied the material – Richard Sparks, Chris Langham, Rik Mayall, Griff Rhys-Jones, Paul Newstead, James Leigh-Hunt, Richard Curtis and Rowan Atkinson.

Behind the scenes, I worked extremely hard to persuade people to assist us for free. I brought in Edwin Shirley and Tim Norman for staging and trucking, and Mick Jackson for security. Also Brian Croft, who I'd worked with numerous times in the rock world. He very kindly volunteered to provide the extra sound and lighting equipment that was required, over and above that provided by the theatre.

These guys helped at all the events mentioned here, generously providing their services and equipment totally free, so none of the charities had to pay for them. They are my unsung heroes – most especially Brian Croft.

All this, and extra props, needed to be trucked in early on the Sunday morning. Rowan Atkinson had apparently always been keen on driving trucks, and had an HGV driving licence, so the Edwin Shirley Trucking Company allowed him to drive one of their massive articulated trucks. Meeting that massive truck at 6am by the loading bay, with Rowan Atkinson driving, was really rather surreal for me!

My brother Mark also got involved as a carpenter for this show, as we needed a large mock electric plug and socket for a sketch with Mel Smith and Andy Summers (Andy being the bass player in The Police). As MK Electric had been our grandfather's company, Mark made a large wooden replica set of an MK three-pin plug and socket. The sketch was Andy pulling

Mel Smith and Peter Cook, Nether Wallop Arts Festival
(Photo from author's personal collection)

the plug out of the socket held by Mel, and the band being 'switched off' and suddenly going quiet. It was funny and worked well. This can still be seen today, on YouTube.

I tended to use the same people as my team of helpers: my friends and family – one was a lawyer, another a travel agent, another an architect, one a jewellery designer. All professional people in their own fields and kind enough to give their precious free time to work their guts out on a charity event. I always said in my normal rock and roll work that 'a happy crew is a happy tour'. And this was the same on all the charity events. I would do my best to make sure they all had fun, meeting all sorts of famous people, with the only benefits being a few sandwiches and copious cups of tea and coffee. I took no payment at all – not even any expenses. That was my way of giving to the charities. (We did not get any credits on the BBC's film of that first event.)

The next one, which many of the same people, celebrities and friends helped out with, was the Battersea Big One in aid of Mencap in August 1982. Then in July 1984 Jane asked me to help organise another fundraising event, but this time the event would be for her own charity, Charity Projects, which she had set up after leaving Mencap. This event was the first International Nether Wallop Arts Festival in September 1984, lasting four days, with many celebrities descending on the Wallop villages in Hampshire, to take part in this extravaganza of comedy, music, dance and acting. Jane's original ethos was amazing. She and any other staff didn't take any salaries or administrative costs from the money they raised, but were funded by individual philanthropists: people like Tim Bell, Richard Branson and the Saatchi brothers.

The Nether Wallop event was unique. How on earth do you get the following luminaries to take part in such an obscure event in such an obscure village as Nether Wallop? Judi Dench, Jenny Agutter, Maria Aitken, Rowan Atkinson, Philosophy Professor A J Ayer (known as Freddie), Billy Connolly, Peter Cook, Sir Michael Hordern, Paul Jones, Andrew Lloyd Webber, Rik Mayall, Marion Montgomery, Jessye Norman, Trevor Nunn, Lynn Seymour, Ned Sherrin, Wayne Sleep, Ralph Steadman, Stanley Unwin, Mel Smith, John Wells, Bill Wyman, Jools Holland, Hugh Laurie,

Stephen Fry, Paul Jones – and many more. And how on earth does one organise such an event?

It had all started when the journalist Stephen Pile wrote an article about the Edinburgh Festival in *The Sunday Times* in 1982:

> Why, the arty ask, do these people bring their inward-looking conference to Edinburgh? What is wrong with having it at Nether Wallop in mid-January?

As he described it to me, Stephen basically thought of the silliest-named place he could think of, and Nether Wallop came to his mind. Well, the villagers of Nether Wallop called his bluff and invited him to do just that. So, Stephen met Jane, and they decided to do this mad event. The next person they needed was an organiser – and that's where I came in.

The planning and organisation needed to put this in place was absolutely massive and complex. Which artist should stay with which villager? Where could we put on a big variety show? The village hall was too small. So, I told them that if we put a marquee on the football field, we'd also need to bring in portable toilets, build a stage and provide chairs, sound and lighting equipment etc. It wasn't a simple or quick job, but entirely feasible. I would never have come up with such a nutty idea, but I knew I could organise it.

Stephen managed to base himself in a caravan parked in someone's garden, which became the festival office for those few months. He even managed to get a phone line put in there, although BT took some cajoling. I would stay down there in Nether Wallop for a few days at a time. ensconced myself, with my trusty electric typewriter, at the home of a local major and his wife, who let me use their telephone. There were no mobiles in those days. No computers or email, either. Jane organised London Weekend Television to film the event for £50,000, which was a vast amount in those days. This was to be split between the village church and Charity Projects.

My technical people from the Fundamental Frolics and Battersea Big One events all came back to help. It was fantastic of them to step in again. My wonderful friends volunteered as my assistants again. We all worked extremely hard, but at least we also managed to have a laugh over those few days. One of our main worries was that news about all the famous people there would leak out to the public, and the village would be inundated.

So everybody – literally everybody involved – was sworn to secrecy. And it worked! Only the villagers and their friends and family came along. It was quite a surreal experience. My family attended, and there are some marvellous shots on a YouTube film of them in the front row of the show in the marquee. I was backstage all the time, but I remember being mortified at the language of Peter Cook and Mel Smith in their sketch about the Raving Lesbians, because my father was so Victorian and po-faced, but I don't think he understood a word of it! I thought it was absolutely hilarious, but many others in the audience weren't so appreciative…! There's a YouTube video called 'Weekend in Wallop' which shows many of the highlights.

Everybody except me managed to be asleep when it was time to empty the contents of the portable toilets into the sewers at 6am on the Monday after the event was over. Nobody ever sees this sort of thing, but of course it's a vital part of an event like this. No wonder we all said, "Never again." We were all absolutely exhausted! But it was all worth it in the end, as this really was the precursor to Comic Relief and all the millions of pounds that have been raised by them in the intervening years.

One thing that also sticks in my mind from the Nether Wallop event was the arrival of Bill Wyman. He was one of the people I'd invited to appear at the festival. Little did I expect him to turn up with a new girlfriend. He had briefly told me about her over the phone, but I honestly didn't expect her to be so young…this was Mandy Smith, who he later married.

I'd booked Bill into the only decent hotel because there was no way I could put Bill Wyman of the Rolling Stones up in a villager's house.

When he and Mandy arrived, I was shocked to the core and said to him, "Bloody hell, Bill. You ought to be careful. She's jailbait."

Bill replied, "Oh, don't worry. She's eighteen."

To which my response was, "What a load of rubbish! You can't fool me."

It was obvious Mandy was very young, not from her looks – she certainly looked over eighteen, with the thick make-up and large hairstyle – but it was her mannerisms and attitude that were the giveaway. Although I never knew for sure her age at that time, Bill was quoted in 2013 as saying that he told the police about 'his affair with a thirteen-year-old, but they weren't interested'. They ended up getting married when she was eighteen, but it didn't last long. And, bizarrely, Bill's son ended up having a relationship with Mandy's mother.

The early 80s were a busy time for me, and not just because of the comedy festivals. I'd first met promoter Paul Loasby in late 1976 when he was organising the Lynyrd Skynyrd gigs at the Rainbow in north London for Harvey Goldsmith. By 1977, I was using a spare desk in Harvey's offices in Wimpole Street to run Five One Productions. Of course, that all came to an end after the Skynyrd plane crash, but it was then that I got to know Paul well. We became good friends and, in 1981, together set up Paul Loasby Productions. We promoted tours for Echo and the Bunnymen, The Thompson Twins, Tears for Fears, Elvis Costello and others. I was mainly responsible for the big open-air shows such as Queen at Leeds and Milton Keynes Bowl, and Barry Manilow at Blenheim Palace. All I remember about the Queen gigs was the hanging around for hours into the wee hours of the mornings to clear up after Freddie's parties!

When Barry Manilow was scheduled to play at Blenheim Palace, I was contacted by a doctor at a nearby hospice. A dying woman there was a very big fan of Manilow, and the doctor asked me if I could help get this lady a decent place to see the concert in her wheelchair. He wondered whether I could organise for her to meet Manilow? I said I would do my best. I got her a wonderful position to see the concert, so that worked well. However, for some reason, Manilow refused to meet her. Sadly, she died a few weeks later without meeting her idol. Think what just a few minutes of Manilow's time would have meant to her. I can never understand why some celebrities refuse to meet their fans.

Another feature I remember of the Barry Manilow concert was the hundreds of presents and cards from his adoring fans. I put them all in his mobile dressing room backstage for him. But, after he'd left, I noticed they'd all just been pushed to one side in a pile. Not one had been opened. I had never known a star treat fans with such apparent contempt. It made me feel sad and put me off him. So much so, that I avoided meeting him in person. Paul Loasby and I were 'summoned' to meet him, but I didn't go. It made me feel I was sticking up for the dying woman and all those fans in some small way.

Paul and I worked well together, and things moved beyond friendship.

Even strong women need a shoulder sometimes and, despite being an extremely independent woman, I wanted a partner who was on my side, a good man who would respect me and stand up for me in any circumstances. I thought I'd found that man in Paul, so, in 1984, we got married. It was a big step for me, especially after losing Dean in the plane crash. Unlike many women, I had never seen marriage and children as the only option, and I certainly didn't need the institution of marriage to validate me. I greatly valued my independence and freedom, so I was very wary of getting married.

I didn't change my name, as I had an excellent reputation as a good tour manager, and I wanted to be treated on my own merits. Plus, I felt that my name was my identity, and I didn't want to be 'owned' by someone else.

We were working hard, not paying ourselves much (£70 a week, I remember, although we made sure the other staff were paid properly) and we ploughed everything back into the company. I was still singing in the LSO Chorus and I met the composer Hans Werner Henze. I told him that I sang with the LSO Chorus, and would love to sing with his Montepulciano Festival Chorus, which was in Italy for a few weeks during the summer. I told Hans that I hated doing auditions, but he replied that if I was with a chorus as good as the LSO Chorus then I wouldn't need to audition for him. But stupidly I didn't take him up on it, as I thought I shouldn't really leave Paul for a jaunt in Italy. I regret that decision to this day. To sing gorgeous music, with like-minded people in the wonderful Italian countryside...

After a few years I realised I was desperately unhappy. I gave up some great experiences for my marriage. My biggest regret, just a few months after getting married, was turning down the job as Bruce Springsteen's tour manager... Bill Zysblat (Stones accountant) had called me from New York, saying he had recommended me to Springsteen. Wow! Nowadays, I think back and I really wish I'd taken that job, but I told Bill that I'd only just got married and that I felt I had a duty to stay at home with my husband. What a massive mistake in retrospect. Paul really had no appreciation of the things I gave up for him.

Paul was drinking a lot, too, and I was a good little wife, doing what I thought I should – clearing up the empty vodka bottles, the overflowing ashtrays every morning. And my husband, like my father, was hyper-critical of my best efforts. Both men confirmed my own self-loathing. We women have been conditioned for far too long into thinking that everything wrong is all our fault…but that's not what a mutually loving marriage should be like, surely? My confidence began to disappear. We tried counselling with a therapist that Steve and Nicole Winwood had recommended to me. We had several separate sessions each with him, then finally one together, where the therapist said, "Your wife is one of the most well-adjusted young women I've ever met."

Well, Paul didn't like that one bit and even accused me of bribing the therapist to say that. He also accused me of cheating on him, continually saying that I would leave him, but he wouldn't listen to me when I said I'd married him because I loved him – what more could I do to prove it? He went on and on so much about me leaving him that eventually it became a self-fulfilling prophecy, and very sadly, I decided I couldn't carry on like this. It's really best to leave if you continually feel let down and judged by people who suck the pleasure out of your life. It is vital to feel enriched and enhanced in a marriage, not diminished. In retrospect I now realise the true meaning of being a victim of gaslighting – which is exactly how I felt I was treated in that marriage.

So, I left my job, my London home and my husband. Luckily, I still had my little cottage in Oxfordshire, where I ended up living. But I nearly lost that last bit of security, as I had agreed some years previously that Paul could have a £25,000 financial charge against it. Thankfully it was removed the following year, but it was an extremely worrying and desperate time. Worst of all was the sense that I had lost my best friend.

Interestingly Paul got a new girlfriend just a few weeks after I left him, whereas it took me nearly a year to find the confidence to even go out with someone new.

It was very cold and depressing for me in my little cottage that winter of 1984. I was probably drinking too much and becoming very low. But eventually I pulled myself together and wrote to a few people, including Pete Townshend, saying I was looking for a job.

A few days later the phone rang. It was Pete. "I can't believe you're looking for a job!" he said. "Come and have a chat with me. I think I've got something for you."

Pete then asked me to run The Who's charity, the Double O, which, coincidentally, I had helped set up some years before while working for Bill Curbishley. I was offered a starting salary of £14,000 a year plus a company car.

At last – a decent salary! Pete Townshend had, quite literally, come to my rescue.

Chapter 18

The Double O Charity

For the next three years, from May 1985 to November 1988, I ran the Double O Charity. Pete Townshend had set it up along the same lines as Charity Projects: every penny I raised went to the charity and its work. Salaries, including mine and that of my assistant, and all administration costs, were paid by Pete himself. I honestly think this is the way charities should be run in an ideal world, but of course it's not an ideal world; some charity CEOs now earn exorbitant sums, which shocks me to the core.

The Double O was mainly helping drug and alcohol addicts. When I asked Pete why he wanted me to run the Double O, he said it was because I had been around many people taking drugs in the bands, and had taken many myself, so obviously had some understanding of the subject and its complexities. My time was filled with visiting various clinics around the country, including Meg Patterson's clinic, where she treated people like Eric Clapton and Keith Richards. (I remember speaking to Boy George's mother, and recommending that she talk to Meg Patterson, who had helped so many people.) I had meetings at the House of Commons and the House of Lords to try and get the drug problems discussed by politicians. And I would also have regular meetings with the probationers at the Inner London Probation Service.

Around this time, I discovered that Jackie Curbishley, Bill's wife, had been up to her old tricks, spreading bizarre lies about me. Apparently, she would go around saying to anyone who would listen that I 'stole other people's jobs'. I have never, ever done anything like that and never would, so I thought to myself, that's classic projection. *You're* the one who took *my* job back in 1976!

When Pete wanted a logo for the charity, I called an old friend, Brian Sweet, a brilliant artist and illustrator who was teaching in the graphic department of Somerset College of Art and Technology. I gave him the brief about the charity's work, and he came back with the most amazing design. Brian remembers me telling him that neither Pete nor I were happy with the designs that some of the best artists in London had come up with, as they were all too obviously using the two Os. So, Brian came up with a white poppy on a black background, explaining his reasoning that the poppy was already used by this country as a war memorial, but that the white poppy suggested the heroin poppy, which he saw as a memorial to heroin victims. It was also the poppy of peace. So very appropriate for the work the Double O Charity was doing with drug addicts. And it did, very subtly, include the two Os in the poppy petals, but not in an overt, obvious way.

Pete and Brian have given me permission to show the logo here, and it can also be seen on YouTube in the TV programme *The South Bank Show*, about Pete and his work as a musician, charity founder and book editor.

Left: The Double O Logo (by Brian Sweet, with kind permission)
Right: Sir Elton John CH CBE with Pete Townshend
(© Richard Young, with kind permission)

The YouTube clip of Pete and me is titled 'Pete Townshend on The South Bank Show', where I'm showing Pete this new Double O Charity logo.

Pete was so sweet and kind to me during the shooting, as I was terrified of being filmed and really didn't want to be included, but he insisted and said he'd help, and indeed he did! At one point in the film you can see he gives me a lovely kindly smile, as he knew I was nearly shitting myself!

During the Double O Charity years I spent a lot of time at Peter de Savary's club, the St James's Club in. I was working closely with de Savary's assistant, Pene Delmage, who went on to marry the actor Albert Finney. Together we put on various fundraising events for the Double O Charity that Peter de Savary sponsored. Peter was generosity personified to the Double O Charity. He's another of my unsung heroes. He did such a great deal for charity, but with no fanfare. In fact, PDS, as we all called him, asked if one of his daughters could come along for some work experience with me, as he wanted her to learn about the dangers of drugs. She was a delight, and I even took her, with a probation officer, to watch the drug dealing going on in Tottenham Court Road and Soho Square, where the probation officer was watching out for any of her clients.

Later, in 1986, PDS gave me a free holiday at his St James's Club in Antigua for three weeks and said I could invite a friend. So, one of my chums from Los Angeles joined me. It was fabulous – truly amazing! Keith Richards was also there, so he invited us to have drinks with him a few times. It was lovely catching up on the news about Marlon and Dandy, and how well they were doing.

What wonderful kindness and generosity from Peter de Savary. He told me he had given me this holiday as he was so impressed by my hard work over the previous year for the Double O Charity. I have never, before or since, had such an amazing present. And I was very fortunate that he helped me out with a personal project many years later when I had just got over breast cancer, by sponsoring a small fundraising event I organised for a cancer charity.

But I'm jumping ahead. Earlier in my time at the Double O, on 14th September 1985 to be precise, I organised a massive charity event, the St James's Square Ball. We persuaded some fantastic people to take part, including Roger Moore, Elton John and The Temptations. Pete Townshend also played a set, although he often used to say he would prefer to stay in the background, while I could totally understand that he was a big draw for supporters and it really was a means to an end – we needed money to keep the work of the charity going.

As well as Brian Croft helping on the technical side, one of my old friends, Robbie Williams, helped as our production manager. Robbie ran Pink Floyd's equipment company, Britannia Row. I was delighted to have him on board, as I simply could not manage to do production management as well as all the other work involved with organising such a huge event. And, again, my loyal troupe of helpers were there too.

To say it was hard work is an understatement. The ball took place in St James's Square right in the middle of the West End of London, so I had to jump through hoops with the Greater London Council. My 1985 diary is filled with numerous meetings with people from various departments, including health and safety, police and fire. The fire people used to come along unannounced and try to set fire to any marquees and tablecloths – just to check they really were fire-retardant.

I had to organise parking spaces for all the workers and participants, sort out space for a generator, hire the marquees, tables and chairs. Then there was the catering, the portable toilets, security…not to mention a big Winnebago changing room for Elton John. I have a lovely photo of me and Elton from that night, where he had just made me giggle. We were standing at the side of the stage, with me holding him back before he rushed on.

The photo was taken just after Elton asked me, "What's happening – is it time for me to go on yet?"

"Hang on a minute," I said. "They're just toasting the Queen."

To which he replied, "Don't they know I'm already here…?!"

Later that year, in November, I organised two big concerts at the Brixton Academy in aid of the Double O Charity. One of the concerts featured Pete Townshend's own band, Deep End. This fairly short-lived group was formed by Pete and featured Pink Floyd's guitarist, Dave Gilmour. Another Deep End musician was John 'Rabbit' Bundrick, the amazing American pianist who I'd worked with in the States in 1977 when he was in Crawler.

I had an odd experience with Pete here. He took me aside one day to say he'd seen me being rude to a black guy... Well, nothing could have been further from the truth. What had happened was that this guy had crept in the backstage door. When I politely asked him to leave, he became very abusive to me saying "Who the fuck are you?" and pushing me up against a wall. So, I put my hand on his chest to stop him coming any closer to me. He was well over 6 feet tall and really scary and intimidating. That was what Pete saw... Luckily, Jim Callaghan, our security guy, arrived in the nick of time to rescue me and throw this guy out. However, Pete had seen everything from a distance and assumed that I was being rude to this interloper. He never apologised for getting it wrong. Those things rankled at the time, and still do to an extent because of the unfairness, but I had to be a professional and move on. I had other things to think about, including the next event I was organising just a month later in December '85 – The Snowball at the Dominion Theatre.

This big event was raising funds for the Refuge Charity (originally Chiswick Family Rescue) of which Pete's wife, Karen, was a trustee. David Frost was the announcer for the evening, and he rushed in to do his bit at the beginning, then rushed out again. There was the usual mix of music and comedy, with Pete and Midge Ure and chums doing the music bit, and Rory Bremner doing some wonderful comedy sketches. Joanna Lumley also helped us, and afterwards she told me she would really like to employ me as her assistant, but couldn't afford me! What a wonderful thing to hear from such an amazing person. She really is one of the nicest people I have ever met, and always did what she said she would do – unlike many others, who offer but then 'forget'...

A month later, in January 1986, we were in Midem, Cannes, with Deep End. Pete says in his memoirs that even though the band was extremely well received, he decided not to continue with it. It was also there in the South of France that I had a quick fling with Dave Gilmour; nothing special, just a bit of fun for us both as he was separated from his wife. He did take me out for lunch a few times after that, but just as friends.

Back in England, not long after, I met two wonderful people who had just started up a new drug charity providing a holistic approach to addiction. They were Jackie Leven and Carol Wolf, and both became close personal friends. They were squatting in the building in Lisson Grove in London that would eventually become the site of The CORE Trust. Jackie and Carol had been in the band Doll by Doll, and had both been heroin addicts, but couldn't afford the cost of going to one of the usual detox places when they wanted to get off it. So, they tried another way – by instead using complementary health treatments such as acupuncture and homoeopathy. The Double O helped them a great deal over those early years, funding individuals to go through their treatment plan. I was immensely proud when Jackie and Carol asked me to become a trustee when CORE officially set up as a registered charity. We also managed to get Princess Diana to be the patron, which was a great coup and helped the charity blossom and grow, thus helping more and more people.

Another Double O event I organised was the St James's Club Ball at Peter de Savary's Littlecote House. It was held in a marquee in the gardens with the jazz musician, Courtney Pine, playing. He was one of the more difficult celebrities I have had to deal with. Nothing specific, just awkward – not fitting in with others. Mind you, he was pretty young then, so maybe it was nerves. But maybe he also didn't really enjoy playing for people who probably didn't listen intently enough to his wonderful music...?

On the night of the event, I stayed overnight at Littlecote sharing a room with Pene Delmage. Well, what a fright I had in the middle of the night. I suddenly awoke to the loudest banging – it was like metal on metal, or metal on stone and it was BANG, BANG, BANG – seven times. Pene slept soundly right through it! I got up and walked to the bedroom door, trying to be brave enough to go out and see where it was coming from. I got as far as the corridor. It sounded as though it was coming from a room downstairs but then it stopped. I rushed back to the bedroom and leapt back into bed. It was truly terrifying. The next morning at breakfast with Peter de Savary and his wife Lana, I told them about it. Peter proceeded to tell us that the room below ours had been used for executions. I was never sure whether he was teasing, or if that was the truth. But whatever it was, that was the only time I've had an experience like that. I really wish I'd been brave enough to go downstairs but, no, I was far too scared!

Work in those days was intense and very full on. I even worked on Sundays. On one occasion I had lunch at the St James's Club with Sir John Mills and his wife, Mary. We got on so well that they invited me to Sunday lunch at their house the following week. Jack Lemmon was due to be there too. I'm not much phased by famous names but, oh my goodness, *Jack Lemmon*! How exciting! But, as was usual for me at that time, I was working that particular Sunday so couldn't go – and once you've declined an invitation, people never seem to invite you again. What a sadness that was to me. I've never been overawed by famous people, but Jack Lemmon was something else! Although, it goes to show how hard I was working for Pete's charity, even on Sundays.

In September 1986, the dancer Michael Clark offered the Double O Charity the proceeds of one of his nights at Sadler's Wells: The invitation reads:

> Sadler's Wells Theatre has pleasure in presenting the Gala World Premiere of a new ballet by Michael Clark and Company at 7.30pm September 17th 1986. In aid of Pete Townshend's Double O Charity.
>
> Michael Clark – the style leader of modern dance – leads his company of eight superb dancers in the World Premiere of his explosive new post-punk spectacular.
>
> In this eagerly awaited new show – produced in association with Sadler's Wells Theatre – Clark's taste for the extreme in dance, music and design sets him apart as a cult figure in the new generation of dance creators.
>
> With the live sounds of rock and the glittering tongue-in-cheek designs of young fashion stars Leigh Bowery and BodyMap, Clark's two-week season at Sadler's Wells Theatre promises to be the hottest property this Autumn.
>
> The Double O Charity was founded in 1976 by The Who, since when it has supported many worthy causes. Following Pete Townshend's cure of heroin addiction, he and his wife took over the Charity specifically to help those people suffering from drug abuse. The Double O Charity helps to fund treatment clinics and rehabilitation centres for chemical dependents and especially supports the work of Dr. Meg Patterson.

It was a fabulous evening, with a large amount raised for the charity, and with the party going on well into the night at the Limelight Club in Soho.

Early in 1987 I read in the Celebrity Bulletin (info that is passed around in the music and film business world) that Paul Newman and his wife, Joanne Woodward, were staying at the Savoy Hotel, which was just down the road from my office in Covent Garden. I knew that his son had died of a drug overdose, so I personally wrote to Paul Newman, explaining the work of the Double O Charity, and was there any way he could help us with a donation or some fundraising? I ran down the road and delivered the letter to the Savoy by hand. I never really expected a reply, but I got one! It was signed by Paul Newman himself on his own headed notepaper – not even company notepaper. I still have it today. It's reproduced here with kind permission from his daughter. He wrote:

February 18, 1987
Ms. Sally Arnold
Director, Double O Charity

Dear Ms. Arnold,

Newman's Own food products is set up in such a way that the profits I contribute to non-profit organisations must come from the country in which the sales are generated.

I don't know that what was made in England will amount to much, but I'll be happy to see that you get what we have.

Very truly yours,
Paul Newman

What an amazing response – far and above what I had expected.

In June that year Paul Newman's daughter, Nell, was coming to London and wanted to present Pete and the Double O with a cheque for £25,000 from Newman's Own foods. This really was a huge amount of money for us. The company that ran the UK distribution asked me if Pete would do a photo op and publicly accept a cheque to the Double O from Nell Newman. This was to be in front of a few invited members of the press, with a big mock-up of the cheque being passed over.

So, I did my usual thing of giving Pete all the details – in writing – asking him if he would be happy to do this. Which he was. We communicated for some weeks about it, with him stating that he wanted there to be no more than three photographers and one journalist there. We held the event at the May Fair Hotel, as Patrick Board, the general manager, had agreed to let us use a suite, including refreshments, as a donation to the Double O. So, there were about ten people in total. Pete, Nell Newman, me, and three people from the food company and only four from the press. Then there would be a lunch for six people – Pete, Nell, me, and three people from the food company.

What happened next was one of the most horrible moments of my working life.

Of course, all the press guys and photographers wanted to get a picture of the cheque being passed over from Nell Newman to Pete Townshend.

But when Pete arrived and opened the door, he took one look inside and shouted, "What the fuck? I'm not doing this. There are too many fucking people in there."

"What are you *talking* about?" I hissed, aware of everyone in the room behind me. "There's exactly how many we agreed on."

"Well, I'm still not doing it," he said and stalked off down the corridor – leaving the hotel.

I was in tears by this time, and Nell came out into the corridor to comfort me.

"Sally, nothing surprises me when it comes to celebrities," she said.

"But I feel I've wasted everybody's time," I replied.

"Honestly, I've seen far worse. You're not to worry about it."

But, of course, everybody was still waiting inside the suite, not knowing why Pete Townshend had slammed the door and just disappeared like that.

Nell then offered to have the photograph taken with her giving me the cheque, but of course that's not what the press wanted. They didn't want me – they wanted the famous Pete Townshend! Luckily, I knew the photographers – Richard Young, Dave Benett and Alan Davidson – who were all kind and sweet to me, and totally understanding, as they had all experienced these dramas from celebrities on many occasions.

I'm still in touch with Nell Newman, and she remembers this event vividly – as do I – and she has given me permission to write about her reaction. She told me recently that Pete had written to her at the time, to apologise to her.

In July 1987 Pete allowed me to help Bill Wyman put on a fundraising event at the Hilton Hotel in Park Lane for Bill's project, AIMS, which was letting young musicians use the Rolling Stones' mobile recording truck for free. It was a very successful event, and Mick Jagger even came along – and greeted me with a kiss and a hug – such a surprise! I had bumped into him occasionally over the years, often at the nightclub Tramp, where I first met Jerry Hall with him, who was cheerful, friendly and a breath of fresh air.

I also had a few meetings at The Prince's Trust, Prince Charles's charity, advising on the work of the Double O Charity. Through those meetings, I met a woman who ran a charity called The Life Education Centres; Prince Charles was their patron, and I would organise some events for them in the coming years.

In October 1987, I arranged the May Fair Ball at the May Fair Intercontinental Hotel for the Double O where some amazing acts took part: members of Dire Straits, Pete Townshend, the magician Fay Presto, Lord Colwyn's 3B Band and Judy Garland's daughter Lorna Luft. Donations came from Keith Richards, Michael Palin and Suzi Quatro. Dire Straits' manager, Ed Bicknell, was a great supporter. As usual my friends helped me backstage, ushering people to their tables, selling raffle tickets, being runners and generally stepping in with anything and everything that I might need help with.

Patrick Board, the general manager at the May Fair Hotel, was again amazingly helpful and generous, especially with letting us use the ballroom free of charge, and providing auction and raffle prizes. We made a great deal of money for the Double O Charity coffers. One auction item went for £25,000 alone. It was a silver replica of a 1932 Alfa Monza racing car designed by Theo Fennell and signed by Mark Knopfler, who drove it in the 1986 and 1987 Mille Miglia race. It had been donated by the May Fair Hotel and Alain de Cadenet. I think it was Mark Knopfler who actually put in that final bid. Pete wrote the following:

Addicted to Helping Addicts

The Charity was originally established in 1976 by The Who. They donated money to many worthwhile causes, but when The Who split up, the Charity lay dormant. However, after Pete Townshend's treatment for heroin addic-

*Top: Left to right: Gary Kemp, Pete Townshend, Bill Wyman and Andy Summers,
Snowball Revue, December 1985 (Photo by Mat Croft)*
*Bottom Left: Pete Townshend and Lady Mary Mills, St James Club Ball, September 1986
(© Richard Young, with kind permission)*
Bottom Right: Sally with Sir Elton John (© Richard Young, with kind permission)

203

tion by Dr. Meg Patterson, he decided to revitalise the Charity in the hope of helping many desperate individuals.

The reason Double O is required is simple – amid all the hysteria and the campaigning, drug abusers and victims need treatment. The NHS currently cannot do very much, for reasons we all know are purely financial. The aim of the Charity is to help provide clinic beds and rehabilitation for addicts. We do this by supporting established foundations and sometimes by paying directly for an individual's treatment. We also fund research into different types of treatment and into endogenous drugs (the body's own drugs, vital in our ability to bear pain and discomfort, but distorted by alcohol and drug abuse); we pay to train counsellors in the Minnesota method of rehabilitation.

We have an extremely high success rate with individuals. As most of our money is donated, we have to make absolutely sure that people are ready for treatment, therefore, we fund people only after advice from their doctors and/or probation officers. We work very closely with many different doctors, probation officers, counsellors and clinics, and we also keep in touch with people we have helped and make sure they are happy in their rehabilitation (with their jobs and families, for example).

We don't align ourselves with any one type of treatment, but support the many we have researched. Our attitude is that no one method works for everybody, but they all work for somebody.

We have been supported by a wide section of the community, from show-business personalities to top business people, from local authorities to the Royal Trusts, from both left and right of the House. As well as dispersal of funds we also do a great deal of research and run our own fund-raising events – ranging from clay pigeon shoots to glittering balls and ballets!

The *Evening Standard* wrote about the May Fair Ball in their Ad Lib column:

Guess Who'll be playing at Pete's party

Amid great secrecy, plans have been underway for the most exclusive rock 'n' roll party of the year to be held next week at the West End's Mayfair Hotel.

Dire Straits fans will gnash their teeth with envy. Appearing in front of just 400 guests in the hotel ballroom will be Mark Knopfler and bassist John Illsley playing a selection of the band's best known hits.

The £100-a-head evening on October 20th is in aid of Pete Townshend's Double O Charity, which rehabilitates drug addicts and alcoholics. Indeed, The Who guitarist will join Knopfler and Illsley on stage.

'It is a very private affair and tickets have only been sold to people on our mailing list,' says the charity's director Sally Arnold.

The Double O's offices and staff expenses are all paid for by reformed heroin addict Townshend.

Money raised, which this year will top £100,000, funds treatment clinics and rehabilitation centres, counselling and educational videos.

I also remember that evening for another, rather sad, reason. The guest list included Steve Winwood and his new wife, Eugenia. As I had known Steve for some years, I made sure I looked after them extra well – but what I hadn't expected was that his ex-wife, Nicole, who I also knew well, would turn up. She proceeded to get extremely drunk and somehow managed to corner Steve and Eugenia round the back of the ballroom, shouting and screaming. Luckily, I heard this ruckus and managed to steer Nicole away, with Steve begging me to keep her away from them. Poor Nicole; her heart was broken, and to see her beloved Steve with his new wife was just too much for her.

I spent some of my happiest years at the Double O Charity. Pete made me a director of the Double O Charity Ltd, and Double O Promotions Ltd – the charity's trading arm. I was there for nearly three years and raised funds for treatment centres and rehabilitation clinics for drug abuse and alcoholism from the ten events I organised. I had total responsibility for both companies, and had to keep all financial records properly and carefully, in case the Charity Commission or HMRC wanted to check anything. This is why I simply cannot understand how people manage to steal from charities, or run them badly, as there are usually so many checks and balances by the various authorities.

Chapter 19

Down to Earth

I was continuing to move the work of the Double O Charity further and further forward. We were becoming very well known and respected in the area of helping addictions. Then, without warning, and just a few weeks after the hugely successful May Fair Double O Ball, Pete called me into his office. He said he was making me redundant.

To say I was shocked would be an understatement. I honestly thought he wanted to keep on the way we'd been going. But no. He said he'd never meant it to go on for so long and that, when we first met up for that coffee in 1985, he'd told me he only wanted it to run for a year.

Well, that's not how I recalled it. I would definitely have remembered if he had said that, as it concerned my whole future. In fact, he even gave me a pay rise on each of the two anniversaries of my starting at Double O – in 1986 and 1987 – congratulating me on my work. That didn't sound to me like a job that was only supposed to last a year…and in those few years I had organised ten extremely successful events for the Double O.

I'll never really understand it, especially as I had raised the charity's profile so successfully. We had an amazing regular sponsor in Peter de Savary, plus I had brought into the mix both Paul Newman and Patrick Board of the May Fair Hotel, not to mention all the voluntary help from people like Brian Croft. I was utterly heartbroken. This was my dream job and, although Pete could be challenging, he was a great boss and I loved working for him.

I wasn't the only person to be made redundant. There were two others, so I know it wasn't personal. To soften the blow somewhat Pete commissioned me, paying me to write a document about all the work I'd done for Double O. It took me many weeks to write it as I only had an electric typewriter, and then he lost the document – after all my hard work.

Pete has given me permission to reproduce the following reference:

Sally Arnold was the Director of Double O's drug rehabilitation fund-raising team for just under three years. In that time she was directly responsible for the generation of more than £240,000 in donations and, through the auspices of Double O's commercial arm, Double O Promotions, generated another £300,000 (much of it royalty based income).

Further to this, she has become an important figure in the group of dedicated individuals who work with addicts, criminal offenders, hospitals, drug companies, rehabilitation units, crisis centres, the Ministry of Health and the D.H.S.S. She has been responsible for helping disseminate information freely among all concerned, and for the correct disbursement of funds for the benefit of both individual addicts and the organisations providing help.

Hailing from the rock business, she is tough and well experienced in dealing with show business egos. She has also proved herself capable of great entrepreneurial versatility, producing events as various as Christmas Variety Shows and Clay Pigeon Shoots. Yet she is also sensitive and demanding, capable of independence but happier in a team. She works best with real responsibility and is effective under pressure. A natural leader, she nevertheless welcomes guidance and direction and responds quickly and efficiently to the changing climate in a volatile area like drug abuse.

If she has a fault, it is that she is too dedicated and can become annealed to the feelings of work-mates when she is at full tilt. But in the field of charity work this is not a bad vice to have; too often the unpleasant work fails to get done because so many charity workers are seeking affection from anyone they happen to meet.

Sally has earned the regard of all the individuals she has assisted. This is because she is able to work in the charitable sector without any hint of patronism or superiority.

I recommend her wholeheartedly in any role that would give her the responsibility and freedom she has enjoyed at Double O, but I also believe she has great potential in public relations and corporate image-making should she feel so inclined.

Signed: Pete Townshend
23rd November 1987

Pete was very wise in many areas. At one point I had organised a large event with another very famous charity. We had an agreement to split the proceeds fifty-fifty. I had done all the preparatory work with the local council, completed the technical work, and obtained the sponsorship and most of the entertainers. But after the event, the other charity refused to adhere to the agreement and refused to give the Double O Charity any of the proceeds. I was distraught and went to Pete in tears, saying, "They lied to us. We must tell the press." But Pete said no, if we did that the other charity people could just lie again. So it was best to leave it. I didn't like it, especially after my months and months of hard work, but he was absolutely right. A big lesson all round – especially to always get everything in writing, even if you think you can trust the people you're dealing with.

So, here I was, redundant. Back down to earth with a bump. But I respected Pete and years later, in 2003, had occasion to help him…

It might be remembered that he had a terrible time with the press with accusations of child abuse, which of course were never proven, and I heartily believe were never true. In March that year, I wrote him a reference for the police, at his request:

Dear Pete,

I do hope the attached testimonial helps. You must have been going through some very deep despair these past few months – which I do understand – albeit for a different reason. But a dark night of the soul it is, nonetheless – and my heart goes out to you.

And my testimonial:

To whom it may concern:

I have known Pete Townshend and his family since 1974 when I was employed by The Who's management company as Tour Manager for this group and many others.

I am also a qualified Norland Nurse, with full NNEB qualifications, so I have been trained to look out for inappropriate behaviour from adults towards children.

When Mr. Townshend asked me to become Director of the group's charity, The Double O Charity, I was thrilled, as this meant that I could become more helpful and proactive in helping young people – as previously I had spent many years helping charities in my spare time. For example, I was one of the founders of Comic Relief/Charity Projects, having produced and directed their first fund-raising events. I was also a Founder Trustee of The CORE Trust, which helps young people with various types of addiction. I also continue to be a proactive Trustee of Between the Notes, a charity helping young people via classical music.

The Double O Charity was set up specifically to help young people – and I think this alone shows that Mr. Townshend has always had a desire to help others who are unable, for one reason or another, to help themselves. For example, we helped many people with drug and alcohol problems who could not afford their own treatment. During the three years I was running the Charity, Mr Townshend and I frequently despaired at the statistics which showed that addicted young people came from homes where physical and sexual abuse were the norm, and who then went into lives of crime and drug abuse. The other statistic that is common in these cases is an 'absent father figure'.

I personally feel it is monstrous that Mr Townshend can be accused of any type of wrong-doing, when all he has tried to do is help people who are less fortunate than himself – the proof of this being the formation of the Double O Charity in the 1970s, and his financial and personal generosity to this charity and many others.

Should anybody wish to speak to me to discuss this further, I would be more than happy to oblige.

In 1988, following my redundancy from Double O, I was excited to be employed by one of the United Kingdom's first satellite channels, Landscape. The channel had been started by Nick Austin, of the Beggars Banquet record label. Mike Appleton, producer of the BBC's Old Grey Whistle Test, was the programme director, and asked me to be his personal assistant. This was a lovely job, as Mike is one of the nicest people I have ever met. My official job title was Senior Programme Executive, although later I was promoted to Deputy Managing Director.

While I was working at Landscape, John Illsley, the bass guitarist of

Dire Straits, asked me to organise a large fundraising evening event. I had originally met John Illsley through The Prince's Trust. He was a trustee of a charity called The Life Education Centres, of which Prince Charles was the patron. This was an Australian charity set up to send specially equipped mobile units to visit schools to educate children about their bodies and the effect of drugs on them – not only drugs, but the effects of everything ingested, including food and drink – and how to respect and treasure their bodies, and not put dangerous drugs into them. So, I organised and produced this event for them at a large stately home in the Hampshire countryside.

The evening ran wonderfully well with Dave Dee as compère, magic by Fay Presto, and Dire Straits providing the music.

My usual crew of unsung heroes helped out yet again.

However, my time at Landscape was coming to an end. Sadly, the company ran out of funding and so most of us were made redundant. I think the company was rather ahead of its time, with people not being used to satellite channels yet.

Sally with dancer Desmond Ledgister and Fay Presto, Charity Polo Match, 1992
(© Dave Benett, with kind permission)

Mike, in his position of managing director, wrote me this amazing reference:

Due entirely to no fault of her own, The Landscape Channel has reluctantly been forced to make Sally's position here redundant.

Since arriving here in September 1988 as the Senior Programme Executive, Sally has progressed to become Deputy Managing Director. She has been responsible for all areas of office and personnel management, which she has carried out diligently with her natural brand of enthusiasm and dedication.

In my absence she has taken the additional responsibility of supervising both programme planning and production.

I have no hesitation in recommending her to any prospective employer; and indeed should the financial situation here change, would, having worked with her for the last ten months, equally have no hesitation in offering her reinstatement in her present post.

After Landscape closed down, I had to go on unemployment benefit, also known as 'the dole', for the first time in my life. But I wasn't down for long because, in 1989, Mike Appleton soon asked me to work with him again. He was back at the BBC for The One World Project, a BBC initiative on the dire state of the world's environment. The BBC was one of the first organisations to be in the forefront of such important environmental and ecological programmes so many years ago. Mike wanted me to be his PA again.

The coordinator of The One World Unit was Ritchie Cogan, with Mike and I organising a live concert in May. Working with Mike again, and with Ritchie and his team, including adviser James Lovelock, was a truly happy experience. No dramas – just plain common sense and hard work from all involved. What a relief after the years of rock stars and their demands and tantrums!

We were struggling to find enough support for a live concert when I introduced a new creative director to the project – Kevin Godley, of Godley and Creme. He came up with the idea of him travelling to wherever the musicians were around the world and recording them in situ, which was a brilliant solution and overcame all the problems of an actual concert.

The project also needed a logo, one that could be automated. So,

I again introduced my artist friend, the illustrator, Brian Sweet (who had designed the Double O Charity logo). Yet again Brian came up with a fantastic design. He told me recently that at his initial meeting with Ritchie, in a pub in Soho, Ritchie had said to him, "I think you're going to make me a very happy man."

Brian designed a simple but effective logo. It was the first of its kind, being digitally animated, with the leaves flying off the tree, which is in the shape of the earth. He said he had the idea from autumn leaves, and the line: 'Good planets are hard to find. One good blow and it's all over.'

Both the BBC and Brian have given me permission to reproduce the One World logo opposite.

Sadly, this project only lasted four months for me, as the following reference from Ritchie explains:

> Sally Arnold joined the One World project in October 1989 and worked from the BBC's coordinating office. The project is a major collaboration of international broadcasters in a week of programmes scheduled for transmission in May 1990. The intended climax to the week was a 10 hour live international concert, and Sally was employed as artists' manager and PA to the Executive Producer Mike Appleton. At the end of January it became clear…that the project could not attract sufficient world class artists to make such a multi-venue event as spectacular as wished, and with reluctance we cancelled it. However, Sally by this time had introduced us to a well-known Creative Director, who came up with an alternative and original proposal which has been adopted with enthusiasm by the international consortium of broadcasters.

> Ironically as this new idea does not call for a live concert element, Sally has in effect made herself redundant, and by mutual agreement we terminated her contract early. Our gratitude goes to Sally, not only for rescuing the One World project but also by introducing us to the designer who has provided us with the international logo

The Dodgy Duke

I don't know whether Pete Townshend had kept up the relationship with Newman's Own food products when he made me redundant, but I continued to have a connection with Paul Newman. Some years previously he had set up the Hole in the Wall Gang Camp in the States. This was a camp for terminally ill children where they could have a great time, all the while still having their chemotherapy or radiotherapy given by voluntary oncology doctors and nurses. The camp was massively successful, and funded by Newman's Own food products. Paul Newman himself didn't take a penny from these products, and channelled all profits into the camp and its work.

Throughout the late 1980s I kept in regular touch with him and his office in the States. In 1990, they contacted me and asked for my help to set up a UK version of the Hole in the Wall Gang Camp. Paul Newman had recommended me to Angus Montague, the Duke of Manchester, with whom he had discussed this UK venture, to be known as The Duke's Trust.

BBC One World logo (By Brian Sweet, with kind permission)

But, oh my goodness, what a very strange man the Duke of Manchester was. He had ingratiated himself into Paul Newman's charitable work in the States, and told Newman that he wanted to start up an Over the Wall Gang Camp in the United Kingdom. And obviously Paul Newman trusted him. Well, why wouldn't he? However, Angus turned out to be a crook – in the true meaning of the word.

We had an office just round the corner from the Houses of Parliament, and I started working there, very happily initially, setting up The Duke's Trust, and organising fundraising events.

But then the doubts started creeping in. Every time I tried to contact any of the aristocracy to become a trustee, none of them would ever respond, or reply to phone calls or letters. I thought this was odd but, at first, nothing more than that…until money started disappearing.

Then, on 22nd June, I was at the Nordoff Robbins Music Therapy lunch, a regular annual bash for the music business where I had volunteered for many years. I got chatting to a journalist from the *Daily Mail*. He asked me what I was doing now.

"I'm working for the Duke of Manchester," I said.

He raised an eyebrow. "Angus Montague? Hmmm, I'm sure we've got something on file about him and his criminal past."

What?!

And this is how I learned about the Dodgy Duke.

We talked a bit more and I begged the journalist to fax me details. Later, I got back to the office to find he'd made good on his promise. There it all was in the fax machine tray. Copious amounts of information. Copies of headlines from the newspapers showing that this man had been in prison in Australia and had, only recently, narrowly escaped a prison sentence here in the United Kingdom on a serious fraud case. The judge had said: "I've never met such a stupid man. On a scale of one to ten, you are minus ten. I am acquitting you because I think you're too stupid to have done it all on purpose."

No wonder none of the other aristocrats wanted to get involved!

Later, I would discover from my aunt in Australia that Montague had been in the prison where she worked in Melbourne. What a coincidence.

Apparently, his grandfather was sent to Wormwood Scrubs, and an uncle was jailed in at least three countries. More recently, I've read that his son has been jailed twice in Australia.

I waited in the office until late one Friday evening, making sure I was alone. Then I faxed all the documentation over to Paul Newman's office in the States, with a note stating my worries. I duly packed it all up in a box and left, never to return. I took everything to my nearest police station in Hampstead on the Monday morning.

(I did however become involved again with the next version of the Over the Wall Gang Camp in the United Kingdom as a trustee at Paul Newman's request.)

So, I had walked away from my job, and had to go on the dole again.

This was the last straw for me. I felt as if I was stuck in a revolving door – either being made redundant, or losing a job like the one with the Dodgy Duke. I was getting thoroughly fed up with being in and out of work. So, after a bit of soul-searching, I decided to sell my lovely penthouse flat in Hampstead, put everything into storage, and go travelling.

It was a great relief to get rid of my mortgage as, at that time, interest rates were horrendous at 17%. But suddenly my fortunes turned around because now I was the one *receiving* interest at 17% on my remaining capital of £50,000.

I felt so fortunate, because this would allow me to travel extensively and in comfort, a far cry from my trips in the 1970s when I'd had to make do with cheap hostels and third-class trains!

Chapter 20

Around the World

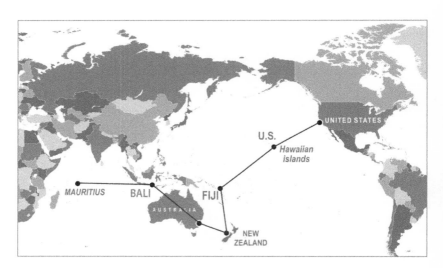

I hadn't had a proper holiday for years, having been on a non-stop hamster wheel, either working or job hunting. So, I used some of my new free time during the summer of 1990 to plan and organise a nine-month trip around the world. Never one to do things by halves, I decided to include the United States, Hawaii, Fiji, New Zealand, Australia, Bali and Mauritius. My trip would start in September 1990 and run through until July 1991.

For the American part, when I wasn't going to be staying with friends, I used various travel books. Back then, there was no internet, emails or mobile phones, and only basic computers to which I had no access anyway. I was on the phone almost non-stop, booking accommodation, car hire, trains, flights etc. I used faxes where possible, so that I had paper copies of all the bookings. I thoroughly enjoyed doing this for myself. It's what I was good at, and now I could do all this planning just for me, instead of for rock stars and their entourages, many of whom had no appreciation of the hard work other people did for them.

For the first week in America I stayed with my old friends Aaron and Elaine Schechter in Connecticut. Aaron was the US accountant for The Who, Stones and Skynyrd, so I knew him and his wife very well. Their house in Westport was one of those beautiful classic New England houses.

While in Connecticut I drove a small distance further north to see Paul Newman's Hole in the Wall Gang Camp, as I was a trustee for the UK branch, which we had eventually set up (despite near disaster with the Duke of Manchester). So at last I could see the original camp with its lakes and wooden cabins and marvellous medical facilities. I was delighted to meet all the staff in the office at last, many of whom I had spoken to on the phone but never met in person.

It was at this stage that I met up again with A E Hotchner, the well-established editor, novelist, playwright, and biographer. Hotch, as he was known, was Paul Newman's friend and partner, having co-founded Newman's Own foods. I was somewhat doubtful about seeing him again, as he had badly misquoted me in his book *Blown Away* about the Rolling Stones. I did briefly bring it up, but he was quite dismissive and said it was too late now. Some months later, when I was in LA staying with Lorna Luft, her father Sid Luft (Judy Garland's second husband) advised me to sue Hotch for misquoting me. But, on one of my long drives in the States, I was listening to the radio and on came Alistair Cooke's 'Letters from America', where he said something along the lines of, never sue anybody unless you really have to, as litigation is never worth the stress, the heartache, the waking up with a sinking heart. Litigation is not for the faint-hearted. So I decided against it.

I drove all around New England where the colours of the leaves were stunning. I saw places like The Mount built by Edith Wharton, my favourite author, in the 1920s, and Chesterwood, the house built by Daniel Chester French, the sculptor who made the Lincoln Memorial.

I have never worried about getting lost, as one always 'finds' oneself again, and one can discover so many exciting things and places. I also never worry about eating alone, as I always take a book with me.

Then I made my way to Concord, Massachusetts. Goodness, what a place! Established in 1635 by a group of English settlers, it grew and developed to become the birthplace of the revolution between Britain and America in 1775, and great authors such as Emerson, Hawthorne and Alcott lived and wrote there.

From Concord it was on to Plymouth to see the replica of the *Mayflower*, and to the Plimouth (correct spelling) Plantation, where the pilgrims first settled. Then to Martha's Vineyard where I hired a bike and cycled around the island. I can certainly see why people love living there so much, but I bet it's a nightmare in summer with all the visitors. Then back to the mainland and on to Newport where all the massive mansions are. I visited the Astor Mansion, and Marble House, which was built by the Vanderbilts. They are utterly fascinating with their over-the-top opulence.

From there, I headed south, taking the Amtrak train from New York's Penn Station to Charleston, via Delaware, Baltimore, Washington DC, Richmond, Petersburg, passing fields of pumpkins and corn. So many houses have flags and colonnades, with corn stalks and pumpkins on their verandahs.

Charleston is a beautiful town. I went to the Preservation Society to watch an interesting film, where I learned that it was originally Charles Town, after King Charles II. He gave a great deal of local land here to many of his favourite aristocrats like Lords Ashley, Cooper and Shaftesbury. While in Charleston I drove out into the countryside and visited two fascinating plantations, Drayton Hall and Middleton Place. Both very 'Gone with the Wind' types of plantations. I then discovered that Savannah is like Charleston's poor, plain sister, with very faded and distressed grandeur.

Next, on to Sea Island to meet up with an old friend. We stayed at the very flash Cloister Hotel for a few days. Then onto my nemesis... Jacksonville and memories of Skynyrd.

Jacksonville was the town of my loves, losses and heartaches. I stayed with Dean's mother, and on this visit I missed Dean even more than before. All the old memories came flooding back. Mrs Kilpatrick told me that I was the only one Dean would have ever considered marrying, and even with all the previous (gorgeous!) girlfriends, she and Dean's father knew I was the 'only one'.

I also met up with Artimus, Leon and Gary of Skynyrd. We all shed tears and memories. They were all the same sweet guys, but with some grey strands now appearing in their hair and beards. They had become Lynyrd Skynyrd again, after trying to make a success of the Rossington Collins Band. But after Allen's death, they couldn't continue with that name.

I also visited Judy and Theresa, the widows of Ronnie Van Zant and Steve Gaines. Judy told me that Leon and Artimus were the only ones who were clean and not taking any drugs.

I had a chat on the phone with Allen's daughter, Allison, who was eighteen then, married and expecting a child. She was so sweet, saying she remembered me because she loved me as I was Dean's girlfriend, and she had absolutely adored him. I always thought she'd end up a mess, but no – she was a sensible young lady, living there with her husband and sister, in their parents' old house. At least Allen had left them with a nice home, if not much else…plus royalties from the Lynyrd Skynyrd albums of course.

Leon told me that Bill Graham, the San Francisco promoter, was managing them now and they all wanted me to be with them for the upcoming shows at Christmas and New Year. I would be meeting up with Bill later on in San Francisco, so we could discuss it and the plan for me to continue being their tour manager in Europe for any upcoming tours. I was somewhat ambivalent about this, and not too sure that I really wanted to do it. It just wouldn't be the same without Ronnie and Dean.

Interestingly, they all told me that I was probably one of the few people that they *all* liked and would talk to – as there's still a great deal of animosity between the band and Judy Van Zant.

I spent a day at rehearsals with them, which was great. It was a wonderful feeling to be back with the guys and to feel so wanted and accepted; it was clear that they all still loved me. Then I spent an evening out with Leon, Billy and Artimus at a bar, and Artimus told me, "You're still as beautiful as ever…!"

Shit – why hadn't he ever said things like that to me before when

I really wanted to hear them?! I'd had such a big crush on him all those years ago!

Eventually, I left Jax and drove on through swamps and sugar cane fields – all very poor and depressing. Then suddenly into affluent Palm Beach on the outskirts of Miami. The first part was quite ugly with hotels, high-rises and skyscrapers everywhere. In Miami I stayed with my old friend Martha, who had originally been married to Gary Rossington of Skynyrd.

Nancy, my friend from LA, met me as we drove down the Florida Keys to Key West. One day, she decided we must pick up a stray kitten she'd found in the street and take it to a vet. So, she was driving, and I had this tiny little thing on my lap wrapped in a towel. Suddenly it leapt up in a frenzy, going totally mad and shrieking and scratching anything that was in its way – especially me! I was scratched all over my arms, but didn't worry unduly until we got to the veterinarian, who told us the cat wouldn't survive as it had some terrible disease, and that we must both get tetanus shots.

He glanced at me and my scratched arms. "Also, if you have been scratched, you might get Cat Scratch Fever."

I didn't think any more about it. Nancy flew back to LA, and I continued driving up the west coast of Florida. Then I started feeling ill – like the flu was coming on. Could this be the infamous Cat Scratch Fever? Thank goodness I'd been warned. I had booked the Ritz Carlton Hotel in Naples. Luckily, they let me keep the room for longer than originally booked, because I ended up staying there for about five days in a stupor of aches and fever. I would never normally stay so long at such an expensive hotel, but I simply couldn't continue driving. I couldn't even manage to lie on the beach and read. I just had to sleep and get over this nasty illness. The hotel staff were very understanding when I didn't even want the room cleaned – I just needed peace and quiet.

When I was better, I headed on to Mobile, Alabama. After a five-hour drive, I arrived at the Hill Ware Dowdell Mansion in Lafayette, Alabama, where parts of *Mississippi Burning* were filmed. Then on via Natchez, Mississippi, where all the big plantations and mansions are. I stayed at the Monmouth Plantation. Very antebellum.

I ended up in Atlanta for Christmas and New Year, staying with an old friend and oh, what a time I had! The parties in Atlanta are quite something, extremely chic, with great perfection shown to the décor, the food and drink – even the cutlery and glassware. They really like to do things nicely there.

And…it was at one of these parties that I saw a gorgeous man across the room and our eyes met. It really was as corny as that. He was quite a famous actor from Los Angeles. We had great fun for a few days in various hotels, and agreed to meet up in LA later.

On 1st January 1991 I got the sleeper train from Atlanta to Chicago, and from there to Vancouver along the Rocky Mountains to Vancouver Island where I stayed with some cousins. My goodness, what a wonderful area. The ferry ride to Vancouver Island is utterly fabulous. The water is so clean, with so much wildlife all around.

From there I hired a car and drove to San Francisco, and stayed at the Archbishop's Mansion. I met up with some old rock and roll friends who worked for Bill Graham. I was supposed to be meeting Bill, but very, very sadly he'd had an untimely death just a few weeks earlier in a helicopter crash. So, I met up with a friend who I had known from the early days in London, and he told me about the ongoing problems with the Skynyrd boys. Many of them were back to their old tricks again with booze and drugs – all except Billy and Leon. We discussed me tour managing them in Europe, but I was beginning to get cold feet by this time. Especially after my disastrous time trying to manage them ten years earlier. All the drug taking just put me off. I found I couldn't work with people like that any longer. It's all so ridiculous and childish. I also met up with my old friend Dave Evans, who also worked with Skynyrd many years ago and was living in San Francisco working at a scientific organisation. He agreed with me – we had grown out of all this nonsense.

From San Francisco, I set off for LA on Highway 1 via many amazing places, first driving along the Monterey Peninsula and on to Carmel, where Clint Eastwood was the mayor. The drive from Carmel to Big Sur is utterly incredible with the most fabulous coastline – rocky, sandy, mountains, blue-black sea. I stopped for a picnic at Point Lobos Park which is another stunning place, where I saw whales' plumes spouting way out at sea, on their way to Mexico to give birth. I checked into the Ventana Inn, a fabulous place, then went down the hill to The Esalen Institute.

I'd been wanting to go to the infamous Esalen Institute for many years, as it was the birthplace of the hippy movement, and the 'human potential and meditation movement' based on the psychology of Freud and Gestalt, and is now into quantum physics. It's right on the Pacific, where the hot tub (nudity required!) looks out over the ocean, with the waves crashing beneath.

I also had a brief stopover at Hearst Castle at San Simeon. It's nigh on impossible to describe, being truly bonkers and very dark and quasi-religious inside. The castle was built over a couple of decades by the newspaper magnate, William Randolph Hearst, for his mistress Marion Davies. It was finished in around 1947. Coincidentally, I had lived in their mansion in St Pierre Road, Bel Air in Los Angeles in the 1970s while nannying for Mick and Bianca Jagger. Of course, then we had all called it the Citizen Kane house, as that film was based on the Hearst story.

Then to the fabulous San Ysidro Ranch Hotel, to meet up with the gorgeous man I'd met in Atlanta. This is an astonishing place, full of history. Once owned by Hollywood legend Ronald Colman, it was the venue for the marriage between Laurence Olivier and Vivien Leigh, and was visited by many famous Hollywood stars. The gorgeous man and I stayed for about three days in a magnificent room with a massive bathtub and huge fireplace, plus a private terrace. Such a wonderfully romantic place. The perfect hotel and location for a dirty weekend! On our return to LA we discussed me staying there with him, but I decided I didn't really want to live there full-time, nor was I madly in love.

Then in LA I stayed with some old friends from my rock and roll days, followed by Albuquerque to stay with other chums. The old town is astonishing, with beautiful adobe buildings, and incredible shops, selling the most wonderful things: lots of hippyish clothes with Native American touches, and turquoise jewellery everywhere. I drove along the Old Turquoise Way to Santa Fe for the day, another astonishing place, and then had a dip in the hot springs in the Jemez mountains.

At Flagstaff, I picked up another hire car and drove on to the Grand Canyon, where I stayed a couple of nights before going on to Sedona, the famous heart of the spiritual world in the States. There are supposed to be twenty-two spiritual vortices in the world, and four of them are there in Sedona. The drive was beautiful with incredible sights of rocks, crags, mountains, rivers, streams and monoliths.

From there I flew to Phoenix and met up with a friend at the Tanque Verde Ranch in Arizona for a few days. This is a dude ranch with cowboys, wranglers, horses and cattle. Wonderful! I was given a gorgeous horse, who went with just the most gentle of squeezes, and was obedient to all commands. I'd had a bad fall some years ago, so this helped me get over my loss of nerve.

I then spent a few days at Deepak Chopra's Maharishi Ayur-Veda Clinic in Pacific Palisades, where I had the full Panchakarma rejuvenation package. Best of all was my Transcendental Meditation teaching and personal mantra, which has held me in good stead all the following years. They say that meditation gives you development of the following qualities: to have an open, receptive, caring attitude; cheerfulness and good humour; predominance of positive thinking; spontaneity and freshness of appreciation; self-sufficiency; loss of fear of death; affective readiness for developing consciousness; discovery of opportunity for creativity; acceptance of self, nature and others; and a conscious sense of destiny; and one can 'dive into the gap that exists between the thoughts'.

Little did I know it then, but the things I learned here would stand me in good stead during the traumas to come.

In LA, an old friend had told me about some friends of his who had a fabulous hotel in Fiji, and I really must go there. I'd booked it immediately, of course, and this was my next destination, after a stop in Hawaii. My first diary note in Fiji says:

> I think I've died and gone to heaven! Thank God I'm here at last and away from Hawaii which I didn't enjoy at all as it rained all the time. Plus it was so touristy and crass and loud. Now I'm in Fiji. Bliss.

I'd flown from Honolulu to Nadi Airport in Fiji, then caught a tiny eight-seater plane to the island of Taveuni. It was all so laid back that the pilot forgot his flight was supposed to leave at 12.30, so we didn't leave until

1pm, when he suddenly remembered! Also, all the people and baggage were weighed, as the plane was so small. My goodness what a wonderful flight – the sea was the most stunning colours – with amazing views and scenery of little islands and coral reefs. A world away from the busyness of the Hawaiian Islands, which were so overrun by tourism.

I arrived at the Maravu Plantation Hotel on Taveuni, the Flower Island, which is green and lush. I was greeted by Ormond Eyre, the hotel's owner, who ran it with his German boyfriend, Hine. As I'd had a personal introduction to them from my old friend in LA, I was greeted like a long-lost friend. They looked after me so well over the next two weeks and I felt I was truly in heaven. Ormond's European family had lived in the Pacific for generations, mainly as plantation owners, and had frequently intermarried with the locals. Hence his gorgeous sultry looks with coffee-coloured skin.

I stayed in a *bure*, a traditional wood and straw hut, which thankfully had a mosquito net, a fan and a fridge – all vital in such heat and humidity. The food was always delicious, with a drum summoning us at mealtimes. The hotel had a lovely swimming pool and was just a few steps from the beach. The sea was wonderful, warm, clear and clean – except for where the fishermen were gutting their catch which attracted sharks! While snorkelling, I saw stunning sea life – including a shark at one point, which looked enormous through a mask, but was, in reality, quite small and not the slightest bit interested in me.

Ormond and Hine took me with them on wonderful trips, and treated me to meals in their private house, where we all smoked some hash, which is highly illegal there, so it rather surprised me.

From Fiji I went on to New Zealand, where I stayed with friends in Christchurch, then hired a car and drove around both islands for about five weeks. I stayed in some horrendous dosshouses…and some wonderfully luxurious places – the main one being Huka Lodge, where the Queen Mother used to stay, for the fishing. It's built on the Huka Falls and is utter luxury, with the rooms looking out onto the river.

I hiked up and down glaciers, walking for miles totally alone. The weather was very different to Fiji, of course, with snow and rain but also lovely crisp, sunny, cold days. I hiked up Mount Aspiring in Wanaka, and drove past numerous waterfalls and stunning scenery on the way to Lake Brunner Lodge, on the Franz Joseph Glacier. The hotel I stayed in was horrid – rather like a 1960s boarding school! I was glad to leave the hotel and move on to Rotorua, which is the main place for Maori art and culture. Then to the Tongariro Lodge at Turangi, which is on Lake Taupo and the most astonishing hotel – a classic wooden building, but massive and very luxurious. From there I visited the thermal pools at Tokaanu, also on Lake Taupo.

From New Zealand I made my way to Australia, where I stayed with my aunt in Melbourne who told me that the Duke of Manchester (then Angus Montague) had been in the prison where she worked. Small world! Then on to stay with her son, my cousin, in Canberra. Then I stayed with old friends in Sydney, Adelaide and Kangaroo Island, where the Remarkable Rocks are just that – utterly remarkable!

After Australia, I had two wonderful weeks in Bali, without friends or family. Just me and a series of beautiful hotels. From there it was on to Mauritius, where I stayed at a friend's hotel, and visited other friends on their sugar plantation. Then, on 29th June I flew home after nine months away.

Phew! Back in England on 1st July 1991 as planned. What a trip it had been, but I was ready to be at home.

Chapter 21

Friends and Unsung Heroes

Back in London, I rented a flat from a friend for a while, and started working part-time for two charities, The CORE Trust and The Life Education Centres. It felt good to be back in the world of fundraising, organising events that would do good. I didn't once regret turning down the old rock and roll lifestyle.

In 1992, Jackie Leven of The CORE Trust asked me to organise a royal event with Diana, Princess of Wales. So, I booked the May Fair Hotel for The CORE Trust's large gala lunch. The organising committee for this event included Jackie's close friend, Richard Olivier, son of Sir Laurence Olivier. For the auction, Richard kindly provided a shirt that had belonged to his father. The programme included the fantastic close-up magician Fay Presto, with my old friend, Lorna Luft (Judy Garland's daughter), singing. The auction and raffle were announced by Shirley Anne Field and Wayne Sleep. Richard Young was the photographer. All of it was emceed by Craig Ferguson, who went on to become one of the biggest talk show hosts in America. I can't remember exactly how much was raised, but I know it was a substantial amount.

Yet again, my old friends and usual crew helped. They gave their services free of charge. There are too many to name individually here, but I was always so grateful to them. I certainly couldn't have managed without their unfailing generosity over the years.

I was sitting next to Princess Diana on the stage during the speeches.

As we sat down, she whispered, "Do you think it's okay that I'm not wearing tights?"

"Of course," I replied. "I'm not either. It's far too warm!"

Then she pointed to the top of her suit jacket and said, "Can you see the safety pin?"

"Don't worry!" I said. "Nobody can see it!"

Considering her status, it was strange to think that it was just like a normal chat between any two women. Both worried and concerned about the same things. Tights and safety pins!

Below is the speech given that day by Princess Diana, which includes her own pencilled underlinings. It is reproduced here by kind written permission of Prince William, the Duke of Cambridge, and Prince Harry, the Duke of Sussex.

Thank you for asking me here, once again.

When addictions accelerated in the sixties and seventies, orthodox medical services were severely challenged. The number of types of addiction increased, with even nastier secondary complications. Up until then many people had felt sorry for the alcoholic because they seemed to be messing up their own lives and those of their immediate families or friends. Cigarette smoking was perceived more as a habit than an addiction.

The term 'addiction' for many people referred to <u>drugs</u>. Drugs tended to attack a young age group and killed them. However, again, the problem was left to the individual and their immediate circle – for a while. Subsequently, secondary effects on the individual cropped up – the brain abscesses, the heart failure for infected valves, the limb loss, Aids – the list is long.

All this began to demand ever larger resources from the orthodox medical establishment. But other secondary effects, outside the addict's circle, were expanding horribly – the crimes of the pushers and the desperately vicious attacks of the addicts to pay for their habit, began to affect whole communities and countries.

Opportunities for addicts to seek help were not driven by public sympathy. Even less was there much common interest in trying to see why so many addicts, not only entered, but <u>re-entered</u> the world of addiction. Orthodox medicine could help the physical problems of drugs just as it can with alcoholism. But escape from addiction only begins when the root cause, such as self-esteem or inability to cope, is addressed for each individual.

Nature has a funny way of sending us what we most resist. None of us can remain smugly immune from addiction whether it is chocolate, cigarettes, alcohol, drugs, or even, work. Many will use these addictive 'tools' to distract them from having to face life in a changing and testing world.

Perhaps there is value in learning to cope with change before it pushes us to addiction? Many believe that addiction can be prevented by attention to spiritual development of individuals, maybe beginning at a young age. The opportunity to discuss a problem with an understanding and experienced individual or group can improve lives enormously; not least by sharing the load.

However, it is hard to find someone to trust. Those at Core have all needed that trust themselves, and understand how much it matters. At Core the mixture of alternative techniques and personal development seems to work rather well – and is adapted to suit each visitor.

Early addicts were often people who were developing faster than their fixed world. Now, however, a much larger group is at risk. These are people who desperately try to remain stubbornly fixed in a changing world. Their materialistic icons are failing them.

An experienced canoeist allows himself to be carried by the current, but used skills to steer his course and harness the stream. There are times in life when it is pointless to try to paddle frantically upstream to the past. But the confidence to face the future does not come easily.

Core is one organisation which chose to explore a holistic route where physical help is combined with attention to the spiritual growth of the individual.

The word 'spiritual' can make people cringe. Notebooks are shut and eyes turn to the skies. However, 'boosting the spirit' within each individual (rather than 'chasing the dragon') teaches them to be independent not only of their drugs, but also of organisational support. The growth of their own self-esteem (or spirit) can lift them out of the quagmire so that they can manage without help.

One of the most striking features of Core is the enormous loyalty and dedication of its supporters. It is not easy to help despairing people back on to their rails. It is no mistake that so many of the support team here have risen from their own ashes and have chosen to support others in doing so. The effort of the supporters is only successful (as they all know) if the addicts' efforts match it. Many people seek spiritual peace and harmony in a wide number of ways – there are even correspondence courses and TV evangelists, but so many of those routes pretend that it can be 'made easy' for the individual. It becomes like the house built on sand. For an individual to re-form, their foundations need to be rebuilt and, just as with a building project, the more skill and effort that goes in (by all parties) the better the result.

In particular, the individual who is being helped faces some painful tasks of inner exploration. For a great house building result, the investment may be painful in the short term.

The life which an addict has lived before addiction was plainly not working. Core will help them to build one which might.

Some wonder why people like Core make such an effort to help addicts. It is common in tricky times that those who have already suffered, and who have previously reached the depths of despair, have most to teach us. A five-star tourist with all his cash can feel pretty safe in a foreign country miles from home – until a 'coup' happens. At those times they may come to develop a deep admiration for the hardened traveller who has already learned to survive. The same hardened traveller might even lead them out of trouble, before disappearing on his independent road again. Reformed addicts are one such group of hardened travellers.

There are some tricky challenges ahead. Many of these crop up unexpectedly; often to those who think that they have life in control. None of us is protected from change. Some of the techniques taught and practised here can reduce the huge suffering which undeserved' changes or challenges might bring. Much of the approach is extremely 'earthy' and direct, re-instating the individual's ability not only to regain their own strength and direction, but also to help others to do the same.

One value of organisations like Core is that they transcend the old-fashioned 'how good they are to do it' ('because we're glad we don't then have to, but it would be awkward if no-one did' approach).

But Core looks hard to see how they can help someone to help themselves. Once that happens, the knock-on effect is huge. The addicts' families, friends and workmates all benefit – ultimately, we all do.

In common with some of the other organisations which I'm involved in, there is a spirit at Core which I find extremely moving. It is refreshing to see a group of people making positive efforts to understand hardship and to recognise and boost the spirits of those who have suffered.

Thank you for stirring my spirit; and once again, thank you for having me here today.

My goodness, how prescient the speech sounds now, since Princess Diana's death and the details that have come out, especially about her desperately unhappy marriage.

Just as she sat down next to me after that speech, I said, "Well done."

"Was it really okay?" she whispered.

"Yes, absolutely. It was an excellent speech," I replied. It was quite astonishing to me that she needed my validation.

I went on to work with Princess Diana at other events and she was always animated and involved with everyone she spoke to. Without fail, she'd spend more time than had been allotted, always leaving later than her prearranged departure time because she would willingly spend more of her precious time with everybody.

Dream Jobs

I was still only working part-time, but at last, in 1994, a couple of exciting things came along. I was offered a job with the Covent Garden Arts Festival *and* – at the same time – was approached to run Michael Jackson's charity in the United Kingdom, which Comic Relief founder Jane Tewson had recommended me for. It never rains but it pours! Nothing for months, then two perfect jobs come along at the same time.

Left: Sally with The Prince of Wales and Marion Board,
Life Education Centres Charity Polo Match, 1992 (© Dave Benett, with kind permission)
Right: Sally with The Princess of Wales at the CORE Charity Lunch, 1992
(© Richard Young, with kind permission)

Stupidly, though, I made the wrong choice and went for the Michael Jackson one, which never really panned out in the end. I seem to remember there was some sort of disconnect somewhere along the line, and that Michael Jackson himself would never make a final commitment to setting up in the United Kingdom. However, in retrospect, I probably had a narrow escape, for reasons that became obvious as the years went on and Jackson's reputation plummeted.

Sadly, I had lost the chance with the Covent Garden Festival, which was heartbreaking, but eventually things changed in June 1994. I got the job of my dreams – at last and about time!

It all started when a member of the board of the Covent Garden Festival, Neville Abraham (founder of the restaurant company Groupe Chez Gérard), got in touch. I'd met him during my interview for the festival, and he then recommended me to John McClaren, a merchant banker who was looking for someone to run his new International Composers Competition.

John and I got on like a house on fire, but then he told me that I had to meet and 'get on with' a woman at Classic FM. My heart sank – not another one! So I met her and, luckily, we got along fine. They didn't have any sponsorship at the time, but she felt sure there would be no problem, as it was such a successful commercial radio station.

I soon settled in to the Classic FM offices in Camden Town, in north London, with a composers competition to run. I started by setting up the database of music academies and colleges worldwide, sending them the necessary information for their students to enter the competition.

I discovered, during a wander around to introduce myself, that somebody I knew was working there. This was Anna Gregory, who was the head of music. We immediately recognised each other – but where from? We spent hours trying to work out how, where and when. Eventually it dawned on us that she had been in the girls' choir that sang for the Mike Oldfield tour that I tour-managed in 1980. Of course, she was only a schoolgirl then, so it wasn't surprising that I didn't remember her at first.

There was no sign of any funding coming in for the International Composers Competition, so I really didn't have much work to do. Knowing I wasn't one to sit back and relax, Anna recommended me to the bosses at

Classic FM and suggested I put on a big event they had been planning. It was to be a fundraising event at the Palace Theatre in London's West End, with a number of famous musicians. They had nobody to organise it, until Anna thought of me, telling CEO John Spearman and programme controller Michael Bukht about my organisational skills and my previous work on such large and difficult events as that Mike Oldfield tour.

So there I was, back in my comfort zone.

I put the event on at the Palace Theatre on Sunday 9th October 1994. The participants were Julian Lloyd Webber, the Royal College of Music Chamber Orchestra, the Birmingham Royal Ballet, Lesley Garrett, Fenella Fielding, James Galway and American harmonica player Larry Adler.

My usual crew and helpers mucked in too.

This was an extremely difficult event to organise, with many weeks of advance preparation, consisting of numerous rehearsals with the students at the Royal College of Music. Despite a couple of hiccups at the rehearsal where two extremely famous classical musicians caused trouble, everything was alright on the night.

After the show, which was a spectacular success, we had a party in the bar at the theatre. I was relaxing for the first time in weeks, when the three big bosses at Classic FM approached me. This was John Spearman, the CEO, Michael Bukht, the programme controller, and the main shareholder, Sir Peter Michael, who I'd never met before. They said how very impressed they were with my work on this difficult event. They wanted to promote me to being the concert manager at Classic FM.

Wow! What a wonderful surprise. I went home very happy but utterly exhausted.

A few days after the big event, Michael Bukht, the big boss at Classic, gave me a copy of a letter he had received. It was from the general manager of the Palace Theatre:

> I'm so glad the evening was a success for Classic FM. I would like you to pass on my thanks to your team from Classic FM, especially Sally Arnold the producer, for her professionalism which is refreshing to meet in this day and age.

And Michael had handwritten on it:

Well done Sally – I think so too!

MB

The accolades were much appreciated. Even Larry Adler contributed after the show by writing the following about me:

> This is less a letter of recommendation than a recounting of a personal experience. Classic FM put on a concert at the Palace Theatre in London with soloists like James Galway, Julian Lloyd Webber, Fenella Fielding and me. In charge of all these egomaniacs was a lady whose job it was to see that the concert ran smoothly. Boy, was I impressed! She was too, it seemed, because she sent me a superb letter of thanks commending me for not being at all temperamental. We've since become good friends. I admire her as a natural executive who follows a project through from conception to completion. In fact, and don't tell Sally this, I'm hoping to persuade her to be my concert manager.
>
> Signed,
> Larry Adler

After the gala show, Larry Adler and I became firm friends, meeting regularly for lunches and dinners as we lived near each other in Primrose Hill. He used to tell me some astonishing stories about his early days. One was that he was a member of the Thursday Club, a weekly dinner and drinking club at Wheeler's restaurant in Soho, with Prince Philip, his equerry Michael Parker, and a number of raffish friends including Baron, the famous photographer. But Larry was the epitome of honour and silence. He would never, ever tell me what went on at these parties, even though he loved gossiping and name-dropping. Good for him – discretion above all.

Larry and I went to various parties together, one being at Sting's house in Wiltshire. Many of my old friends were there, like Eric Clapton and Harvey Goldsmith, but I was far more excited by meeting Alan Rickman, who was sitting next to me at dinner, and chatting to Tom Hanks and his wife, who were both charming and very friendly.

At Classic FM, the founder and programme controller, Michael Bukht, was one of the few men who appreciated efficient women, and he showed it.

I always held him in the highest esteem, and we always got along extremely well. Outwardly, he was a rather bluff man who didn't suffer fools gladly. He became a father figure for me, and I'm sure for many other people at Classic FM. He was half-Welsh and half-Pakistani, a devout Muslim and a family man. He had started up Capital Radio, where he was programme controller, but he was incredibly versatile. At one point their on-air chef hadn't turned up, so Michael ended up doing the slot and became known as Michael Barry, the Crafty Cook. I got to know him better on our frequent travels to meet up with various orchestras and musicians.

My new job as concert manager was very hard work. I thought I had worked hard in the past, but this truly was something else. My responsibilities were to organise all the live music that would be broadcast on Classic FM: negotiating with the orchestras, the soloists, the venues etc. Plus, there was the technical side of getting the recording mobile and crew organised for either a recorded programme or a live concert, even live New Year's Eve broadcasts. Luckily, I knew many of the orchestras, agents, managers and soloists from my days doing PR for Harrison/Parrott and singing with the LSO Chorus.

But one part of my new job was unfamiliar to me, involving something I had never done before – selling airtime slots. They were usually short advertising slots to promote upcoming concerts. I was given a financial target for the year, and at the end of my first year I had exceeded it, so I got a lovely big bonus payment. However, I learned the hard way that when you exceed targets, the target is then increased exponentially. My work rate went up another notch. I was allowed to do deals at my discretion – so I happily did deals to advertise charity events.

This is the point where the karma comes in concerning the woman at Peter Gabriel's office who had scuppered my job at his WOMAD organisation. While working as concert manager at Classic FM, I was approached by a charity to promote an event for them. I invited them to come to the office for a chat with me and my boss, Michael.

When I approached the boardroom, which was all glass, I could see that *there she was* – the same woman who had lied about me over the WOMAD job! I went to Michael's office and quickly told him the saga.

He was utterly amazing and wonderful. During the meeting he said to her that if we, Classic FM, decided to help them then it would be, "Totally up to Sally. She makes all the decisions on these things."

He really was my knight in shining armour. And, of course, I decided to help, as I'm a sucker when it comes to helping any worthwhile charities, but at least I was vindicated and had my revenge – so to speak. It was a good feeling – especially to have someone of Michael's standing and stature supporting me like that.

During my days at Classic FM, Michael and I had to spend quite a lot of time together, and it was fascinating chatting to him about his Muslim faith. He was another of my unsung heroes, and supported me through thick and thin, to the extent that he became a financial backer of my new company sometime later.

Around this time, I could now think about buying another flat and settled on a lovely one-bedroomed garden flat in Gloucester Avenue in Primrose Hill. Luckily it was just a short walk to the Classic FM offices, so I didn't need a car. But, a year or so later, they made me and two other senior staff redundant. There were mutterings about selling the company and needing to make the bottom line look better, hence the need to trim some of the higher paid staff.

So here it was again – another redundancy.

Chapter 22

Sally Arnold Events Management

What now? I asked myself. It was 1996, I had been made redundant again, and I was totally fed up. I needed to take some control over my own job prospects. I decided the only way forward was to be my own boss and set up my own company.

As I lived in Primrose Hill, I contacted Camden Council, my local council, because they offered a number of excellent courses. I took a few computer and financial courses, and one on how to write a business plan, as I needed financial backing for the necessary office rental, a computer, headed notepaper etc.

I was amazed and proud when my business plan won the North London Business Plan Competition. The prize was a (then) state-of-the-art fax/copier/phone machine. As Sally Arnold Events Management, I got financial backing from Camden Council, plus from three other wonderful backers. One was a friend, and the other two were Michael Bukht, the programme controller from Classic FM, and Sacha, the Duchess of Abercorn. I bought my first computer – a laptop which cost a massive £1,000 despite being second-hand! I had a lovely little wooden summer house built in my garden, and dug up the lawn to lay electricity and telephone lines, and ran the office from there.

The first event for my own little company was an evening concert to celebrate the 75th birthday of Prince Philip, the Duke of Edinburgh. A friend had recommended me to the Duchess of Abercorn, who was looking for someone to help urgently with an event she was planning to celebrate the prince's birthday and to benefit his charity, Arts for Nature. The prince's usual organiser, Major Michael Parker, had gone into hospital when the event had just started being organised. They already had the venue, the Royal College of Music, with its Britten Theatre for a stage show – plus most of the artistes – and a dinner was planned for elsewhere in the college.

When I met Sacha, the Duchess of Abercorn, we got on very well indeed. I then had a number of meetings with the organising committee of the upcoming event. Quite daunting to say the least, but I knew I was good at what I did, so it all went well. I proceeded to organise the event that took place in the Britten Theatre.

Sacha and I agreed that I would be responsible for all technical production, staging, sound and lighting, the preparation of costs and budget, liaison with venue, artistes, managers etc. Alongside that I coordinated rehearsals, organised the security in cooperation with Buckingham Palace and the Britten Theatre, arranged refreshments for participants and working personnel, and sorted the insurance in cooperation with the Britten Theatre. Then there was travel and accommodation for visiting artistes, backstage crew, hospitality and dressing rooms, running order, PRS etc. Not forget-

Sally introducing Prince Philip to members of the Birmingham Royal Ballet
(Photo by Sacha Gusov, with kind permission of the Duchess of Abercorn)

ting cleaning up afterwards! The few elements I wasn't responsible for were the mailshot, although I was always happy to help, the advertising, ticket sales and the dinner.

Before the event, I had a number of meetings with Ted Hughes, the Poet Laureate. Well – what can I say about him? What a man. What a voice. I am more proud of having worked with Ted than anybody else, ever. Mick Jagger? No! The Who? No! Ted really was a magnetic person, and also great fun. We had a few nice coffees and lunches in London over the weeks preceding the event, and I enjoyed myself immensely. We often chatted about Pete Townshend of The Who, as Ted had worked with him on *The Iron Man*, and we both agreed that Pete could be a very difficult person to work with.

The event itself was held on 13th November 1996, entitled 'Gala Performance in Celebration of the 75th Birthday of His Royal Highness The Duke of Edinburgh'. The participants were Melvyn Bragg, the Birmingham Royal Ballet, singer Ruby Turner, comedian John Wells, male Russian soprano Oleg Ryabets, Ted Hughes, Maria Friedman and ballerina Briony Brind.

The invitation read:

Proceeds from the Gala will support the Arts for Nature Project, an educational enterprise that will stage performances and exhibitions throughout the country, with links to schools and with competitions and exhibitions.

Arts for Nature was founded in 1989 by its Patron, HRH The Duke of Edinburgh, to re-establish the relationship between mankind and nature, the Trust seeks to appeal to the human spirit through the language of the artist.

Special Gala Supper in the presence of HRH The Duke of Edinburgh with an art exhibition from Prince Philip's private collection of wildlife paintings.

The Arts for Nature Trust: Through Prince Philip's inspiration, Arts for Nature serves as a catalyst, encouraging artists who seek to convey to the general public not only the beauties of nature but also the perils we face.

As Prince Philip has said: 'We are under threat of serious and irreversible damage to the environment through ignorance, thoughtlessness and selfishness. Rational argument can achieve a certain amount to halt and reverse the damage, but it is going to need much more than that. We need to arouse popular will and commitment and I believe that creative artists have the power to stimulate a positive awareness of, and love for the world of nature. Their work can engage the emotions and create the vision which is so desperately needed in the struggle to halt and reverse the damage that humanity is doing to God's creation.'

The programme notes:

The Arts for Nature Trust. Patron: HRH The Prince Philip, Duke of Edinburgh, KG, KT. Gala Committee: Chairman: The Duchess of Abercorn.

About our Patron by Ted Hughes, The Poet Laureate: Prince Philip is well known throughout the world for his work as President of the World Wide Fund for Nature. Another aspect of his efforts for the same great cause is less familiar.

The Environmental Movement has always met strong opposition – understandably. A civilisation that has developed and still largely sustains itself on a determined exploitation of the natural world cannot be expected to change its attitudes easily. At every level the vested interests have a powerful voice. And in verbal debate the weighty arguments of the environmentalist are neutralised without too much trouble, as a rule, by the equally weighty arguments of the opposition.

The Environmental Movement's greatest problem, perhaps, has been to get past that inevitable argumentative resistance and to reach the hearts and souls behind it in a way that will change attitudes.

Prince Philip understood this problem all too well. But then in 1986 he saw a partial solution. It had occurred to him that there exists a well-tested, universal means for transmitting the necessary change of attitudes at the deepest psychological level – in a form that would be unquestioned and would reach vast numbers of people. That year he invited representatives of the world's religions to meet in Assisi. The purpose was simple: to discuss the possibility of giving environmental awareness a more urgent priority in their teachings. Five major religions – Hindu, Buddhist, Moslem, Jewish and Christian – saw the importance of the idea, and agreed to put it into practice. As a result, hundreds of thousands of religious communities became directly involved. Following this success, other religions are now joining the network. As Prince Philip had divined, religious feeling and spiritual values are the natural mother and father of both environmental awareness and the willingness to change a way of life.

In a similar way, the language of art bypasses argumentative, self-serving resistance and unites the feelings of very different people at a deep level. Accordingly, Prince Philip brought together representatives of the various arts to discuss how art might be used to help the environmental cause. Out of this meeting came The Sacred Earth Drama Trust, which collects and publishes plays on environmental themes to be performed by children, The International Sacred Literature Trust, which edits and publishes sacred texts of the world's religions as selected by each religion's own spiritual leader, and The Arts For Nature Trust.

Tonight's event has been devised by Arts for Nature. It brings us together to celebrate the seventy-fifth birthday of Prince Philip and to pay tribute to his very great contribution to global awareness, not only in practical and political matters, but in the deeper spiritual understanding of what is now required to save the Earth.

Ted Hughes

[Courtesy of The Ted Hughes Estate and Mrs Carol Hughes.]

Being responsible for all the above, the production, stage management and direction was a truly massive job. I was grateful that the dinner wasn't my responsibility as well! Thankfully everything went extremely well. John Wells, the comedian, even praised my competence, because he had lost his wife's ticket. I habitually always kept a list of seat numbers for special invited guests to any big event (extra work, but worth it), so I was able to show her where to sit. John said he was hugely impressed!

One thing I remember vividly from that evening was shocking and frightening – we had an IRA bomb scare. The police, dogs and security people had obviously checked the venue for days prior to the event, but on the actual day, about halfway through the rehearsal, I was taken to one side by the police and the theatre manager. They told me the IRA had phoned with their 'code' saying there was a bomb in the theatre. They stressed that the only people who knew were us, the police, Prince Philip's security people and the Duchess of Abercorn. We didn't tell anybody else, so as not to cause any panic or worry.

We had to decide there and then whether to go ahead with the evening's entertainment. I had often wondered how I would react to such information, but we were all in agreement that we refused to be bullied and threatened like that. The evening would proceed as planned.

The other thing that I remember was helping Prince Philip fit a radio mic inside his dinner jacket. He was charming and humorous throughout the fitting, thank goodness, as I was a nervous wreck!

The event went without a hitch – and no bomb! I had actually forgotten about it until the end, because my attention was utterly focused on the job in hand. Especially as I was also calling the lights from the side of the stage as well as being stage manager and director – so I needed to be on my toes, both mentally and physically at every second.

Some of us were given a wonderful book as a memento – a copy of a special limited edition of *The Lizard's Question*, with a foreword by

Sally with Poet Laureate Ted Hughes (centre)
and broadcaster and writer Melvyn Bragg
(Photo by Sacha Gusov, with kind permission of the Duchess of Abercorn)

Ted Hughes. In mine he wrote (in proper pen and ink!) and I reproduce his words here by kind permission of The Ted Hughes Estate, Mrs Carol Hughes, and the publisher The Press at Colorado College:

For Sally, the midwife of the evening. Greetings from Ted.
13th November 1996.

Inside it states:

On the occasion of the 75th birthday of His Royal Highness The Duke of Edinburgh and in recognition of his inspiration for faith and the arts to work together for nature conservation through Arts for Nature Trust, International Sacred Literature Trust, Sacred Earth Drama Trust. Foreword by Ted Hughes, Poet Laureate. Published through the generosity of Leonidas and Alexander Goulandris. The Press at Colorado College. Summer 1996.

Readings from The Faiths. Selected from well-known sacred texts and from those that have been translated into English for the first time for the series of the International Sacred Literature Trust.

Foreword by Ted Hughes
Once Moses was sitting in a house when a lizard scuttling across the road urinated and a few drops fell on Moses.

Irritated, Moses raised his hands to God and asked, 'For what purpose did you create this creature?'

God replied, 'Do you know Moses, every day this lizard asks me, 'Why did you create that man and what is his purpose?'

Sufism: Solomon's Ring.

Ted then wrote:

This fable is a little drama of two points of view. Moses, from his point of view, sees only a small corner of Creation. God, from His, sees the total picture. Implicit in Moses' question is the statement: 'If this creature has any value that I can convert somehow to my own profit, by hunting or farming, I will convert it. If it has no value, then I would prefer to see it exterminated as a nuisance and a pollution.' Implicit in God's answer is the statement: 'My Creation is a single balanced assembly. If you disturb any corner, you unbalance the whole – including yourself.'

The fable is also the story of Moses' enlightenment. Reading the story gives us a glimpse of that. First we see Moses' fragmentary picture of the Creation, and we recognise it – because it is ours. It is the fragmentary picture on which almost the whole of our commercial enterprise and scientific activity has been concentrated. We understand the implications of the question, because so much of our civilisation is founded on them.

But then we see God's total picture and realise just how it corrects Moses' fragmentary picture, and thereby corrects Moses and us.

The fable is old. And human beings have asked the question posed here by Moses from our earliest days. And now and again during our brief history, we have, like Moses, heard God's answer.

Insofar as humanity has heard God's answer we have tried to hang on to it – in the rituals of religion, in sacred texts and songs. But insofar as our wits have been confined to the hungry scrimmage and exciting profits of our fragmentary picture, we now find that we have unbalanced the whole Creation, which is consequently falling to pieces round our ears and under our feet.

Quite suddenly, humanity has seen its mistake. The question is: what can we do about it? How can the tremendous physical energies of commercial enterprise and scientific activity adapt themselves to the total picture of Creation? For this realignment to happen, human beings will have to change. But how can we change? How can the mysterious biological and psychological compulsions that drive commerce and science be made to see Creation from God's point of view?

The response to the crisis is global. We are all in the environmental movement – some more persuaded than others. The decisive arguments, no doubt, will have to be presented by science. The inevitability of catastrophe, or the avoidance of catastrophe, are matters of cause and effect. In religious terms 'as we sow, so shall we reap'. At the same time they are processes that can be described, step by step, in terms of hard science. But hard science will never see these processes until it looks at the total picture.

This science of the total picture, the necessary science of the future, the science of repairing and maintaining the balances of life on earth, which will modify our control of how we live and how commerce exploits earth's riches – this science will inevitably coincide with one aspect of God's point of view.

Among those who are trying to orchestrate the world-wide response to the emergency, the Duke of Edinburgh is pre-eminent. His attitudes are practical, but one of his most practical inspirations was to see that our total picture of the Creation is first of all a spiritual vision. He then saw what could be done about it.

All religions have at least this in common: a vision of a sacred Creation, seen from God's point of view, and taught to their worshippers. (I use the words God and Creation here and elsewhere simply as symbolic indicators of the ultimate and the worldly reality, respectively, to which all religions relate in some way.) The Duke of Edinburgh saw how the different faiths of the world might be united on this common ground, in such a way that their immense powers could be brought into the environmental movement. Accordingly, under his initiative as President, the World Wide Fund for Nature has established an international network in which religion and conservation actively cooperate. Following from this, His Royal Highness was a catalyst for three more initiatives: the International Sacred Literature Trust, Arts for Nature and the Sacred Earth Drama Trust, each working to make the essential visions of the total picture accessible in fresh ways and to raise them to the forefront of awareness.

The new scientific grasp of the total picture and the spiritual vision of the total picture are not antagonistic to each other. Without the first, the job cannot be done. Without the second, we cannot understand what the job is or why it should be done.

The two need equal investment of energy. The global effort to recover and enhance our human vision of the inner meaning of the total picture is as important as the global effort to find a science that can grasp the material constitution and interconnections of the same.

In both efforts, we are doing what humanity has always done, but pushing it a few steps further: trying to raise our awareness to a perfect understanding of life on this earth – so that we can look after the whole thing and incidentally ourselves.

Ted Hughes, Poet Laureate, June 1996

The book consists of quotations from the world's major religions juxtaposed with twenty-one of James Trissel's drawings of insects, birds, moths and butterflies.

The next day the *Evening Standard* wrote:

Philip at 75

Country Life scoops *Hello!*

It isn't often that *Country Life* scoops *Hello!* Magazine, but it happened last night at a belated party to celebrate the Duke of Edinburgh's 75th birthday. The party, held at the charming Britten Theatre in The Royal College of Music, was pictorially the exclusive domain of Country Life.

Prince Philip, who wasn't accompanied by the Queen, was as handsome as ever, in black tie, was apparently enjoying himself so much he retired almost a quarter of an hour later than intended.

The event, which raised money for the environmental trust Arts for Nature, of which the Duke is patron, was followed by dinner at the college in Kensington.

The Duke, the very personification of nobility and decorum, was actually 75 in June, but that didn't stop two of his favourite artistes, jazz singer Ruby Turner and comedian John Wells turning in performances and there was a recitation by The Poet Laureate, Ted Hughes.

The Poet Laureate paid tribute to the Duke opining that he had a superb understanding of environmental problems. 'The event brought us together to celebrate the 75th birthday of Prince Philip and to pay tribute to his very great contribution to global environmental awareness, not only in practical and political matters, but in the deeper, spiritual understanding of what is now required to save the earth', said Hughes.

Prince Philip's contribution includes inspiring a conference in Assisi 10 years ago to discuss the possibility of giving environmental awareness a more urgent priority in Hindu, Buddhist, Muslim, Jewish and Christian teachings – following its success other religions are joining the network.

Ted's testimonial for me, below, says in a nutshell what was going on with the event before I arrived on the scene. Reproduced with kind permission of The Ted Hughes Estate and Mrs Carol Hughes.

Dear Sally,

I thought you brought off the 'Arts For Nature' concert brilliantly. When the organisation had ground to a halt, you came in, picked it up – the whole merry complication of it – straightened it all out in no time and set it on the stage that night running like a flawless machine. I was just immensely impressed. And you did it so smoothly and coolly – no fuss, no stress, no pressure. Everybody commented on it. In future, I shall know who to recommend.

Thanks again and all the very best,

Ted.

Sacha Abercorn's testimonial to me, dated 15th November 1996, said:

Dear Sally,

That was an <u>extraordinary</u> evening by any standards! Thank you, Sally, on behalf of 'Arts for Nature' for your faultless production of the show.

Your clear focus, superb communication all the way along, and your professionalism on the evening itself spelt out SUCCESS in large letters!

You made everyone feel confident, from us in the charity to the artists themselves and that can only be achieved by someone who is 100% competent themselves.

On top of all that it was fun and enjoyable and your astonishing energy kept us all in top gear!

Thank you more than I can ever say – and I look forward to the next venture one of these days.

Well, I have to say that that event was probably the highlight of my career, until I was later nominated as one of the Women of the Year. I discovered that Sacha Abercorn nominated me, so I am eternally grateful to her for that. There were many rumours around that she had had an affair with Prince Philip. Sacha herself is quoted as saying: "Our friendship was very close, but I did not go to bed with him." Whereas the author Sarah Bradford says: "Philip and Sacha certainly had an affair, without a doubt."

Some of my friends urged me to ask Sacha outright, but I would never have done that. For a start it was none of my business – and also I didn't want to spoil our friendly relationship.

Chapter 23

I am one of the Women of the Year 1997

Quite unexpectedly, in July 1997, I had a letter from the Women of the Year organisation. It read:

Women of the Year Lunch 1997. As Honorary Officers for the Lunch, we are delighted to tell you that you have been nominated by our Committee to be invited as a Guest to the Women of the Year Lunch. The Lunch will be held at the Savoy Hotel on 6th October 1997, in the presence of our Royal and International Guest of Honour Her Majesty Queen Noor of Jordan.

Established as the leading annual event which brings together outstanding women from every walk of life, each one distinguished in her particular field, this unique occasion also raises considerable sums for the blind.

Numbers are strictly limited so if you wish to attend, could you please apply as soon as you can. Every year there is a waiting list.

The press release accompanying it said:

This is the forty-second year of the Women of the Year Lunch which annually gathers together leading women in Britain from all walks of life who have distinguished themselves by outstanding achievements. Nominations are submitted by a committee with special expertise in thirty six categories of work and this ensures a representation by women across all regions and including all ages and ethnic communities. The Lunch has become one of the most important occasions for women in the world.

The Royal and International Guest of Honour in 1997 is Her Majesty, Queen Noor of Jordan, who is being recognised for her untiring efforts to improve her people's welfare and to highlight their rich cultural heritage. Fellow speakers are the Right Honourable Harriet Harman MP, Secretary of

State for Social Security and Minister for Women, and Vivienne Westwood, top British fashion designer. The theme of the Lunch this year is 'Making a Difference'.

Among the 550 guests this year will be Shirley Conran, novelist; Caroline Hamilton, Polar Explorer; Darcey Bussell, Principal Ballerina, Royal Ballet; Ann Gloag, Executive Director, Stage Coach; Lisa Potts, Nursery Nurse; Rita Restorick, Peace Campaigner; Doreen Lawrence, Civil Rights Campaigner and Liz Paver, President National Association of Head Teachers.

Hosting the occasion is Lady Lothian, Founder President Women of the Year Lunch, who is serving as Executive Chairman for the second year.

The Lunch raises funds for the Greater London Fund for the Blind. A visually impaired woman achiever is selected each year to receive the coveted Frink Award for 'outstanding achievement in overcoming visual disability'.

The organisation instructed us nominees to contact our local press to try and get some publicity. So I had some photographs taken of me by my old chum Pattie Clapton, and I contacted the *Evening Standard* in London, which wrote:

Fame at last for the woman who's lived with the famous

From Princess Diana to Mick Jagger, Sally Arnold has worked with some of the most famous people in the world – but it's taken over 25 years for her to find herself in the spotlight. She has now been selected as one of the 500 Women of the Year and she's finding it hard to adjust.

'I hate being photographed. I've never chosen to be up front. I've always been in the background putting the nuts and bolts together,' she said.

Mind you, she must have learned something about self-promotion from Mick Jagger. Her business leaflet talks of her 'formidable organisational skills' and 'unique career'.

That has included keeping the Rolling Stones on the road while they partied through the wild years of the seventies and making sure Poet Laureate, Ted Hughes, had a bottle of water while reading at the Duke of Edinburgh's 75th birthday concert last November.

Ms Arnold, an events producer, was selected from 1,200 nominees for the award, to be held at The Savoy Hotel next week. She is not sure why.

'Some of the others will be women who have saved lives or set up hospices. I suppose it's because I've done a lot of voluntary fund-raising work for charities,' she said.

From her small office in Primrose Hill she masterminds the production of charity events, including Paul Newman's summer camps for terminally ill children, and a Montserat Caballe concert at the Royal Festival Hall next year.

She has staged a polo day with the Prince of Wales, and fund-raising evenings for drugs charity Core with Princess Diana, and gives an expert's assessment of their respective performances. 'Prince Charles is very good and very professional, but it's a job to him. With the Princess you could tell she really enjoyed it, she was really engaged. She was more human.' Ms Arnold's career began when Mick Jagger invited her to become tour manager for the Stones in the seventies. A trained Norland nanny, she had been looking after his baby daughter Jade – which made her the ideal candidate. 'After all being a tour manager is really like nannying overgrown kids,' she said. 'You have to deal with so many different egos and make all the detailed arrangements. The band liked me and importantly so did their wives.' There followed years on the road with the archetypal wild men of rock – the Stones, the Who and Lynyrd Skynyrd.

However, Ms Arnold, 48, says the sex, drugs and booze passed her by. 'I was too busy working. While the bands were partying I was writing them newsletters of the next day's arrangements, which they probably never read! At the time I was the only female Tour Manager in Europe, but because I came across as very schoolmarmish I never had any trouble from the men.

When I said the bus would leave without them if they were late, the bus left without them.'

The Eighties saw her working for Who guitarist Pete Townshend's charity for drug addicts, Double O, and staging concerts with Queen, Barry Manilow, Dire Straits, Elton John and Comic Relief.

Not that she is ever daunted rubbing shoulders with the stars. 'I'm the boss. It's an equal relationship and I never think of them as stars. Mind you, telling the Poet Laureate to speak up at the sound check was a bit stressful.'

The Women of the Year Lunch is to be attended by Queen Noor of Jordan, and dozens of other female success stories, including Minister for Women Harriet Harman, novelist Shirley Conran and designer Vivienne Westwood.

Which leaves Ms Arnold ambivalent about the need for such an event, now in its 42nd year. 'I've never had any problems working with men, but women are still not recognised in a lot of areas. What I want to do is pass on my skills and experience to other women,' she said.

Wow! How amazing! At last I was being recognised for all the charity work I had done over the years.

I then put on a massive event for the thirtieth anniversary of Chrysalis Records. It took place on 18th September 1998 at a wonderful venue in central London. One Great George Street is in the heart of Westminster, just minutes away from the Houses of Parliament. It is a Grade II listed building, an Edwardian mansion built in 1910 as the Institution of Civil Engineers. It is a four-domed building, with a massive marble staircase. Very imposing and with many gorgeous, large, light and airy rooms which we used for different entertainment and refreshments.

I had my usual team of helpers of course. Afterwards, I had a fantastic letter from Steve Lewis, who I had originally met at Virgin Records while tour managing Mike Oldfield, and who had recommended me to the Chrysalis chairman, Chris Wright.

Steve wrote:

The sheer scale and ambitious nature of the event resulted in a mammoth undertaking for whoever was charged with the organisational responsibilities. Having known you for 20 years and worked with you previously, I was confident that you could pull it off better than anyone else. I can tell you now that not everyone on my Board was as confident as me! Nevertheless, they have all told me how impressed they were with the party and the organisation. I have also received a number of letters and telephone calls from the guests I invited myself and all of them reflect how much everybody enjoyed what was a great evening.

Thank you again and congratulations on the high standard that you and your team achieved. You were a vital part of the success of the evening and as I was the person who recommended you to the Chairman I should also add that you made me look good as well!

What a fabulous letter!

Around this time, I was recommended as manager to Geri Halliwell soon after she had left the Spice Girls. I flew out to the south of France for a couple of days to meet her. She was staying with George Michael, and we met for lunch and got on alright but – and this is just my opinion from that one meeting – I didn't see any driving desire in her to do anything in particular. Personally, I thought her single 'Look at Me' was very good, but that was about it. I decided against this job, as I really couldn't see myself managing her and having to jump to another star's inevitable demands, queries and requests.

I really was past looking after celebrities and their never-ending dramas. Besides, Sally Arnold Events Management was beginning to flourish. I had numerous events lined up for the future, and even a grand gala evening at Le Manoir Aux Quat' Saisons in Oxfordshire for millennium night, for chef and owner Michel Blanc. I had two lovely overnight stays there at the hotel for meetings with Michel and his staff, which was heavenly – to stay at such a wonderful hotel, for free! Furthermore, I was appointed to organise the new, revived Carl Flesch Violin Competition, which was to be headed by the German virtuoso violinist, Anne-Sophie Mutter, whose own teacher had been taught by Carl Flesch. I had some wonderful meetings and meals with Anne-Sophie, which was thrilling. I am in awe of women like her. The talent, the brain, the work ethic – not to mention her beauty too. I felt utterly privileged to work with her, even for a short time. Sadly, it transpired that nobody actually managed to get enough finance for this project, despite having some really big names on the board.

It really felt as if my fledgling company was on its way to being established and permanent. But it wasn't to last. Before long, the newspapers started announcing that a recession was on the way. Soon, Sally Arnold Events Management started to suffer… One by one, all my upcoming events were cancelled – this will feel very familiar to hospitality companies who endured COVID-19 and the lockdowns during 2020–21, of course.

Back then, the recession was starting to hit. I began to struggle financially. I soldiered on for as long as I could, but I could see the writing on the wall. I could tell bad times were coming, as the first things to go in any financial recession are the charity events, and the celebratory events that some financial companies like to put on. These, of course, were my bread and butter.

My final event was for Mikhail Gorbachev's Green Cross Charity. This was an evening gala dinner at the May Fair Intercontinental Hotel in London, with the usual entertainment, raffle and auction. Again, my regular team was on hand.

When I was introduced to Mr Gorbachev at the drinks reception beforehand, I remember him being extremely grateful to me for putting on such a prestigious event for his environmental charity. All of this was said via an interpreter, who was a very friendly and cheerful man. Gorbachev himself was extremely charming and charismatic; I would have loved to talk to him properly, but that could never happen, so I had to be grateful with just this small chat.

So, my little company had started with an event for Prince Philip and ended with one for Mikhail Gorbachev – not bad really.

Closing my business was devastating. This time I really thought I had reached rock bottom. But worse was to come. I'd always had my health, but suddenly even that deserted me...

I became extremely unwell and discovered I needed a radical hysterectomy. I won't go into detail, but this is a major operation for a woman. For me, it was the final straw. That shocking diagnosis finally made my decision for me. I would close my company permanently, sell my flat, pay off my debts and have the operation in Devon, where I could recuperate with my family. The post-operative period would entail six weeks of near inactivity. No driving, no rigorous exercise. I promised myself that, after I'd recovered, I would go travelling again.

So, I sold my garden flat in Primrose Hill to a member of the pop group The Cure. I made a good profit, and invested my capital of £50,000, while leaving myself £20,000 to travel on. I put all my belongings into storage, as I had done so many times before.

Things happened then just as planned. The operation took place, and I was a good patient – faithfully settling myself for the required six weeks' post-op inactivity. Then, after a good long recuperation, I set off for three months travelling around Jordan, India, the Maldives, and the Seychelles.

In hindsight I wish I hadn't sold that lovely little flat, but had just rented it out, as the London property prices have since gone through the roof. But I can't dwell on things like this. It is what it is. We make decisions based on the information we have at the time. And, at that time, I was planning to do what I had always done in the past – sell up, have a break, return, get a new job, get a mortgage and buy somewhere new.

But sometimes things just don't work out how we expect.

Chapter 24

Wonderful World Travel

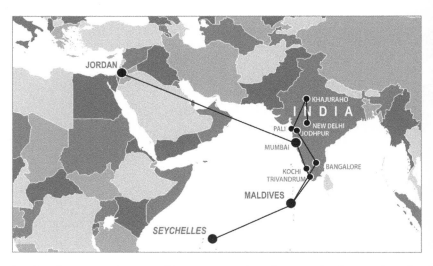

In October 1999 I went off on my travels, taking in Jordan, India, the Maldives, and the Seychelles. It took me months to organise and luckily I found Captain Padam Singh, who runs Paddy's Treks and Tours, to organise the Indian part of my trip. He is a font of knowledge about India and made sure I was looked after every step of the way.

I had decided to do this trip first class where possible. So, I flew club class on Royal Jordanian Airlines to Amman in Jordan. I had been given one contact there – Queen Noor. This was from an old friend who had been at school with her when she was Lisa Halaby. But when I got to Jordan and called the number I'd been given, I was told the Queen was away in Lebanon. So that was that.

Obviously, I did the Petra touristy thing, travelling through the most amazing desert scenery with very few buildings, via Wadi Mousa which has a shrine to Aaron, the brother of Moses. I also did the one-hour climb to see the famous monastery high up in the mountains.

Strangely Amman and other towns were very clean, but the countryside was littered with rubbish, tattered old black bags and their contents spilling out. My taxi driver told me that rubbish was a massive problem, but then I noticed him chucking tissues out of the taxi window...

I flew to India with my first stop being Bombay (now Mumbai) for one night. The next day I flew to Goa, where I stayed at the Taj Holiday Village, right on the beach, for about a week, from where I went on various trips with my driver in his ubiquitous little Oxford air-conditioned car, which all tourists use.

My next destination was Cochin. There was no first class on the train, so I was in second class with air conditioning, but even so, there were no doors, just curtains. I noticed a massive difference between the trains and stations from my first visit to India in 1973 when I had travelled as cheaply as possible. There were many more shops and stalls on the stations now, where you could get bottled drinks of every kind, fruit, packed meals, crisps and snacks. Previously it had been hawkers selling just chai (tea), and bananas if you were lucky. Now they had efficient young men in neat uniforms selling all these goodies. I also noticed many more men were wearing Western-style clothes, but not the women though.

The Malabar Residency Hotel in Cochin was wonderful – a true haven of peace and tranquillity. Now it's the Malabar House Residency, and Cochin is Kochi. It's a fabulous place to stay for a few days to look around Cochin, which is a strange mixture of Christian, Jewish and Chinese influences. There's the St Francis Protestant Church, Jew Town, and the famous Chinese fishing nets. But the humidity was 100%!

Next, I headed to the High Range Club in Munnar. This was a taste of real old colonialism, high up in the hills surrounded by tea plantations. The club itself was like an old-fashioned English boarding school. I was given a special trip to the Kundali Club, another taste of old colonialism, nestled in a peaceful valley. It is how I imagine Shangri-La – a lush, green valley, with a river and streams running through it, surrounded by tea plantations and a haven for wildlife, like elephants, deer, boar and bison. But then the peace was broken by a helicopter landing with five very noisy, and obviously very rich, Indians getting out. This turned out to be the chairman of the club, with his wife and a VIP Indian – manager of some company that produces and sells machinery to the massive Indian Tata company, plus his family. We all sat and had drinks together, but they were *so loud*. The Kundali seemingly only allows very rich, upper-class Indians to belong to it. The caste system is still going strong in India.

In Periyar, at the Taj Garden Retreat, I did a tour of a spice plantation. This was fascinating, seeing tamarind root, cocoa plants, nutmeg/mace, cloves, pepper, coffee, cinnamon and tapioca (who knew it was a root?!) all growing. A boat ride on the Periyar lake followed, where I saw a herd of wild elephants drinking. This lake had been made by an English engineer in 1895 for irrigation and power for the locals.

At another Taj Garden Retreat, in Kumarakom, I began to feel extremely ill, with my right arm swollen and aching badly. I later discovered from a doctor that I had been bitten by a spider, which had caused a mild paralysis. The manager at the hotel took pity on me and put me in a Superior Cottage on the lake, instead of my normal room, where I could just be quiet and recover.

I then spent a few days on a boat on Kerala backwaters. The boat was extremely large, made of reeds, and surprisingly luxurious with dark wooden panelling, proper lovely clean white cotton sheets on the bed in the beautiful bedroom, and a little shower room just off to the side. A lovely, kind Indian couple looked after me. The backwaters are a 1,000-mile network of developed canals, rivers and lakes, with numerous islands. These waterways were part of the ancient spice route, developed many years ago by a wealthy maharajah. There were no roads, so this was the only way for the trade of coir and spices. Life was reliant on these waterways, which became known as the 'Venice of the East'.

The boat dropped me off at Mankotta House, on Mankotta Island where I had the most wonderful time. Mankotta House Hotel was (and maybe still is) run by Jay and Leila Chacko, who were the kindest of hosts.

They invited me to join their large family celebration luncheon where seventy people celebrated Mrs Chacko senior's seventy-fifth birthday. This was really a great privilege. Even more amazing was that I was seated next to the guest of honour, Duleep Matthai, a cousin who had been a Member of the Government with Nehru. More recently he had been running the Indian World Wildlife Fund. Well, to say I was blown away would be an understatement – he was gorgeous! Even when he just walked into the room I had noticed him – his bearing, stature and clothing spoke of a most unusual and interesting man. He was also extremely handsome, despite being seventy-five years old. During the meal we talked and talked non-stop, both being interested in each other.

I began to fall in love there and then, but doubted it would be reciprocated. But over the next few days Duleep would hunt me out, whether I was in the hammock reading, or sitting by the water cooling off. We chatted about everything – he told me that he was a Christian, which was rather unusual in India. He was divorced and lived in genteel retirement in Bangalore, but was still helping the WWF. We became extremely attached to each other, until it was time for me to leave, and I thought that would be the end of it. But no! As I was leaving he gave me a big hug and a note with his address and phone number. He told me to contact him when I was in Bangalore, and invited me to stay with him there. This was the first time that I had even vaguely fancied an older man. It was a great relief to feel that I could be attracted to men closer to my age, instead of always lusting after long-haired young men in their twenties and thirties! I was fifty after all and it was time to stop seeing the toy boys!

After that reluctant leave-taking, I travelled further south to Trivandrum, staying at the fabulous Surya Samudra Hotel, where the beach is just a few minutes' walk through the gardens. Trivandrum is an area that had originally been quiet and peaceful although not prosperous, with local trade being fishing, coir rope making and coconut farming. Then in the 1960s the hippy tourists came. Now there are three types of tourist: the rich, the middle class and backpackers who all come *en masse* – too many wanting drugs and sex.

I spent millennium night in the Maldives. I was in Nakatchafushi from

21st December 1999 to 5th January 2000, in the North Atoll. It really is the archetypal desert island – palm trees, azure blue sea, coral reefs, soft white sand and flowers like bougainvillaea and frangipani growing profusely. The rooms are thatched bungalows each with its own private bit of beach. The millennium New Year's Eve there was fantastic.

Then onto Thulhagiri, with a lovely chalet-style room right on the water's edge, surrounded by clean, white sand. Each chalet had its own sunbathing furniture, so no arguments with anybody about sharing loungers or chairs – all so sensible and logical. The restaurant and food were stunning, as was the swimming pool. My sister-in-law flew out to join me with my seven-year-old niece, plus another little friend of hers. Even though the hotel was full, the management agreed to put two extra beds in my room, so we managed very happily and had the best week together. It was such fun swimming with the kids and collecting all sorts of shells, and looking out for all the wonderfully colourful exotic fish and feeding the manta rays, which the kids loved.

I can't recommend these two Maldive islands highly enough. They are fantastic. They are not advertised over here much, probably because they are not in the expensive bracket, but nonetheless they are absolutely amazing. They have all the same things as the very expensive ones, namely the same sea, sun, sand. So why pay through the nose? I would go back to either of these in a heartbeat.

My next stop was Bangalore and the Taj West End Hotel. I had initially wanted to go there so that I could get to Puttaparthi to see Sai Baba, the well-known spiritual guru. I wasn't exactly a follower of his, but knew some people who were. I was mostly just curious. I stayed at a hostel in Puttaparthi, decent enough and close enough to walk to the Ashram for Darshan prayers for 6am. I sat among the Indian women, who were so nice and sweet to me. After about another hour some music started and Baba came in. I was sitting only about six rows back, so I saw him quite close up. He was so small, and looked much older than I expected. He walked very slowly, among the women first (we were segregated), and he produced some *Vibhuti* for some, took letters from many, then blessed us all before he left. Vibhuti is an ash-like substance which Baba produced from his hands, with no obvious supply. A miracle? A trick? Who knows. For the curious, there is plenty of information about Baba and his Vibhuti online.

Puttaparthi itself is a mass of shops and stalls devoted to Sai Baba, selling incense, saris, scarves and silver jewellery – almost all with a Baba picture on them. It's the usual Indian craziness! Hot and dusty too. Thankfully my funky hostel had a sweet little roof terrace which caught the breeze, when there was one. One evening up there, I met a young man who was studying with Baba, and he told me he had seen some UFOs above the Ashram. He said that our Christian archangels are the same as all the Hindu gods. Interesting.

Although I was never really sure what to make of Sai Baba, my Indian friend, Duleep Matthai, had told me an interesting story about him. He had met Sai Baba once, and they had driven together to an animal sanctuary. Now, Baba was always saying that he could tame any wild animal, but when they were shown a small, tame bear by the organisers, Baba just ran away in terror!

On my return to Bangalore I stayed with the lovely Duleep for about a week. He had been an MP for years, and there were photos of him with Nehru, Earl and Countess of Mountbatten and Mrs Gandhi all around his apartment. He knew Prince Philip as well because of his WWF connection. He helped start up the Tata company, and the Taj and Oberoi hotels. He was passionate about the preservation of wildlife in India, and had set up the Duleep Matthai Nature Conservation Fellowship in the 1950s.

After a week with him, he asked me to move in and live with him, but I really could not live in that heat and humidity. It made me sad to say no, as he was such a wonderful man, and just what I was looking for, and needed. Intelligent, interesting, passionate, well educated, well read, kind and loving. But, I had to get back on the road, so Duleep gave me some contacts for my further travels through India – various maharajahs and retired government ministers.

Back in Bombay I visited the Malabar Gardens, where Salman Rushdie's book *The Moor's Last Sigh* is set. I also visited the most astonishing Jain temple and went to the Hanging Gardens where the Jains leave their dead to be devoured by the birds.

The next stop on my journey was Udaipur. The Lake Palace Hotel is the stunning hotel in the middle of the lake, which is so often shown in photographs of India. It really is astonishing but, yet again, demonstrates the imbalance between rich and poor and the horrendous caste system. For some reason, I was given a suite – it was massive with a little gazebo balcony/terrace which hung out over the lake.

I was in Rajasthan for my horse safari week, riding a Mawahi horse over the deserts of Rajasthan. I hadn't ridden for some years, and had rather lost my nerve, but the minute I was introduced to my lovely mare it all came back to me – the smell, the noises, the feel of a horse's muzzle in my hand, everything that I loved about horses. The safari was run by two young men, who both accompanied me on horseback, with another, older man, driving our belongings to a stop somewhere midway. We would arrive at the stop after a wonderful ride through valleys, desert and villages, ready for some food and gallons of water. And there, under a tree, or a makeshift shelter, would be the driver with lunch already prepared and cooked. We ate delicious Rajasthani dishes, mainly peasant-style food, which I absolutely loved. Nothing flash, just chapattis, dahl and some vegetables, and occasionally some meat. Then back on the horses for another few hours to our stop for the night.

The next stop on my itinerary was Sardar Samand Lake Palace Hotel at Pali. This was an astonishing place. The palace was once owned by the Maharajah of Jodhpur. It is now a Heritage hotel, with part of it kept for the royal family's personal use. Built on a lake, it is absolutely stunning.

That evening, as I was having my meal, one of the staff came to me with an invitation to join the maharajah and maharani for drinks that evening. It seems Duleep had contacted them to tell them I was staying there, and asked them to look after me! I was ushered into a very grand room where both the maharajah and maharani and their son were waiting for me. What charming people they were. He is the most handsome man, and she is a very striking woman, and the son – well, what a gorgeous young man! (Sadly, since then, he had a terrible fall when playing polo and, as I understand it, is somewhat brain-damaged, which is heartbreaking, because he was obviously such a vital young man.)

One thing I found very uncomfortable was the fact that whenever either the maharajah or maharani got up to get another drink or something, this very old, tiny woman – who seemed permanently bent double – would sweep the carpet in front of them with a broom of twigs, going backwards as she did it. It was obviously quite normal and went on all the time, but I did find it wrong, especially as the royal family are obviously so well educated and seem to be very decent people. I imagine she was happy to do this, and felt honoured to serve them in this way. So, who was I to question a centuries-old custom?

That evening, I ended up drinking with them for about two hours, by which time it was 11pm. I was exhausted, but on and on the drinking and chatting went! The maharajah asked me if I could organise events for them – as early as next year. Like an idiot, I said yes. But after a few days of serious thought I realised that I did not want to be rushed into anything, so I wrote to them saying that I was sorry but I couldn't help.

After that fantastic week, I ended up in Jodhpur, at another fabulous

Sally with Maharaja and Maharani of Jodhpur,
with their son and heir, Shivraj, February 2000
(Photo from author's personal collection)

hotel, the Khimsar Fort, where I had a much-needed Ayurvedic massage to knead away my poor old overused muscles from the long days of riding.

After the Khimsar Fort were the Bal Samand Lake Palace Hotel and the Samode Hotel, old palaces that had been transformed into luxurious hotels. Sheer opulence, if somewhat over the top. But however luxurious some of these old palaces are, many were actually very dank and cold. At one of them I got chatting to a young English couple who were on their honeymoon, and talk about coincidence – the young man had been in the army fighting in the Gulf War with my cousin, Philip Marques. What a small world.

The last leg of my wonderful trip took in Khajuraho, where I saw the famous erotic sculptures. My guide explained they are part of the tantric/kundalini tradition. Then Jaipur and, on the train, I sat with some sweet Indian kids who spoke with American accents, having been living in New York. Their father was one of those Indian men who smother themselves with strong, overpowering aftershave. It made me feel quite ill. I wonder why men do this? Maybe to show their wealth?

Finally, my Indian travels came to an end. My last stop was New Delhi. The last time I had been to Delhi in 1973 I had stayed in the youth hostel, but this time I was in the Imperial Hotel!

I had promised myself that I would return to India one day and do it in style – and I did! What a few months it had been, from leaving England in October 1999 to back home in March 2000. I was feeling fit, healthy and happy, no longer exhausted and worn down with endless work.

Immediately on my return – literally in the car from the airport – my sister told me that the chairman of the Over the Wall Gang Camp charity desperately needed to speak to me.

Chapter 25

Cancer, and Recovery

The Over the Wall Gang Camp UK, the sister charity to the Hole in the Wall Gang Camp in the States, had been set up by some other people who had approached Paul Newman, after the debacle with the Dodgy Duke. Mr Newman had recommended me to the chairman, so I had been a trustee for some years. We'd hired a married couple to be the working directors and to run the day-to-day affairs of the charity. Now, though, the chairman told me that there were suspicions and allegations that this couple was taking money, so please would I consider taking over the post as director? I agreed. I had to resign as a trustee, obviously, because a trustee cannot receive any remuneration, and the post of director was a proper salaried post.

Bizarrely, even though Paul Newman himself had recommended me twice for positions in his charity over here, and we communicated via fax, letters and email, I never actually met him!

On YouTube there is a film called 'Genesis, The Hole in the Wall Gang Camp', which was first produced in 1999, and tells the 'hole' story of the camp's creation:

> Founder Paul Newman, architects, construction workers, medical professionals and others share exciting accounts of their efforts to build a hideout in northeast Connecticut for seriously ill children to 'raise a little hell'. Viewers see how, in an astonishing nine months, a 344-acre Camp emerged from the woods featuring 35 buildings – including 15 cabins, a swimming pool, horse barn, recreation center, and a Shaker-barn dining hall. The Camp, which has grown from a summer camp for children into a year-round organization that serves the entire family, provides 'a different kind of healing' to more than 25,000 children and family members annually. All of Camp's programming is free of charge.

The UK camp was in progress initially only in the summer holidays at a school for the disabled in Hampshire, which had the necessary facilities. So, I decided to rent a cottage nearby, then buy something once I knew the area better. The salary was a considerable drop from what I had become used to at Classic FM and from running my own company, but that didn't worry me. Money has never been my driving force. Job satisfaction is far more important, and this job would hopefully be just what I wanted, being able to organise things as well as being helpful to those desperately sick children.

I rented a little cottage about five miles away from the school. My income was a small salary, plus half the rent for the cottage as I had to have the office there. All was going well. The camp was underway that summer. Then I was diagnosed with breast cancer.

I had been visiting my parents some weeks before in Devon and a letter from the NHS was waiting for me offering me a free mammogram. I had no idea that they offered these free to all women at the age of fifty. I said I wouldn't bother to have it, as I'd had one privately just six months previously. I had always been vigilant about my health, going regularly to my doctor in London for regular Well Woman Check-ups – which included regular smear tests, and mammograms at the Portland Hospital every three years.

That year, 1999, everything had come back clear, as usual.

But – and this is what saved my life, *again*, after Dean had saved my life by stopping me being on the Skynyrd plane in 1977 – this time, my mother nagged and nagged at me to go for the NHS mammogram. It was as though she had a premonition...

So I went along to have it, and was called back for a biopsy, which confirmed the cancer suspicion. To say it was a shock is an understatement. There had never been any breast cancer in the family. And I didn't have any symptoms. No lumps, nothing unusual at all in fact.

I went to see two different consultants, and I chose Mr Gerald Gui at the Royal Marsden Hospital in London, as he was so kind, and told me to email him any time I needed to.

I explained to the chairman of the charity that I'd been diagnosed with breast cancer and would be off work for two weeks to have my mastectomy and to recuperate, and that I was happy to take it as holiday time. Then I'd be back at my desk, raring to go. To me I wasn't ill – I just needed an operation.

But then came a massive shock – which was nastier than anything else ever done to me in my life.

The next day I received a very formal letter from the charity's accountant telling me my salary would be stopped *retrospectively for the previous month* and for the next month to come. Retrospectively? Why? I had done my normal hard work for that past month. I was to be put on statutory sick pay of £12 a day – nowhere near my salary. And the share of the rent for their office would be stopped. Suddenly I had no proper income, and no help with the rent for the office. What was going on? Talk about kicking someone when they're down. I vividly remember the gut-wrenching feelings of total and utter dismay.

I couldn't believe this was legal, so my first call was to my solicitor and he told me that indeed it was legal, as the Disability Discrimination Act did not apply if there were fewer than fifteen employees. I'm sure things are different now, as I read recently that companies owe a duty of care to their employees, particularly when they are on sick leave. But I wasn't shown an ounce of compassion or care. What they did to me was perfectly legal. But to me it seemed immoral or unethical at the very least. All I know is that it was unkind in the extreme. I was utterly bereft. My world had come crashing down. Okay, they weren't exactly sacking me, but that's what it felt like. And at that stage I didn't even know that I needed chemotherapy. So I wasn't even ill. I was just going to have an operation.

I certainly couldn't live on £12 a day. That was an insult, especially the retrospective bit. I just wanted to get away from these people, who I had thought of as friends over the past few years that we had all been trustees together. So, I resigned. But I was stuck in a cottage that was far bigger than I needed. I had signed an eight-month rental agreement, so I obviously couldn't move out without causing all sorts of legal problems. And I would never do that to my lovely elderly landlady. I was stuck there, having to pay rent for the charity's office out of my own savings. Paul Newman was so shocked at the way I had been treated that he sent me a personal cheque for $10,000. He couldn't believe that such a thing was legal over here, as it certainly wasn't in the States. He also mentioned something about closing the charity down. But I begged him not to, as the work was the most important thing.

Besides, I had other things to occupy me: I had a full mastectomy of my right breast, with some lymph nodes taken, which showed the cancer had spread in the blood; vascular invasion, rather than lymphatic invasion. I needed six months of gruelling chemotherapy. I decided not to have a reconstruction, as I knew the terrible problems that my sister-in-law had had with hers. She was in constant pain and, even after all that, nothing would look normal anyway. So, I am left with a flat side, and use a prosthesis – which is fine, other than when swimming, as it tends to float away!

On chemo days, I would drive up to the Marsden Hospital in London, spend the day there having the chemo, and drive back. This was okay for the first couple of sessions, but after that I needed friends to help out. And thankfully they all rallied round. The chemo was horrendous, giving me violent nausea, exhaustion and a horrible taste of metal. It was like nothing else I'd ever experienced. Just a total takeover of my body. No control left seemingly. The continual nausea was the worst thing, with terrible pain in the oesophagus every time I ate or vomited.

After the chemo sessions, I was usually very poorly for the first eight to ten days, then I would feel somewhat better – until the next round. I would carefully organise everything in advance: do my laundry and shopping, have everything prepared so that I would hardly need to go out. My landlady was wonderful and would let me use her beautiful indoor swimming pool.

I had become friends with a senior staff member at the Connecticut Over the Wall Gang Camp's office, and he emailed me:

First, please know that you have been in my thoughts and prayers these past weeks. I am still finding it difficult to find the right words to express my feelings at the treatment to which you have been subjected. Please know how deeply sorry I am for how the events have transpired and for all the added stress that you do not need in your life, especially right now, but that you don't deserve at any time, not just now.

But I hope and pray that you will be somehow protected from this added stress during your chemotherapy and that it will not affect your outlook on your recovery and your outlook on who you are as a person.

I am so sorry for the turn things have taken – I don't understand either, and I wish I could do something more, but please know I am always here to listen.

This is a letter I wrote to the chairman about a year later:

I have now got past the anger stage, but I confess to being totally bewildered as to why I was treated so very badly by you and the other Trustees – especially at such a horrendously low point in my life.

Think about it: I was diagnosed with cancer on 4th July 2000; I had a mastectomy 2 weeks later; I took 2 weeks off work. I returned to my desk after those 2 weeks because my doctor passed me as fit and well.

But then you all – in your wisdom – put me onto Statutory Sick Pay of £12 a day, one month retrospectively and for one month further – without any warning or discussion whatsoever. You also withdrew the office rental being paid to me for running the office from my home.

So – suddenly I had no salary and no help with the rent – but I still had to live and obviously then had to pay the full rent myself. All this after you had promised me I wouldn't lose my job. But Statutory Sick Pay was an insult and indeed felt like I had been given the sack. You must, surely, understand that there was no way I could continue working with you all after such an uncaring and thoughtless attitude?

I ended up losing a great deal of money because of this unkindness. For example, I had spent in excess of £2,000 on removals to take up this post. I had signed an 8 month rental agreement on the cottage I had moved into in order to be closer to the Camp – and being a decent and honourable person, I did not want to be in breach of that rental agreement – so I had to pay out £900 a month for the next 7 months out of my savings – as I had no income. I also had, obviously, all the other normal living costs. So all in all you have cost me a very great deal and I am having immense difficulty getting myself back onto an even keel.

I went out of my way to help you over the years, only to be kicked by you when I was down. I think that gives me the right to be angry and hurt, don't you?

I am now at a clinic being treated for clinical depression due to all this. And in fact the cavalier attitude towards me by you has hurt and upset me far more than the cancer ever did. That I could deal with – but I was utterly distraught when I received those cold, clinical letters from the accountant on behalf of all the Trustees.

I didn't hear back from him. Thankfully the charity now seems to be flourishing under new trusteeship and management.

I went to the Optimum Health Institute near Austin in Texas to detox from the chemo, and again in 2005 for a top-up of healthy living. It's the most amazing place – all raw food and wheatgrass juice, fasting and colonics. Wonderful. I learned such a lot about health there and would recommend it to anybody looking for somewhere to detox from chemotherapy like I did, or to diet, or just for a break. They also have great success in helping people with diabetes and even various autoimmune diseases. I truly think this type of treatment and therapy, where the body is given a chance to heal itself, will become more and more relevant in our world, where we all take far too many medications, prescribed and unprescribed. For many years the Optimum Health Institute – and others – have been recommending a change of diet, for example, to help with diabetes, and only recently has the medical profession concurred. The clinic helped me continue with a healthy lifestyle. I stopped having my hair highlighted, as it seems the chemicals could be carcinogenic. I try to stick to an alkaline diet, mainly fruit and vegetables. I also try to stay calm and mindful.

At this point I had no home, so I ended up staying with various friends and family and living out of a suitcase. Not the ideal for someone just getting over chemo. But I had no choice. I couldn't live with my parents as I didn't need my father's constant criticism. Thankfully, my friends were wonderful – well, some of them. It's amazing how you discover who your real friends are when in dire need. And it's often not the ones you think it will be. Human nature is most odd sometimes.

Actually, in a strange way, the whole cancer experience has been quite rewarding. It certainly jolted me into a different state of awareness, away from the busy London life I used to lead, and towards a much more rewarding, quieter, more peaceful, less frenetic life.

During and after chemo I continued with various complementary treatments, like acupuncture and homoeopathy. Plus using Sea Bands on my wrists which genuinely helped with the nausea. But I continued to have horrendous side effects for many years afterwards. Indeed, I still suffer from extreme exhaustion, and ongoing pain in my oesophagus. Also the brain fog known as 'chemo brain', which meant that I would never be able to do the sort of work I had done in the past, where my brain needed to be razor sharp, on the ball and quick to react to anything and everything. That was all gone.

But I had to find work. My old friend John McLaren, who had started up the original Composers Competition at Classic FM, asked me to join him again. The competition had now been taken over by BBC Radio 3. I explained that I couldn't manage the immensely challenging work I had previously done. So we agreed I would just be a 'junior' and input the information into the database.

As I no longer had a home in London, I had written to some old friends and colleagues asking if anybody had a room to rent. And good old Alan Dunn came to the rescue. He'd been Mick Jagger's assistant and I'd known him since being Jade's nanny nearly thirty years earlier. He let me stay in his wonderful Thames-side penthouse apartment in Battersea. He didn't want any rent, just something towards the bills. This is what a real friend is. It was truly heart-touching and I'll never forget his generosity at my time of great need.

The office was based in the Royal College of Music, which I loved. Arriving there in the mornings and hearing all the students practising – some piano here, a violin there, then a clarinet, a soprano or tenor – all these wonderful sounds drifting along the corridors was sheer heaven for me.

But, but, but… I simply couldn't hack the work. Even though it was minimal, it was just too much for me. I would sit in front of the computer in tears at the frustration of my mind *just not working*. What was wrong with me? I was also permanently exhausted. So, sadly, I had to explain to John that I just couldn't manage any longer. Thankfully, he was extremely understanding, which was a massive relief, as I hate letting anybody down.

I ended up seeing the psychiatrist at the Marsden Hospital. I was in despair. What was happening to me? He told me I had to stop working. I was pushing myself too hard and needed to slow down. I had to give the chemotherapy time to do its work. He also warned me that chemo can stay in the system for many years. And here was me thinking I was going to be fine immediately after it. No such luck. I also discovered that this terrible brain freeze is actually a 'thing' called 'chemo brain'. Your brain just will not work like it used to.

I was desolate at not being able to work. All my life I'd worked my socks off. Now I couldn't even do a simple secretarial job. What was to become of me?

Alan, very kindly, let me continue to stay at his flat for a few months more, even though I wasn't working. Alan, Mick Jagger's long-term right-hand man, is one of the most kind and generous people I know. He has always helped his friends and family when they have needed jobs, or whatever it may be.

I just rested and recovered while reading books for the first time in years, overlooking the busyness of the Thames. It was the most healing time and place. I had never lived in London without being frantic with work before, so now I had time – time to visit the wonderful art galleries and museums and wander around the parks.

But then came the hardest realisation of all – if I couldn't work any longer, at least for the time being, then I couldn't own a home again. I'd come off the London property ladder expecting to be able to get back on it, as I had done so many times before. I had travelled extensively, either renting my flat out, or selling up and putting all my things in storage, then returned, started another job, got a mortgage and found another home, or just moved back in when rental tenants left. I had done this about six times over the decades, and had always assumed I could carry on doing this indefinitely.

I had always wanted to continue working and had never envisaged having to stop. I loved my work and was good at it – organising events from inception to the final show. I had even become a Woman of the Year because of my charitable work. Yet here I was now unable to do it any longer.

To say I felt sorry for myself would be an understatement...

So I moved to Devon and rented a tiny little cottage about two miles

Sally with mastectomy scar tattoo
(© Laura Yabsley, with kind permission)

away from my parents. I also started working again, taking on small, unpressurised jobs such as housework in a small B&B and some administrative work. Plus, I was doing more and more for my elderly parents – cleaning, cooking, shopping, paperwork, numerous trips to the doctor, the hospitals, dentist, anything they needed really.

But even this ended up being too much for me. It would take me twenty minutes to put a pillowcase on. Ridiculous. But whatever it was, I just couldn't hack it. Again. I went to my GP. What was this? Exhaustion? Being under the weather? Again, he told me, in no uncertain terms, *to stop work*. He suggested I might be heading for a breakdown if I didn't stop pushing myself.

Obviously, I couldn't give up helping my parents, but I had to stop the other little jobs. I was distraught and desolate. I couldn't even do the simplest things. I felt a total failure, a waste of space.

In the meantime, it dawned on me that I wouldn't have needed the chemo if the cancer had been noticed and reported from the previous X-rays in 1999. *Because it was there in those X-rays.* I only found this out because two separate consultants commented on it in 2000 when looking at these earlier X-rays. *It had been missed* by the Portland Hospital in 1999, when they had given me the all-clear.

Shocked, I found a local legal aid solicitor who specialised in wrongly diagnosed/missed cancer cases. We were going to sue the Portland Hospital for £100,000 in lost earnings.

However, I simply wasn't strong enough to keep jumping through all the hoops and complications that the other side kept putting up. The legal advisors to the Portland Hospital kept demanding I go up to London for numerous psychological tests. The paperwork was also excessive and time-consuming. I was regularly exhausted from working on this, plus caring for my parents. I was permanently in tears. Something had to give. My GP told me I had to cut something out of my life, as I was just doing too much.

I couldn't stop caring for my parents, so the court case was the only thing I could stop in order to alleviate the massive stress. My solicitor dealing with the court case was furious with me. After two years of hard work I was just giving up – or so it seemed to him. But I simply was not well enough to continue with all the stress that it entailed. I was, quite literally, close to completely cracking up, when I would have been no good to anybody.

So I gave up the legal action. Luckily my solicitor did manage to get me a small sum in damages, but nothing like the £100,000 we had initially been aiming for.

The problem with renting a home is that one is at the mercy of the whims of a landlord. And now I had to move out of the little cottage I had been renting, as the owner wanted to sell it. I found another one nearby, where I lived happily for about eighteen months, when the same thing happened – the owner wanted to sell up, so I had to move *again*. This was becoming a pattern, and one that I would have to live with. I ended up moving six times in ten years. It was truly a nightmare. I wasn't able to settle, and now that I could never afford my own home again, I was permanently at the mercy of landlords. Not to mention the costs of all these enforced moves.

A Buddhist quote helped me:

> Suffering is resistance to what is. If you want to suffer less, you have to come to grips with what is.

I found this quote to be by far the most helpful, especially when I lost everything – job, home, savings etc. I just had to come to terms with the situation I was in now – not yearn for the old days – to cut my cloth, so to speak. I have many inspirational quotes that helped me through these dark years, which are on my website. These are some I can legally quote here:

> **Nietzsche on cancer**: Some situations are so bad that to remain sane is insane.

> **From Kalidasa in 4th century**: Please subdue the anguish of your soul. Nobody is destined to only happiness or to pain. The wheel of life takes one up and down by turn.

I decided to do something positive, and so I went to see a tattooist in Totnes in Devon, which is a hippy little town. I asked him whether he'd ever tattooed scar tissue before. No, he said, but he was keen to have a go.

I chose a pattern inspired by an Aubrey Beardsley illustration, of trailing leaves which entwine in and out of the scar. It didn't hurt at all, just tickled and we were both hooting with laughter throughout! At the time, I didn't analyse the reasons I was doing it. I just knew I wanted to do something to make me feel better about this great barren space. A part of my body that used to be a source of pleasure and beauty had become just empty. But when I think about it now, there was an emotional gap I needed to fill too.

As soon as I left the tattoo parlour, I knew I'd made the right decision. I felt proud of my battle scar rather than ashamed of it. I no longer wanted to hide my body away (I'm always lifting up my bra and showing people!). I want women to know there are other options beyond having reconstructive surgery.

My sister-in-law, the photographer Lorna Yabsley, did a photo shoot of me with the tattoo very prominent for her photographic project on breast cancer.

I was interviewed by the *Sunday Times* for their *Style* magazine, which included some of Lorna's photographs. The article came out on 26th October 2003. It attracted a massive amount of interest, and I am still, many years later, contacted about it to talk on the radio or be interviewed for magazines. Lorna and I were inundated with emails and letters saying how helpful her pictures of my tattoo were. Lorna's photos can still be viewed on her website: lornayabsley.co.uk/breast-cancer.

If you'd like to see all these lovely letters and emails, please head over to my website: www.rocknrollnanny.co.uk.

Even in 2015 I was asked to go on BBC Radio 4 in the 'Something Understood' slot. The journalist who approached me wrote:

> The edition is called 'Mending Cracks with Gold' and takes its central idea from 'Kintsugi', the ancient Japanese practice of using gold lacquer to repair broken ceramics, thus increasing their beauty, strength and value. The image is extended to us, the damage we sustain and how we can see our wounds as an opportunity to strengthen and beautify ourselves, and how we can value the uniqueness of a person/object with history above something shiny and flawless. Your decision to tattoo your scar strikes me as a potent image of a 'Kintsugi' life.

The journalist also told me that there was also to be a lovely reading in the programme from a book called Six Names of Beauty which links the Japanese aesthetic of wabi sabi (of which Kintsugi is a manifestation) with the Rolling Stones track, 'Down Home Girl', so the programme would also have a burst of that, considering my background with the Stones. I happily did this broadcast, where I also recited the poem 'Normal' by Alicia Suskind Ostriker, which is beautiful.

And in 2021 I was mentioned on Zoe Ball's show on Radio 2 concerning the tattoo, my work as the first female tour manager with the bands and this book.

Chapter 26

Life's Lessons

Since the early 1990s my parents had a very interesting book on their kitchen table. It was *The Natural Death Handbook*. (Edited by Stephanie Wienrich and Josefine Speyer of The Natural Death Centre. Ebury Publishing. ISBN 9781844132263.)

My parents had insisted that we, their children, should do exactly as they requested for their funerals, which they had read about in this book. They didn't want us to spend masses of money on their funerals by using undertakers or funeral directors of any sort. This wasn't due to any lack of funds, but because they felt that these funerals were all so impersonal. And to have your loved ones' bodies in an undertaker's premises for days was such a horrible thought. I think they both got this attitude after organising the funerals for their own parents, and seeing just what a 'business' it all is, and lacking in any depth or genuine feelings. So we did as we were told. I'm grateful to them for being so sensible about the whole thing. It meant we talked about it openly and discussed all the options.

Both my parents ended up in nursing homes, so I moved into their home with my new partner, who was an old friend of twenty-five years. My father died first in March 2005. My brother went with my partner in a van, and I drove there in my car with my twelve-year-old niece. We carried Daddy down the stairs, me holding his head, the men carrying his body, with Grace holding the doors open, and we put Daddy's body in the back of the van. I know this might sound bizarre or disrespectful to some, but this is what he wanted. And even though she knew exactly what would happen, the manager of the care home was still a little uncomfortable, saying, "Nobody has ever done it like this before!"

But of course it was all totally legal, and we had cleared it all with her previously, and also with the GP, so all the necessary people knew what we were doing. I suppose it was just a shock to actually see it happening, especially when you're used to having undertakers doing this particular job. As we were leaving, my niece said to me, "What happens if the police stop the van and find a dead body in the back?" Oh goodness! I hadn't thought of that! But hey – it was all legal and above board.

We'd got my father's garden shed all ready for him – his favourite place – with a trestle table covered with nice blankets, photographs all around, candles and incense lit and classical music playing.

He lay in his shed for a few days as we organised his funeral. We ordered a disposable balsa wood coffin off the internet, which arrived in a flat-pack the next day. My brother dug a 12-foot-deep grave in a field near his house, with the permission of the landowner, of course. We organised for a humanist celebrant, who was an old school friend of my mother's, to preside over the funeral. We held it at my brother's house, in his large courtyard, with Dad's favourite Mozart clarinet concerto wafting over the courtyard. It was extremely moving. The only desperately sad thing was that our mother was unable to be there. She was too poorly even to be brought over in an ambulance.

I think the main reason my father wanted this, apart from not being very religious, was that he was a farmer at heart, and loved the land and all things in nature. Humanist funerals focus on the individual's life, celebrating their life as well as expressing sadness, without any religious undertones.

My brother and five other strong male friends carried the coffin up the hill to the field, where the grave had been dug and prepared. The site is in a beautiful place, overlooking a valley, surrounded by fields and nature. We had all chosen this place together, as it was so reminiscent of our years on the farm in Wiltshire.

Bizarrely, there are very few legalities to burying human bodies. All this is laid out in *The Natural Death Handbook*. The main conditions being that they must not be buried less than a certain depth below the surface, and a certain distance from any running water. Probably fewer rules and regulations than for burying animals!

When I went to register the death with the registrar, I told him that we were doing our own funeral and burial, and he wasn't in the least surprised, saying, "Oh yes, many more people are doing these funerals now. The only thing I have to confirm is that you have the permission of the landowner."

When it came to my mother's death eight months later, we did exactly the same. My sister came over from Canada and together we prepared Mummy's body for burial. She too was laid out in the garden shed, with her favourite music playing, photographs all around with candles and incense. Our brother had arranged Daddy's body for his burial. None of us ever noticed any odd smells or anything nasty. We then buried her in the same grave as my father. So, they were together at the end.

Being squeamish never crossed my mind. It was a truly special thing to be able to spend time with both my parents' bodies. I was able to make my proper, heartfelt goodbyes. Yes – of course it's sad, but they had both lived long and happy lives. I put a lovely photo of their wedding on each of their hearts before they were put into their coffins. All in all, we did exactly as they wanted, and it was beautiful. A true life lesson.

And what of my other life lessons?

I had a lovely final love affair, with a Buddhist antique-dealer friend who I had known for about twenty-five years. He even found my lopsided body beautiful. We were together for ten years and had some lovely holidays in Sri Lanka and Egypt, both places where he had travelled frequently and had many friends. In fact, we even had a Buddhist wedding in Sri Lanka in 2015, organised by all our wonderful friends there; but very sadly he died of a sudden heart attack in 2017.

I have a hunger for knowledge, and I suppose I first became interested in the 'other' when we had crop circles on our farm in Wiltshire in the 1950s and 1960s. They piqued my interest, as I just knew there was more to them. Although nobody really knows what causes them, there is a theory that they are caused by some type of electrical reaction between atmospherics and water, as they always occur where there is water (either in underground aquifers as in Wiltshire, or even on ice). Another thought is the use of magnetic resonance of applied sound waves to create designs. Some think they are caused by intense microwave plasma. Or scalar energy/electromagnetic waves.

All fallen stems have some radioactivity in them and changes in the nodules which explode and are elongated. There are some films on YouTube showing bright orbs seemingly making a formation – the patterns usually incorporate sacred geometry designs, as seen in nature – and films of cymatics, which are studies of wave phenomena and vibration, similar to when iron filings go into geometric patterns depending on what is used to make them. For example, with music each note has its own specific pattern. Some mathematicians even say that these crop circle formations incorporate higher mathematics, and that new mathematics have been discovered this way.

Some years ago, I knew a Wiltshire farmer, who was a true sceptic and hated the 'people' who made the formations on his land. Then one day he was driving his tractor past one of his fields – pristine in the early morning sun – but on his return journey some fifteen minutes later, there was the most massive and intricate formation, which had most definitely not been there before, and no 'person' or 'people' could have made it in that short time. They are also a worldwide phenomenon, not just seen in the United Kingdom. The scientific company BLT Research in the United States has some interesting information on them.

This then led me to becoming more and more interested in the mix of science and spirituality, the sacred, the esoteric, Hermetic philosophy, Kabbalah, and the mystery schools. These allow one to find one's 'tribe', although some people think you're crazy of course! These studies also go into synchronicity and numbers, and the sacred geometry which is all around us – in nature, music, science, and the arts. I fill my retirement by studying all these fascinating topics.

I went on to study the sacred geometry of Chartres Cathedral with the architect Dr Keith Critchlow some years ago, staying in the cathedral's Pilgrims' Hostel for a week. He used sacred geometry for much of his work: for example, a building in Prince Charles's garden at Highgrove, and a hospital in Puttaparthi, in India. Through Dr Critchlow I discovered the Temenos Academy, the Kairos Foundation and The Prince's Foundation School of Traditional Arts and have studied with them all.

A quote from the Temenos Academy's website, reproduced here with their kind permission:

The Temenos Academy is an educational charity which aims to offer education in philosophy and the arts in the light of the sacred traditions of East and West. The word Temenos means 'a sacred precinct'.

And Kairos looks at:

> ...the traditional values in the Arts and Sciences – the Unity of Being. An understanding of the relationships between arithmetic, geometry, music (harmony) and astronomy (cosmology) which are the universal language of humankind.
>
> [Permission to use this quote kindly granted by Amanda Critchlow.]

Keith Critchlow's hero was Buckminster Fuller, the American engineer, architect and futurist, who said:

> Keith Critchlow has one of the century's rare conceptual minds...he is one of the most inspiring scholar-teachers I have had the privilege to know.

How very lucky I was to be able to study with Keith. When we were at Chartres, he told us about Plato's quote above his door:

> Let no man ignorant of geometry enter here.

And:

> Geometry will draw the soul toward truth and create the spirit of philosophy.

I have done many courses on sacred geometry at The Prince's Foundation School of Traditional Arts in East London, spending many hours drawing the actual detailed diagrams of the various geometrical designs of Islamic art – far more complicated that we at first realise. On one course there I became friendly with a Muslim woman, who has since sent me a copy of the Koran, pointing out the chapters I should read which mention Mary and Jesus, who are both revered in Islam.

I'm also fascinated by Christianity and studied for many years at the Marlborough College Summer School in Wiltshire, studying St Paul, St Augustine, and topics such as 'The Bible: a guide for the perplexed'. I especially like the quote: *'Belief is a cop-out of intellectual truth seeking.'*

Then there are people like Rudolf Steiner's work to discover. And the fact that many teach the deep esoteric meanings and mathematics behind Jesus's parables. Thank goodness for the internet, which makes it all so easy these days to look up just about anything.

I study with the Francis Bacon Research Trust, run by David and Sarah Dawkins. It goes into great intellectual, spiritual, psychic depth about Sir Francis Bacon, who some think may have written the Shakespeare plays and sonnets. Even the famous actor, Mark Rylance, turns up at seminars and study groups. I love the mix of deep intellect, the esoteric and hidden meanings, which are revealed to those who search.

As Shakespeare said:

> There are more things in heaven and earth, Horatio, than are dreamt of in your philosophy.

About fifteen years ago I started studying with the Academy For Future Science who are striving to bring science and religion together. This is utterly fascinating, extremely complicated, but deeply rewarding. It is run by the linguist and scientist Dr J J Hurtak, who teaches religion, philosophy, Kabbalah and the quantum world. Indeed, he instructs all new students to study physics before doing his courses. It has just what I love in its mix of science and spirituality. In fact, there is a fascinating talk by one of their physics teachers called 'The Wave Genome, Quantum Holography of DNA' that can be found on the website of the Solari Report.

I also have a passion for botanical painting. I know – a classic middle-class and middle-aged hobby! Things finally came full circle for me when Anita Pallenburg, Keith Richards' partner from the 70s, was at the same botanical watercolour course at the Chelsea Physic Gardens in London. We spent the week nattering about the old days, and how their children Marlon and Angela were doing, and about her allotment. One of the most famous rock chicks in the world now loved cycling to her allotment to do some gardening!

So where am I now as I come to the end of writing my memoir? I'm retired! Retirement is bliss. Initially I was dreading it, as I always liked to work and keep busy. But I'm now able to do the things I love, like reading, painting, going to the cinema in the daytime (which feels so decadent!). This is all a real gift for this final part of my life. There are just so many exciting things to discover out there. It's utterly thrilling – who knew retirement could be so exciting! In fact, I really have lived the good life that Germaine Greer foretold in *The Female Eunuch*. To sum up: do what you want, and want what you do.

I have learned to live on my state pension and benefits. A word of advice to all young people: get a private pension. I had a very small one but rarely paid into it, thinking I could work until I died...well, I certainly worked until I dropped, that's for sure, but it all ended far too early. My private pension only provides me with about £600 a year, on top of my state pension. But despite having to survive on these meagre pensions, I cut my cloth to suit my income, and I'm grateful for what I've got. As Epicurus, the Greek philosopher, says: "...having enough, but not too much, is a source of pleasure. Wanting more causes trouble and pain."

I still do some charity work, helping put on fetes for a local church; organising garden parties for the local RNLI and a hospice in Plymouth; plus Shakespeare productions with the Live Literature Company in aid of RNLI and Age UK, and garden parties at the Dartington Estate.

When I look back on my life, I am amazed that I got through it being as healthy as I have, both mentally and physically, as I was often in some quite dangerous situations. And interestingly I never had any sexual abuse problems with the men I worked with – apart from that one time with the roadie from The Meters on the Stones' tour. In fact, I was treated with respect at all times.

Epilogue

Some important things I'd like to pass on to younger women…

- Listen and be kind.
- Be honest. People don't expect perfection, but they do expect honesty.
- Take up your free NHS mammogram at fifty.
- Take out a private pension.
- If you lose a job, sign on for benefits *immediately*, as they only start paying the day you sign on, not the day you lose your job.
- If you do lose a job and have a mortgage, benefits might help with mortgage payments.
- Take responsibility for your actions.
- Be able to take criticism.
- Don't think the world owes you a favour.
- Accept that life isn't fair.
- Offer to help others.
- Stand up against cruelty.
- Respect the other's point of view and be polite.
- We tend to keep the faults of others before our eyes, our own behind our back…beware of this.
- An apology never diminishes – it elevates.
- Avoid malcontents and pessimists; they drag you down and contribute nothing to your well-being.

- Don't make promises you can't keep.

- Have a sense of humour, and laugh loudest when the joke is on you.

- Please don't complain about us oldies having had things easier and better – we did not! For example, we experienced inflation above 20%; petrol prices rocketing 70% in one year; mortgage interest rates of 18%. It was – and is – all relative.

Phrases that have helped me through the years

Always, and in everything, strive to attain at the same time what is useful to others and what is pleasant for oneself.
– Gurdjieff

Care about people's approval and you will be their prisoner.
– Lao Tzu

To call women the weaker sex is a libel; it is man's injustice to women... If by strength is meant moral power, then woman is immeasurably man's superior... If non-violence is the law of our being, the future is with women.
– Mahatma Gandhi

May we be guided by truth. May we have beauty revealed to us. And may it result in the Good.
– Keith Critchlow's Pythagorean Invocatory prayer
[Permission to use granted by Amanda Critchlow]

Final Word

So finally – despite all the entitled, narcissistic, and addictive personalities I have met and worked with, I've survived with no horrendous addictions and with my sanity intact. Many others didn't. It was a rollercoaster ride, but I'm glad I got out of it and that I am able to enjoy the last few years of my life knowing I did my best at all times.

Appendix 1

From Professional Builder 24th May 2019

We celebrate the remarkable achievements of MK Electric

It's a name which readily trips off the tongue when anything remotely electrical is being discussed, the iconic plugs, sockets and wiring devices a familiar feature of just about every UK building of note. However, the company we know today as MK Electric began life exactly 100 years ago as the rather more cumbersome Heavy Current Electric Accessories Company, with second hand machinery and just three employees.

One of those was the visionary gifted electrical engineer Charles Arnold, whose entrepreneurial career began in 1912 when he teamed up with another Charles, in this case Belling, to begin a venture into electric fires. With the outbreak of war two years later, Charles Arnold enlisted and sold his shares to his business partner who, as we all know of course, would go on to become a household name in domestic appliances.

Returning home four years later as Captain Arnold, his old friend highlighted a need for a business producing bespoke switches and sockets, if only for his own range of Belling fires.

Interestingly, when electricity was first introduced into domestic settings in the 1880s it was primarily used for lighting. One common approach for other appliances (such as vacuum cleaners, electric fans, smoothing irons and curling tong heaters) was to connect to light bulb sockets using lamp holder plugs. In fact in Britain there were recognisable two pin plugs and wall sockets appearing on the market in 1885, but made from thick gauge slotted brass tubes they afforded almost no flexibility. Plug pins were split to offer compression but they often led to a loose fit and poor contact whilst large pins on the other hand needed too much force to insert and remove them.

As electricity became a common method of operating labour-saving appliances it was evident that a safer and better way of connecting to the electric system was required. And so the Multy Kontact socket was invented and patented by Charles Arnold, a key feature being its numerous flexible spring tongues which actually grip the pin in much the same manner as "the legs of two caterpillars on opposite sides of a flower stem", according to an original patent in April 1919. Such flowery language is unlikely to hold much sway with current patent applications, one would imagine!

Multy Kontact immediately proved better and, importantly, safer to use and was instrumental in the British Engineering Standards Association (BESA) revising its standards, effectively making MK the industry norm.

In 1926 a small electroplating operation was added to the factory and the company purchased its first delivery van. No one was more delighted than right hand lad Jack Brett, who had joined at just thirteen on tuppence farthing an hour, working six and a half days a week and was required to push a barrow four miles daily to the electroplaters in Ponders End.

By 1928 the company was using the revolutionary new insulating material Bakelite, the same material old radios were made of. It led shortly after to the introduction of the first ever shuttered socket, concealing the socket tubes and eliminating the alarming flash invariably accompanying plug withdrawal from old fashioned sockets.

During the Second World War, MK switched most of its production from sockets, switches and plugs to detonators, firing systems and centrifuges needed for the war effort, with Spitfires, Hurricanes and Lancasters all employing MK products. The devastation of the war encouraged progress in many areas of society, including the establishment of universal healthcare and the birth of the NHS. The massive programme of building required also presented an opportunity to improve and standardise wiring and electrical outlets with updates to British Standards.

The British ring final circuit system and BS1363 13a plugs, socket outlets, connection units and adaptors were introduced into the UK in 1947 following many years of debate by the IEE which was formed by the then Minister of Works and Planning. Over the ensuing years, MK evolved its shuttered socket design culminating in the development of Logic plus – a range of wiring devices which are widely regarded as one of the most advanced and safest on the market.

In the early sixties the company opened a factory in Southend, where it continues to be based and Charles Arnold continued to guide the company for more than five decades, until he died at 83 in 1969.

The 100 millionth safety plug rolled off the production line as long ago as November 1984 and manufacture of all of its subsequent products is undertaken in the UK with another factory in St Asaph. Anyone with an MK product in their home, and there are literally millions, is in good company, the business holding the Royal Warrant of Appointment by the Queen for more than thirty years.

Today, of course, with the proliferation of the internet and influx of mobile devices, all with different plugs and charging requirements, the socket has further evolved to include USB charging ports and is a world away from the original split pin design of the late 19th century. Charles Arnold quite literally helped us to make that switch and subsequently harness one of our greatest resources in an altogether safer and more sophisticated manner than we could ever have imagined.

[Reproduced with permission of Hamerville Media Group, publisher of *Professional Builder*]

Appendix 2

Brian Croft's history of the technical information in the early days of rock and roll

The following is an article by Brian, who has given me permission, along with the publisher, to reproduce this piece about the early days of sound and lighting in rock and roll. I've known Crofty since my early days with the Who in 1974, and he's always been a firm friend and mentor. I have produced the article in its entirety as I'm sure many people will be interested in this fascinating information about the early days. There was no rock and roll business in the UK prior to what is related here by Crofty. And, as is made clear, pretty much all of the crew came from the theatre world. There were very few technical providers then, too. Just one trucking company, Edwin Shirley Trucking; one sound company, Marshall Equipment Hire; and one lighting company, ESP. These days there are probably hundreds of such companies.

Fifty years ago, an enthusiastic young man entered the world of show-business and went on to play a leading role in changing the face of concert touring. Jerry Gilbert celebrates the legend that is Brian Croft...

Right in the front line of many early technology-pioneering tours was Brian Croft whose classical upbringing in mainstream theatre was traded for rock'n'roll at the end of the 1960s when the Rolling Stones gave him his big break. His career began in 1959 as the assistant stage manager at Perth Repertory Theatre, and in 1968, whilst working for the National Youth Theatre, he had been contacted by Michael Kustow, artistic director at the ICA, for whom the move from Dover Street in Mayfair to The Mall would set in train a change to more experimental artistic direction.

As the ICA's new technical director, Croft enjoyed an amazing three years pursuing all forms of art — including a memorable night with avant garde artist and liquid light specialist Mark Boyle, when Soft Machine supported Hendrix. At the same time he started to do liquid light shows of his own, with partner John Brown, with whom he went on to form ESP.

The Nice and Bonzo Dog Doo-Dah Band played at the opening party of the new ICA in 1968, followed by Julie Driscoll & Brian Auger (with The Trinity), who brought in their own sound. All manner of acts would pass through, including The Doors and Country Joe & The Fish, and one day E.H.B. Monck — a.k.a Chipmonck — arrived with the Chambers Brothers. Monck went on, shortly after, to put together all technical operations at Woodstock and then to be the Rolling Stones' right hand production man.

Having established a good relationship with Monck, Croft received a fateful call from the Stones office in December 1969, a few days after the much-publicised tragedy at Altamont, to say the band were planning to play some pre-Christmas London dates at very short notice and asked Croft if he could do some groundwork. "They did one show at the Saville Theatre and one at the Lyceum — so my first ever rock'n'roll gigs were for the Stones. Chip brought some of the lighting with him, which we hung on the theatre flying bars," remembers Croft. "We used Century tungsten 2kW fresnels, as PAR cans didn't exist then." Century was a Broadway theatrical lighting company that was eventually taken over by Strand.

A few days later, in January 1970, Crosby Stills Nash & Young played the Royal Albert Hall using Bob Stern's own PA system. Once again, Chipmonck asked Croft (moonlighting from the ICA) to take care of the lighting, using the same rig as the Stones' shows. He enlisted the help of Roy Lamb "who at least knew a little bit about electricity" for the London date. Production manager on that three-date European tour was Leo McCoter. Monck was eager for Croft to source a lighting desk and dimmer system and so he approached the newly-set up Electrosonic, run by Bob Simpson. They already made thyristor dimmers for house lights and Croft's team asked if they could also make a lighting console... which led to the birth of the Rockboard. "So we ended up touring a standard 19" rack, wrapped in a blanket, with thyristor dimmers and wired the snake in on a terminal block each day with a screwdriver, working from Roy's crib sheet," says Croft. "The control was a very simple two-scene preset board, comprising two rows of 24 faders."

Croft also put an eight-man lighting crew together to do the Stones' 1970 European tour, taking four months leave from the ICA. "The architect-designed structure was made by Access Equipment and it was the first tour with proper ground support," Croft explains: "But we only put up 48 Century 2kWs and a bunch of velour drapes, lit by striplights, while outfront there were seven carbon arc followspots, five Super Troupers and two Gladiators from Strong, hired via Altman."

The PA was supplied by Charlie Watkins' WEM, with Ian Stewart in charge of the back-line, and Croft says it was a largely ground-breaking tour because it was being made up as they went along. "That's where I cut my teeth. We had 70,000 in Helsinki — and just added a few more 100W WEM columns! We carried with us our own gas-powered forklift truck. Three artics took the lighting, set and ground support system but Johnny Thompson, who worked for WEM, insisted on driving the PA in a two-tonne van. and Ian Stewart drove the back-line in his own little VW van — they didn't trust those big bendy lorries or the lighting crew, I guess."

Croft left the ICA in 1971 and rejoined the National Youth Theatre to open the Shaw Theatre, after doing a short UK Stones tour with the aid of a 16-tonne 22' straight truck that hauled all the gear — lights, sound and back-line.

The '71 tour was promoted by the father/son partnership of John & Tony Smith. "Tickets were a princely £1, hence just the one 16-tonner," says Croft, whose next few years were largely taken up producing liquid light shows around the then obligatory Aldis projectors. He remembers (with some embarrassment) lighting The Who at an Oxford Poly ball using only six of the 1kW Tutors!

With John Brown, who had left the ICA shortly after Croft, he had formed the fondly-remembered Extra Sensory Projections (ESP), opening a shop in the Wandsworth Road, south London. Brown fronted the operation with the third partner, Alastair Robertson taking care of the creative side until there was sufficient capital build-up for Croft to bid farewell to the theatre once and for all. "Whatever we needed we rented from Theatre Projects — fresnels, followspots plus the Electrosonic Portapak dimmers and Rockboard. It was a big wrench to leave theatre but there just wasn't sufficient money to be made," he confesses.

Aside from early rock'n'roll, disco was proving big business at the time and Brown started doing gigs with Cerebrum's John Lethbridge, which brought them into contact with desk specialist Graeme Fleming, who subsequently went on to start Britannia Row Lighting.

In 1973, the newly-formed ESP Lighting Ltd landed tours with The Who, Elton John and the Stones — which was the first time they used PAR cans as we know them today, produced by Charlie & Ronnie Altman in Yonkers. Touring clients who followed would include David Bowie, Deep Purple, The Moody Blues and Joni Mitchell. "Previously short-nosed PAR cans had been used only in the film industry, in open white, but they needed snoots to make them longer so as not to burn the colour filter — so Altman started making 'real' PAR cans. The Centurys were cast, but the Altmans were made out of sheet metal and were lighter."

Newly relocated to Blackfriars, ESP was doing good business importing PARs from Altman and selling them on. "For six months or so everyone thought we were the authorised distributors because we were importing them by the hundred," recalls Croft. "We must have stuffed thousands of PAR cans into the industry."

One of his main customers was Eric Pearce, an electrician on the West End production of Oh! Calcutta, who set up Key Lights as a rental company, and later Showlight. Pearce eventually moved to Dallas and took on the sub-contracted lighting from Showco after it became a dedicated PA outfit.

MONSTER TOUR: While Tychobrae was the chosen sound contractor for the Stones' 1973 tour — for which it used the blue carpeted Cerwin-Vega! speakers — the contract for the band's '75 tour moved to Clair Bros, and later again to Showco. Brian Croft was stage manager, Patrick Stansfield was production manager and Peter Rudge, tour director. The set design was by Robin Wagner and the lighting design by Broadway theatre specialist, Jules Fisher. "It was a monster 30-truck tour – the first really grown-up tour, I think," says Croft. "But the costs were enormous and it didn't make much money. For the next European tour in 1976, Peter Rudge was much more cost-conscious and asked me to be production manager, and for my company, ESP Lighting, to be the overall production controller. We reverted to Chip's famous mirror out front/Supers on-stage format, except for the Earl's Court gig where we used the mechanised 'lotus' stage from the '75 USA tour.

"I think we brought in the whole 10-week tour production — stage roof, sound and light, trucking, crew transportation and hotels — for about £300,000. That wouldn't go far these days.

"The lighting control desk and dimmers were built by an ESP staffer, Paul Ollett. They were the prototypes for the hugely successful Avolites range.

John and I decided to let Paul take the designs — at no cost — to Ian Whalley at Avo because we weren't into manufacture, man!

"The audio was subbed out to Joe Browne's Tasco [crew chiefed by Keith Bradley] who at that time were using the big old Roger Harvey-designed Harwell system."

The outdoor gigs interspersed amongst the indoor dates made use of a highly innovative canopy – the famous Orange roof, used at the 1976 Knebworth Fair and later acquired by the Roskilde Festival – operated by Bill Harkin's company.

A key member of Harkin's team was an ex-ESP staffer, Jeremy Thom, who went on to design Live Aid (Wembley) and U2's Joshua Tree tour. Whilst the Stones tour progressed, John Brown handled the rest of ESP's roster of acts from HQ, including Elton John.

ARRIVAL: After the culmination of the '76 Stones tour at Knebworth, Croft moved on to ABBA's Arrival tour, using many of the Stones team. Jimmy Barnett, who had been the Stones' board operator, became lighting designer and when he moved on to become ABBA's production manager, he handed the LD mantle to crew member Patrick Woodroffe, who had already cut his teeth doing the lights for The Heavy Metal Kids, managed by Rikki Farr. Patrick was younger brother of Simon (of the Yo! Sushi restaurant chain fame), who had left ESP to set up the lighting department of Electrosound. But in January 1977, several things happened at once. John Brown was fast losing interest, having found the nightmare of day-to-day live production too great to bear. Then Croft received a call from Farr who wanted to buy the company. This was a pivotal point in the development of concert production as Farr – the promoter, manager and impresario behind the Isle Of Wight Festival – was the junction that many people passed through on their way from A to B. He now had Electrosound, which was based near Borough Market, south London. The name ESP was abandoned and Croft took over as MD of the UK operation.

In the summer of '77 Croft supplied Gerry Stickells with lighting for Queen's shows at Earls Court. It was the start of a long-lasting relationship.

Farr had already moved to the States and bought the Boston-based lighting company, Tom Fields Associates (TFA), who had provided all the lighting equipment for that 1976 Stones tour, and custom-built all the trusses.

TFA's healthy artist roster had also included The Beach Boys and Chicago, and when Tom Fields disappeared into the film industry, the logical move was to merge TFA and Electrosound, with Croft installed as the London-based MD and Farr running the show in California.

Farr first established the audio side of TFA Electrosound in Los Angeles and very soon shut down the Boston-based lighting operation and relocated to LA (turning Ivy League staffers into instant California beach-bums overnight).

Farr also set up a management company in Beverly Hills called AIM (Artistes International Management), enjoying success with The Tubes. He had secured serious financial backing from city brokers Norton Warburg, run by Andrew Warburg, who in turn were reinvesting some of the profits back into the music industry.

In 1982, Norton Warburg went bankrupt, almost taking Pink Floyd (one of its premier customers) with it, as co-founder & bassist Roger Waters explains: "We lost a couple of million quid – nearly everything we'd made from The Dark Side Of The Moon."

ACQUISITIONS: TFA Electrosound (London) had expanded its client roster by 1982 to include Bob Dylan, Neil Diamond, Rod Stewart, Elvis Costello, Ian Dury, The Pretenders and Madness, at which point the company was absorbed by Theatre Projects, with Croft becoming administration director of the newly-formed Theatre Projects Services.

Two years later, the publicly-traded Samuelson Group had taken over Zenith Lighting, Rainbow Lighting and Theatre Projects/TFA. Samuelson Concert Productions (known as Sammy's) was created, headed by Croft, and some of the greatest names in concert touring were all under one roof. Bruce Springsteen and Tina Turner joined the client roster, and in 1985, Croft was one of four stage managers working on the historic Live Aid event at Wembley Stadium. Croft would return to Wembley the following summer as the pre-production co-ordinator for what would be Queen's final tour with Freddie Mercury.

Croft describes the period between 1989 and 2003 as his 'golden years'. At the dawn of the Nineties, Samuelsons' lighting entities were combined in Greenford with Croft overseeing operations as general manager. He then became MD of Vari-Lite Europe (later Vari-Lite Production Services, VLPS) after Vari-Lite Inc acquired the lighting divisions of the company in 1994.

The man who, as far as the great Chip Monck is concerned, will always be known as 'Crofty' Croft, successfully survived a couple of "serious but quite short" illnesses in the late '90s to take the chairman's role at VLPS.

"That was an amazing and very profound time for me," he recalls. "The company was flying, mainly due to the fabulous Vari-Lite products.

"We also had major world tours by Paul McCartney, Pink Floyd, Genesis, Simply Red, Robbie Williams and, of course, the blessed and saintly Rolling Stones."

In 2003, Croft officially retired but his passion for the world of entertainment production shows no sign of diminishing. He remains active on the board of the National Youth Theatre and regularly attends major industry events including the ABTT and PLASA shows, and the annual TPi Awards. Mr. Croft, we salute you!

[Printed by kind permission of Brian Croft, publisher TPi and the author, Jerry Gilbert]

Acknowledgements

This book would never have come into being without the help of the following fantastic friends:

Lin and John Brady	Helen Hawkins	Bea D'Aft
Bryan Walters	Roderick Packe	Beth Coombes
Mike Wood	Brian Sweet	Lorna Yabsley
Chris Sadler	Ems Coombes	Nic Joss
John Paul Forestal	Nancy Sain	Sylvi Brown
Liz Wilkinson	Dave Evans	Dean Goodman
Nell Newman	Edward Rennie	Mike Smith
Sal Wood	Scarlett Hoskyns-Abrahall	

Also, my regular volunteers for the charity events: my sister Faith, and brother Mark, Leslie Rainey, Simon Wakeford, Anna Gregory, Beth Rainey, and so many others – all of whom worked their socks off.

And my unsung heroes who – without fail – helped me with my numerous charity events:

Brian Croft	Peter de Savary	Fay Presto
Lord Colwyn	Dawes Press	
Michael Bukht	Sacha, Duchess of Abercorn	

Robbie Williams (of Pink Floyd's Britannia Row)
Edwin Shirley, Roy Lamb and Tim Norman (of Edwin Shirley Trucking)
Jimmy Barnett of Samuelsons
Mick Jackson of Jackson Security Services

As well as photographers Michael Putland, Richard Young, Alan Davidson, Kate Simon and Dave Benett.

Not forgetting my wonderful editor Helen Hart and the very creative Lucy Reynolds, both at SilverWood Books; Debra Penrice for her sage advice on book promotion; Helen Lewis for my PR.

With special thanks to the family of Dean Kilpatrick.

Very special thanks to Pete Townshend of The Who, Gary Rossington of Lynyrd Skynyrd, and my old friend, Alan Dunn, for their wonderful generosity over the years when I was at my most desperate.